THE   COMPLETE   BOOK   OF

Cake Decorating

© Orbis Publishing Ltd 1995

Published By Grange Books
An Imprint of Grange Books PLC
The Grange
Grange Yard
London SE1 3AG

This edition published 1995

This material has previously appeared
in the partwork *Cake Decorating*

ISBN 1 85627 725 9

Printed in the Republic of Slovakia
51635

THE COMPLETE BOOK OF

Cake Decorating

PROFESSIONAL SECRETS, SKILLS AND TECHNIQUES, CREATIVE IDEAS

Grange BOOKS

Contents

Classic Cakes

Cocoa-painted cake

Raise a smile with this endearing picture of two sleepy hedgehogs charmingly hand-painted in cocoa.

This delightful cake depicts a simple woodland scene and is beautifully hand-painted in cocoa, giving the effect of an old-fashioned book illustration. It requires subtlety and skill, but the end result makes it a special and unusual cake.

A CAKE FOR ALL SEASONS
It just goes to show that you can bake a cake for any occasion you choose – the inscription on this one reads 'Wake up, it's spring!'. The beginning of spring is special, and in days gone by was often celebrated with dancing and games in villages up and down the country.

The design is painted directly on to the top of the cake using a special cocoa mixture, and it requires delicate brushwork. The effect of the colouring is that of a sepia tint, and it is most effective when painted on to a pale background, such as cream or white.

PAINTING THE DESIGN
The picture is built up in layers, using differently sized paintbrushes and a mixture of cocoa and vegetable fat. The design is begun by painting in the lighter shades, letting the cocoa solution dry as each part is finished. Darker hues are required as the picture is developed, and so the amount of cocoa in the mixture is increased. When you have finished painting the picture, you can go over some cocoa-painted lines in places with a scalpel, slightly scratching the surface. This gives the effect of reflected light and adds texture and depth to the cake. Brushwork is an important factor to consider in this design, which can either be painted directly on to the cake itself, or on to a plaque. It is a good idea to practise beforehand. The ingredients for the cocoa solution, and the method of making it, are given on page 8

FURRY ANIMALS
Cocoa painting is one of the most effective ways of painting feathery or furry animals – such as owls, cats, dogs or bears. It is ideally used on a cake for an animal lover when you do not want the design on the cake to seem too childish, although the scene on this particular cake will appeal to all ages.

STEP-BY-STEP GUIDE

1 Marzipanning the cake: Brush the surface of the cake with apricot glaze and cover it with a layer of marzipan.

2 Covering the cake: Cover the cake with a layer of rolled sugarpaste and leave it to crust over for three days. As it dries, cover it with a sheet of greaseproof paper to prevent dust accumulating on it.

3 Covering the cake board: Cover the cake board with sugarpaste and set aside to dry.

4 Attaching the cake: When both the cake and board are dry, attach the cake centrally on the board with a few dabs of royal icing.

5 Piping a row of shells: Using white royal icing and a no. 2 piping tube, pipe a row of small shells around the base of the cake at the point where it meets the cake board.

6 Scribing the top design: Using the template provided, scribe the top design – the two hedgehogs on the bench – on to the top of the cake.

7 Scribing the side design: Place the cake on a tilting turntable and secure the template around the side then scribe the side design.

8 Making the cocoa solution: Make the cocoa solution from cocoa powder and white vegetable fat. Make sure that you have some extra cocoa to hand before you start to paint.

9 Painting the top design: Paint in the top design using a fine, rounded (sable) paintbrush. This is done in several stages.

10 Painting the side design: With a fine, rounded paintbrush, paint in the hedgehogs on the side of the cake as shown using cocoa solution.

11 Adding the hearts: Paint the hearts on to the cake, with a mixture of petal dust and clear alcohol.

12 Painting the flowers: With a fine, rounded paintbrush, add the roses to the side design.

13 Fitting the ribbon: Fit a narrow green ribbon around the base of the cake, securing it at intervals with small dots of royal icing.

14 Piping the inscription: Pipe the inscription on to the cake with a no. 1 tube and green royal icing.

15 Attaching the ribbon bows: Make two green ribbon bows and attach them to the sides of the cake on either side of the hedgehogs.

16 Decorating the board: Add a wide green ribbon around the circumference of the board.

PAINTING THE TOP DESIGN

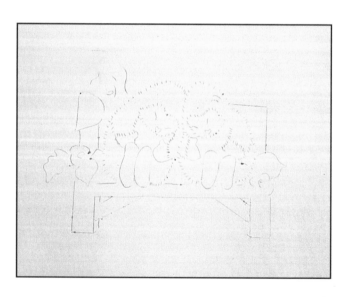

1 Tracing the template: Trace the template of the two hedgehogs on the bench on to greaseproof paper. Cut out the design and scribe it gently on to the cake.

2 Painting in the outlines: Paint in the outline with a fine, rounded brush. Use tiny broken lines to outline the hedgehogs to give a spiky impression.

3 Blocking in the colour: Paint in the leaves, the bench and the fur on the hedgehogs (leaving their tummies) in a pale brown colour with a thick, rounded brush.

4 Adding definition: Darken the cocoa solution. Add the rose petals and features. Begin to paint the spikes on top of the hedgehogs' heads with a medium, rounded brush.

5 Completing the spikes: Finish the spikes, making sure that the lines move in the direction of the fur growth. Add some darker leaves.

6 Adding the leaves and foliage: Add the veins to the leaves and paint in the additional foliage. Add shading to the bench and the hedgehogs' feet.

helpline — CHOOSING PAINTBRUSHES

All cake decorators need paintbrushes among their equipment, and as you become used to using them you will see that different brushes produce various effects on icing.

Brushes are made from a range of materials: sable is very expensive, while synthetic fibre is much cheaper, and there is a range of other materials in between.

If you can, invest in two or three sable brushes. They really are very good quality and will help you advance your skill. The way in which brushes are sized varies too, but generally speaking, small, fine brushes start at the 0 mark and get bigger as the number gets higher.

Brushes can be shaped differently at the top, and it is this shape that determines the effect on your cake surface. Some brushes are long and flat, some short and flat, some round, and some are even fan-shaped. A filbert shape is in between round and flat.

For this particular cake, three brushes were used: a fine rounded, a medium rounded and a thick rounded sable brush. For cocoa painting, choose a watercolour brush rather than one used for acrylics or oils.

At times you can improvise with brushes – petal dust, for example, can often be effectively applied with a blusher brush.

Experiment a little with your brushes before you begin to paint directly on to a cake or plaque, and remember: when using food pastes and petal dusts, use clear alcohol mixed with your colour, rather than water, since this can have a detrimental effect on the surface of your cake.

PROFESSIONAL SECRETS

Making the cocoa solution

Ingredients:

White vegetable fat
(or cocoa butter)
Cocoa powder (or powder colour)

Method

• Melt a teaspoon of white vegetable fat on to a plate which sits over a pan of hot water.

• Add a little cocoa to the fat to produce a very pale shade of brown and begin your work.

• As your work progresses and darker shades are called for, continue to add more cocoa to the fat.

• If you make a mistake, paint the area with melted vegetable fat, using a clean brush.

• The hot water will keep the mixture melted without the heat actually being turned on. If the mixture starts to set, take the plate off the heat, re-heat the water, turn off the heat, and place the saucer back on top of the pan.

• If you want to go over an area that you have already painted, wait for it to dry and then add more cocoa. You can almost achieve black in this way, which is useful for the features.

• When the hedgehogs are dry, complete the effect by scratching out bits of cocoa from the spikes – this will give the appearance of reflected light.

PAINTING THE SIDE DESIGN

1 Tracing the templates: Trace the side templates of the smaller hedgehogs, the hearts, the flower and the butterfly and scribe them on to the surface of the cake.

2 Building up the design: Paint in the smaller hedgehogs on the side of the cake in the same way as on the top, but using a tilting turntable.

3 Adding the hearts: Mix petal dust with clear alcohol. Using a fine brush, paint the hearts red, the butterfly blue and the flower yellow.

4 Painting in the roses: Finally paint on the tiny roses with a little cocoa solution. Add green leaves and some tiny, decorative spots in pale blue.

Embroidered book cake

**Book cakes have always been a popular idea in cake decorating.
Here, for an extra-special effect, brush embroidery has been incorporated.**

HAVE TO HAND

Ingredients: *25 x 20cm (10 x 8in)
rich fruit cake • apricot glaze •
marzipan • sugarpaste • gold, beige
and brown petal dust • gold lustre
powder • dark blue, yellow and pink
paste food colours • royal icing.*
Equipment: *30 x 25cm (12 x 10in)
cake board • book-shaped cake tin •
ruler • sharp knife • greaseproof
paper • pencil • scriber • no. 2 piping
tube • fine and large paintbrushes •
narrow ribbon.*
Main skills: *covering shaped cakes •
piping brush embroidery.*

DIFFICULTY	TIME	SUITABILITY

This versatile cake is suitable for a wide variety of occasions, since you can alter the decoration and inscription to suit. Here, it is decorated for a combined first birthday and christening, but it could be made to suit any occasion – birthday, anniversary, christening, wedding, coming of age, or even a degree ceremony.

SHAPING THE CAKE
The unusual shape is achieved by hiring or buying a book-shaped cake tin. Or it can be shaped by baking the cake in a large, deep, rectangular tin, then cutting it to the shape of the open book when cool. It is important to keep the shape symmetrical. The cake is coated with marzipan and sugarpaste, which must be pressed down firmly in the centre of the cake to keep the shape of the open book.

The effect of the edges of the pages is produced by scoring the sides of the cake, then colouring them with a subtle mixture of petal dust so that they look like the leaves of a book edged with gold. Reproduce the cover of the book with a thin sheet of coloured sugarpaste, and rest the cake on this.

BUILDING THE DESIGN
The design and inscription are first traced, and then scribed on to the top of the cake. Brush embroidery has been used for the flowers and leaves: first the outline is piped with a no. 2 piping tube and royal icing in the appropriate colour.

Then, delicate lines are added with a fine paintbrush and royal icing, to represent the sewing stitches in embroidery.

A final authentic touch is provided by the ribbon bookmark. Here, a narrow strip of ribbon has been cut to use as a book mark, but you could use one made from coloured sugarpaste if you prefer.

ALTERNATIVE DECORATIONS
As an alternative to the brush embroidery design we have used here, you could just as easily use a flower spray, made from silk or sugar flowers. Small roses or pulled blossoms teamed with appropriate foliage could be shaped into a decorative arrangement to cover one page, with a suitable inscription piped on the other.

STEP-BY-STEP GUIDE

1 Baking the cake: Use a fruit cake mixture and a book-shaped cake tin to bake the shaped cake.

2 Shaping the cake: Alternatively, if you do not have a book-shaped cake tin, make a deep, rectangular fruit cake and allow it to cool on a wire rack. Use a sharp knife to cut away the centre in a sloping 'V' to resemble the centre of a book. Shape the sides of the cake by cutting a triangular shape sloping out from the top.

3 Preparing the cake: Fill any holes in the top of the cake with marzipan, to give a smooth surface for covering.

4 Applying the glaze: Brush the cake with apricot glaze and cover it with marzipan, smoothing it carefully around the shape.

5 Shaping the spine: Cut small semi-circles out of the top and bottom of the cake, in the centre, to represent the spine of the book. Pack in some marzipan to prevent the cake from staining the sugarpaste coating.

6 Applying sugarpaste: Cover the marzipanned cake with a layer of sugarpaste, making sure you mould the paste into the holes cut for the spine.

7 Making the pages: Use a ruler and a sharp knife to score the edges of the cake to represent the pages.

8 Applying colour: Brush on a subtle blend of gold, beige and brown petal dust to the edges of the pages.

9 Making the cover: Colour some sugarpaste dark blue and roll it out thinly. Cut a rectangle to act as the book cover, and place it on the cake board.

10 Positioning the cake: Place the cake centrally on to the coloured sugarpaste. It is important that you do this carefully. If the book is placed incorrectly on the coloured cover, it will spoil the finished results.

11 Starting the design: Trace and scribe the floral design on to the top left-hand surface of the cake.

12 Applying brush embroidery: Starting at the top of the design and using a no. 2 tube, pipe on the brush embroidery. You cannot do all the outlines at once as the royal icing will dry quickly, so do one flower at a time.

13 Attaching a book mark: As an extra touch, make a book mark from suitably coloured ribbon and attach it to the cake with a small dab of royal icing.

14 Finishing off: Place the cake on a foil-covered cake board, or on a cake board covered with a layer of suitably coloured sugarpaste.

MAKING THE BOOK

1 Preparing the cake: Prepare the fruit cake by coating it with a layer of apricot glaze. Any indentations in the cooked cake should be plugged with marzipan prior to the glaze being applied.

2 Covering with marzipan: Cover the cake with a layer of marzipan. Cut out small semi-circles of cake centrally from the top and bottom edges of the cake. Cover the exposed areas with marzipan to prevent staining.

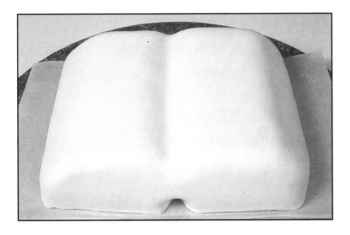

3 Covering with sugarpaste: Cover the entire cake with a layer of rolled sugarpaste, making sure that you mould the paste into the semi-circular indents made to represent the spine.

4 Scoring the pages: Using a ruler and a sharp knife, gently score straight lines along the side edges of the cake to represent the edges of the pages. At the top and bottom edges, curve the lines slightly on each side of the spine.

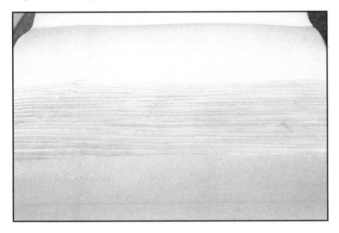

5 Colouring the edges: Using a large paintbrush, dust the scored edges of the cake with a mixture of pale brown and beige petal dusts, with the addition of some gold lustre powder to add the sparkle of gold leaf.

6 Making the cover: Colour some sugarpaste dark blue and roll out thinly to a size slightly larger than the cake to represent the book cover. Position centrally on a cake board and place the cake on top of the rolled sugarpaste.

helpline   BRUSH EMBROIDERY

Use freshly-made royal icing, made to full peak consistency. Add one teaspoon of piping gel to each four tablespoons of icing. This will slow down the drying time and give you a little longer to work on your design.

Pipe the outline of each flower or leaf, one at a time, then use a fine sable paintbrush moistened with a little water to draw lines of icing down from the piped outline into the centre of the design. Do not attempt to outline the entire design at once, as the icing will dry before you can brush it into the centre of the flower or leaf.

Use the brush to add a little more icing if necessary, but retain the heavier outline of the design.

The centre of the design should be subtle and give the impression of fine embroidery stitches.

Have piping bags made up and filled with all the colours required for your design in advance, so that you can move quickly from one colour to the other. To prevent the tips of the tubes from drying out, place them in a piping stand or cover them with a clean, damp cloth.

APPLYING THE BRUSH EMBROIDERY

1 Scribing the design: Trace the design from the template on to a rectangle of greaseproof paper cut to the correct size. Use a scriber to go over the outline of the design, transferring it on to the cake.

2 Working the brush embroidery: Starting at the top of the cake, pipe in the outlines of the design, using a no. 2 tube. Use a fine paintbrush and royal icing to draw in the design, using fine lines so that it looks like embroidery.

3 Completing the embroidery: Continue working down the cake – so that your hand does not disturb the finished design – adding leaves and flowers one at a time and varying the colours. Pipe in stamens with yellow royal icing.

4 Scribing the inscription: Trace the chosen inscription on to a piece of greaseproof paper the same size as the right-hand 'page' of the cake, or draw it freehand. Hold in place and scribe on to the surface of the cake.

5 Piping the inscription: Pipe the inscription in white royal icing and a no. 2 piping tube. Leave it to dry, then overpipe it in pink royal icing, lifting off any mistakes as soon as you make them.

6 Completing the cake: Use part of the template and the scriber to mark a final flower in the top right-hand corner of the cake. Pipe the outline with a no. 2 tube and fill in the design with brush embroidery. Attach ribbon with royal icing.

A special cake for Christmas

**This beautiful cake celebrates Christmas with a traditional
theme that everyone will love.**

HAVE TO HAND

Ingredients: 20cm (8in) square fruit
cake • apricot glaze • 1kg marzipan •
royal icing • white, black, brown, red,
green and blue paste food colourings
• green petal dust • gold paint •
clear alcohol.

Equipment: 28cm (11in) cake board
• side scraper • nos. 0, 1, 32 and 44
piping tubes • waxed paper • fine
paintbrushes • pencil • small pair of
scissors • palette knife • red or green
ribbon (optional).

Main skills: making runouts •
colouring runouts.

DIFFICULTY	TIME	SUITABILITY
✓✓		🍾

Our featured Christmas cake has a beautifully classical look to it which makes it very distinctive and unusual, yet it is quite simple to create and sure to be admired.

The theme is one that everyone will recognise, since it is based on the traditional Christmas carol, 'The 12 days of Christmas'. The top of the cake features the partridge in a pear tree, while each side depicts a different verse: in this case, two turtle doves, three French hens, four calling birds, and five gold rings.

MAKING THE RUNOUTS
The success of the design lies mainly in preparing attractive runouts and making sure that they are correctly positioned on the cake. We have provided the templates, and you might like to practise so that your runouts are perfect. When you have achieved the correct shapes, paint them as we have shown.

BEGINNING THE CAKE
Make a rich fruit cake in advance so that it has time to mature, and store it in a sealed container. Both the cake and board are royal iced. Give the cake three or four coats, leaving it to dry overnight in between each layer. For the final coating, use a softer consistency icing to give the cake a glossy sheen.

The shells that decorate the top edge of the cake and the base are first piped free-hand, and then attached to the cake with royal icing. They are then overpiped with a line of white royal icing around the top surface of each shell. When this has dried, a line of green royal icing is overpiped on to one half of each shell.

DECORATING THE BOARD
We have used a 28cm (11in) cake board, but you could use a larger one if you wish and decorate it with holly leaves and berries. Feel free to alter the design and the inscription to suit your own taste, but remember that part of the charm of this cake lies in the perfect positioning of the runouts and lettering, and in the fact that, in many respects, it is a simple cake. Don't be tempted to overload it with decorations.

STEP-BY-STEP GUIDE

1 Marzipanning the cake: Brush the surface of the cake with apricot glaze and then coat it with a layer of marzipan.

2 Icing the cake: Royal ice the cake and board, then leave them to dry.

3 Piping the shells: Using nos. 32 and 44 tubes, pipe shells free-hand on to greaseproof paper. When dry, attach in place around the cake base and top.

4 Overpiping the bulbs: Overpipe the shells, first in white icing with a no. 1 tube, and then in green icing with a no. 0 tube. Leave them to dry.

5 Tracing the templates: Trace the templates that you need on greaseproof paper. Cut them out and keep safely.

6 Making the runouts: Run out all the figures and the inscription on to waxed paper. It is up to you whether you pipe around them first.

7 Painting the runouts: Paint all the runouts, and leave them to dry. Use food colouring mixed with a little clear alcohol in a saucer. Use a dry, fine brush (sable if possible) to apply the colour.

8 Attaching the pear tree: Position the pear tree on the top of the cake. Gently attach it with royal icing.

9 Piping in the branches: Using a no. 1 tube, pipe in the branches in brown royal icing.

10 Positioning the partridge: Place the partridge on one of the branches, and attach it to the cake.

11 Adding the pears: Colour the pears with green petal dust, and attach them to the tree, one by one, with white royal icing.

12 Adding the snow: Using white royal icing and a no. 1 piping tube, pipe

the snow on to the branches and the trunk of the tree. Then, place a little snow on the soil in the tub.

13 Petal dusting the inscription: Dust the lower half of the letters in green petal dust for a graduated effect.

14 Attaching the inscription: Place the letters on the upper half of the cake, making sure that they are evenly spaced. When satisfied, attach with icing.

15 Attaching the side decorations: Position the hens in a line on one side of the cake, and attach with royal icing. Do the same for the calling birds, turtle doves and five gold rings on the remaining sides.

16 Adding a ribbon: If you wish, and for an extra Christmas touch, finish the cake by adding a red or green ribbon to the edge of the cake board.

COMPLETING THE DESIGN

1 Piping the shells: Pipe the shells, some with a no. 32 tube, and some with a no. 44 tube. When dry, attach the smaller shells to the top of the cake and the larger ones to the base. Overpipe shells with white and green royal icing.

2 Adding the tree: Position the painted pear tree centrally on to the top of the cake and attach it with royal icing. The placement of the tree is very important. Make sure you have sufficient room at the top for the inscription.

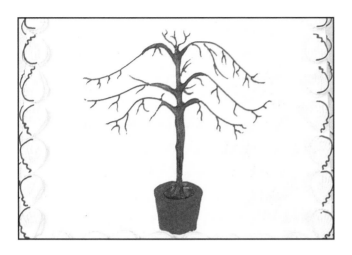

3 Piping the branches: Lightly scribe in the main branches, making sure that you create a good balance. Then pipe them on, using brown royal icing and a no. 1 tube.

4 Adding the partridge: Place partridge on a branch and attach with dots of royal icing so it appears to be raised from the cake. Pipe feet in brown icing with a no. 1 tube.

5 Adding the pears: Attach the pears to the tree with a tiny dot of royal icing. At this stage, if you wish, you could also pipe in some leaves with a no. 1 tube and green icing.

6 Adding snow: Pipe the snow on to the branches of the tree, the trunk, and on top of the soil in the pot. Use white royal icing and a no. 1 piping tube.

7 Placing the lettering: Petal dust letters in green, creating a graduated effect from bottom to top. Position the letters carefully, and attach them with icing when satisfied.

8 Placing side designs: Position the two turtle doves on the side of the cake, and attach with royal icing. Paint in the holly leaves and berries.

THE SIDE DESIGNS

1 The pear tree: Run out the pear tree. Use a fine, dry paintbrush to paint the pot red, and the trunk of the tree brown.

2 The four calling birds: Run out four calling birds, and paint them dark blue and green. It is up to you whether you pipe in the outlines before flooding.

3 The French hens: Run out the three hens, and paint them brown. Paint the combs and wattles in red as shown. The feet are piped in later.

4 The partridge: We gave the partridge realistic colouring – brown feathers with a coloured chest.

5 Two turtle doves: Run out the two turtle doves and attach them to the cake. Paint little holly sprigs and red holly berries by their beaks.

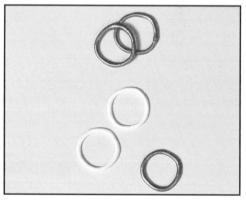

6 The five gold rings: Run out the rings and colour them with gold paint (remember that this is inedible). Run out more than you need as they are quite fragile.

Alternatives

CHOOSING A THEME FOR YOUR CAKE

The beauty of our featured Christmas cake is that it can be used as a starting point for other ideas while providing a useful method of cake decorating. If you are familiar with using templates, you can alter the design of the cake to suit your own tastes. Some of you may prefer to use different verses of

'The 12 days of Christmas' – perhaps seven swans-a-swimming, or eight maids-a-milking. However, the difficulty with these verses is that the cake may appear overcrowded, thus losing some of its appeal.

Those of you who are keen to maintain the religious nature of Christmas could

develop a nativity scene, depicting the birth of Christ and the three wise men. You could also choose a favourite Christmas carol. Find some illustrations that you like, then simply trace them and use them as a templates. You can then run these out and decorate the cake in the way that we have described here.

Sumptuous swags

Thinly rolled sugarpaste can be pleated into opulent-looking swags that are ideal for decorating formal celebration cakes.

HAVE TO HAND

Ingredients: 20cm (8in) petal-shaped fruit cake • apricot jam • 875g marzipan • clear spirit • 1kg sugarpaste • flower paste • egg white • yellow petal dust • yellow paste colouring • white vegetable fat • royal icing • gypsophila.

Equipment: 28cm (11in) petal-shaped cake board • nos. 1 and 4 piping tubes • medium knitting needles • scalpel • bone tool • scriber • orchid throat former • orchid cutter • 28g floristry wire • paintbrushes • gypsophila • 1m (1yd) cream ribbon • 1m (1yd) white ribbon.

Main skills: moulding sugarpaste • making a flower-paste orchid.

DIFFICULTY   TIME   SUITABILITY

Festooned swags and bows, usually associated with curtains and other home furnishings, are used to opulent effect on this cake. The technique demonstrates just how well sugarpaste can create an impression of heavy folds of draped fabric.

The flower paste bows create the illusion of the draped fabric being caught up around the scallops of the petal-shaped cake, producing a striking creation suitable for a formal occasion.

The swags can be made in the same colour as the cake covering, then decorated with piped flowers in a contrasting colour. Alternatively, the swags can be made from a contrasting-coloured paste, although it is best not to use too strong a colour, as this may detract from the formality of the cake.

In the case of a wedding cake, the swags and bows could be decorated to match the fabric of the bride's gown.

FINISHING TOUCH
The main feature of this cake is the ornate side decorations, so be careful not to over-decorate the top, or it could end up looking fussy.

Our cake is topped with a delicate orchid, so cleverly created in flower

paste and dusted with a subtle blend of petal dusts that it is hard to tell whether or not it is real. The orchid is a large blossom and only one flower is required, so take your time over making it, in order to achieve the best possible result.

Another option would be to create a small, floral decoration, comprising half roses and foliage. The roses could be coloured to match the flowers in the bride's bouquet. For an even simpler effect, you could omit the flowers altogether and simply pipe small blossoms over the top of the cake to match the design on the swags.

The only other decoration needed is a row of small shells or bulbs around the base of the cake. These should be piped before the swags are attached.

STEP-BY-STEP GUIDE

1 Marzipanning the cake:
Glaze the cake with boiled apricot jam and cover it with marzipan.

2 Sugarpasting the cake: When it is dry, brush the marzipan with clear spirit. Then, cover the cake with sugarpaste, moulding it carefully around all the scallop shapes.

3 Covering the cake board:
Cover the cake board with a layer of white sugarpaste, and trim the edges carefully. Position the cake centrally on the cake board.

4 Piping the shell border:
Using a no. 4 piping tube and white royal icing, pipe a row of shells around the base of the cake.

5 Making the swags: Using the template provided, cut out rectangles of sugarpaste one at a time for the swags. Form each rectangle into pleats by laying it over two medium-sized knitting needles, and then pinch it together at each end to form a swag.

6 Attaching the swags: Attach the swags to the cake with royal icing, positioning them so that they curve around each scallop shape.

7 Making the bows: Cut bows out of thinly rolled, white flower paste. Form the strips into loops and attach them to the cake over the joins between the swags with dabs of royal icing.

8 Finishing the bows: Add tails of thinly rolled flower paste to each bow. Finish them with a rounded centre, held in place with a dab of royal icing.

9 Making the orchid petals:
If you are making the orchid decoration, roll some white flower paste out thinly, cut it into three small petals and two larger petals, using an orchid cutter.

10 Making the throat and tongue: Use an orchid throat former to shape a throat piece. Form a small ball of white flower paste into a teardrop shape to make the tongue. Assemble the pieces to make the orchid.

11 Colouring the orchid:
Dust the orchid with petal dust, and add details using petal dust mixed with a little white spirit.

12 Attaching the orchid:
Coil up the wired stem of the orchid, and press it into a small, flattened ball of sugarpaste. Position the orchid on the centre of the cake, and attach it with a dab of royal icing.

13 Adding additional decoration: Arrange loops of wired cream ribbon and gypsophila around the orchid, pushing the ends into the ball of sugar paste − not into the cake. Trim the cake board with white ribbon.

MAKING THE SWAGS

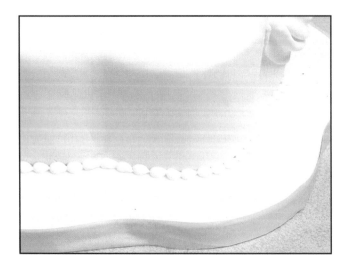

1 Piping the shell decoration: Using white royal icing and a no. 4 piping tube, pipe a row of shells around the base of the cake. Do this before attaching the swags, in order to avoid damaging them.

2 Cutting out swags: Roll the sugarpaste out thinly on a lightly greased surface, and cut a rectangular shape. Make the swags up one at a time; otherwise, the paste will dry out and be difficult to to work with.

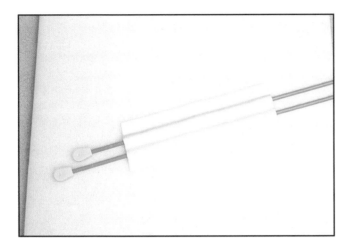

3 Forming the pleats: Lay a sugarpaste rectangle over a pair of lightly greased, medium-sized knitting needles, evenly spaced. Pinch the paste gently to form two pleats.

4 Attaching swags: Pinch the pleats together at each end, and drape the rectangle around one of the scallops. Attach the ends with dabs of royal icing.

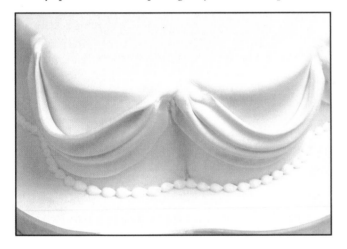

5 Draping the cake: Repeat this process five times, draping swags around all the other scallops on the cake. Any roughness where they join will be hidden by the bows.

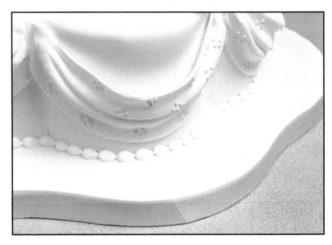

6 Piping the decoration: Using a no. 1 piping tube and yellow-coloured royal icing, pipe a pattern of tiny dots at regular intervals on the swags.

---

helpline

USING A PASTA MACHINE

If you have a pasta machine, which is designed for both rolling out and cutting sheets of dough, you can also use it to roll out very thin sheets of sugarpaste – ideal for making swags or drapes that will look exactly like fine fabric. The cutting blades can be used to reduce the thinly rolled sugarpaste to neat, even strips for making realistic-looking bows quickly and easily.

You can use either an electric pasta machine or a hand-operated one, but with the latter you will need someone to turn the handle while you are feeding the sugar paste through the rollers.

Begin by rolling the paste out into an oblong shape with a small, non-stick roller. You can use either sugarpaste, or a mixture of equal quantities of sugarpaste mixed with flower paste or Mexican paste.

Start with the machine set with the rollers at their furthest distance apart, then progressively alter the setting to bring the rollers closer together until the paste reaches the required thickness. For making swags and ribbons, it should be thin enough to drape well, but thicker than the minimum that the machine can produce. (This setting can be used to produce sheets

of sugarpaste for making flower petals, which should be almost translucent.)

Lay the rolled-out paste on a board, and trim off any irregular edges with a rotary cutter or a sharp knife to obtain a neat rectangle. Make pleats in one or both ends of the rectangle, pinching the paste firmly between fingers and thumbs, depending on whether you want a swag or a drape.

To make narrow ribbon bows, roll out the paste as before, then switch the machine to the tagliatelle setting and run the sheet through the cutters to obtain long, perfectly regular strips.

DESIGN TOUCH

A swag is normally a length of fabric or sugarpaste, pleated at both ends, and draped in a curved shape. A series of swags, caught up with ribbon bows, form a festoon. By varying the length of the swags and the depth of the curve, you can achieve a wide variety of different effects.

A drape usually refers to a length of fabric or sugarpaste pleated at the top and left free at the base, like a curtain. Drapes can look very effective as decorations on a multi-tier wedding cake, falling gracefully from the top tier.

Swags perfectly complement round and petal-shaped cakes. When used on a wedding cake, they can also echo the shape of any real fabric swags used to decorate the buffet table.

Our swags are white to match the cake, decorated with small yellow flowers, but they would look equally effective in pastel-coloured paste, perhaps with bows in a paler shade.

For a more delicate coloured effect, brush the swags with petal dust, allowing the colour to build up in the pleats to emphasise their depth.

Both drapes and swags can be embellished with lace and broderie anglaise patterns using embossing and crimping tools.

MAKING THE BOWS

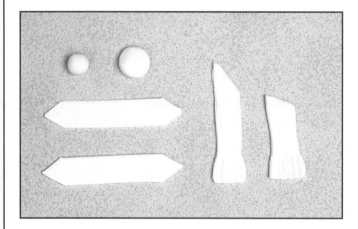

1 Cutting out: Roll some flower paste out thinly and cut four pieces for each bow. Mark a pattern on the tails with a scriber. Mould the centres out of small balls of sugarpaste.

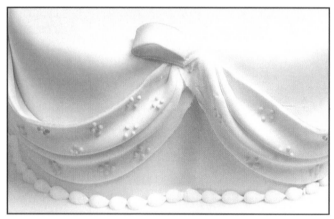

2 Making bow loops: Fold the longer strips point to point to form bow loops, and secure them with a dab of royal icing. Then, attach the loops centrally over the joins between the swags with royal icing.

3 Attaching tails to bows: Position the tails on the bow loops at a slight angle. Attach them with dabs of royal icing.

4 Adding the centres: Flatten the small balls of sugarpaste. Position them so that they hide the joins on the bow loops, and attach them with blobs of royal icing.

Beautiful bellbine

This beautiful cake, topped with a trailing bellbine flower,
is ideally suited for a couple marrying for the second time.

HAVE TO HAND

Ingredients: *30cm (12in) hexagonal fruit cake • apricot glaze • 1 kg marzipan • 2kg sugarpaste • royal icing • flower paste • egg white • green and ivory paste food colours • pink petal dust.*

Equipment: *38cm (15in) hexagonal cake board • nos. 0, 1 and 2 piping tubes • pair of dividers (optional) • waxed paper • fine paintbrush • pencil • small pair of scissors • 1m (1yd) 7mm wide raspberry-coloured ribbon • 1m (1yd) cream velvet ribbon • ribbon insertion tool or knife • floristry tape • 28g floristry wire • scriber • ball tool • piece of sponge • tilting turntable.*

Main skills: *wiring flower-paste sprays • ribbon insertion • bridge and extension work.*

DIFFICULTY	TIME	SUITABILITY
✓ ✓ ✓	⧗ ⧗ ⧗	🍾

If you have ever been faced with the problem of making a cake for a couple who are tying the knot for the second time around, you will know how hard it can be. The bride and groom will probably not want a very grand, tiered cake, but they would appreciate a special cake to mark the occasion. The cake featured here is ideal for a small or a second wedding, or even an anniversary.

TRAILING BELLBINE
The cake is decorated with bellbine, a gloriously pretty wild flower which is sometimes called bindweed. Gardeners will be familiar with it since it has a habit of growing very rapidly and climbing up other plants. It is pink and white and fragile-looking and gives no hint of its real strength, rather like the blushing bride herself perhaps!

The flower has a five-petal funnel shape, and can be teamed with a variety of other flowers. It should be especially pleasing to someone who has a love of wild, uncultivated flowers.

THE SIDE DECORATIONS
Each side of the hexagonal shape features bridge and extension work sweeping up the cake on an angle. If you

work on a tilting turntable, you can pipe one line of the bridge first, and then turn to the next side of the hexagon and do the same. Keep going around the cake in this way until you have built up all the bridges. This will take about six lines of piping. The bridge is then painted with runny, pink royal icing to match the ribbon inserts on the top of the cake.

MAKING THE FLOWERS
Each spray should contain leaves, buds and fully opened blooms. They are wired together, and then bound to another spray so that their stems cross and are hidden by the blooms. They are placed at intervals around the base and top of the cake. The finished effect is one of femininity and grace and is sure to be appreciated at any special occasion.

STEP-BY-STEP GUIDE

1 Marzipanning the cake: Brush the surface of the cake with apricot glaze and then coat it with a layer of marzipan.

2 Covering the cake: Sugarpaste the cake and board in the usual way.

3 Piping a row of shells: Using royal icing and a no. 2 tube, pipe a row of ivory-coloured shells around the base of the cake.

4 Marking the ribbon inserts: Make the inserts, using a set of dividers (or a template smaller than the cake) and a ribbon insertion tool. Leave the cake to dry for two days.

5 Inserting the ribbon: Go over the inserts with the insertion tool once again, and then insert a 7mm wide ribbon into each slot around the cake.

6 Adding the tube embroidery: Using a no. 0 tube and ivory-coloured royal icing, pipe tube embroidery between each ribbon slot.

7 Scribing the design: Pin the template into position. Working on a tilting turntable, use a scriber to scribe in the upper line and the lower scallop on each side of the hexagon. The straight edge on the left-hand side should sit at a right angle to the base of the cake so that the template curves up the cake.

8 Piping the bridgework: Using a no. 1 or 2 tube, pipe along the bottom scallop on each side of the hexagon until you have the required depth, and then leave it to dry.

9 Piping the extension work: For the extension work, use a no. 0 piping tube and fresh royal icing with egg white, sieved through muslin. Keep the extension lines straight, tidying them with a brush. Use a small straight edge to guide you, and start from the centre.

10 Piping the lace pieces: Using the template provided, pipe some lace pieces (more than you will need) with a no. 0 tube and ivory royal icing. Leave to dry, and then petal dust them in pink.

11 Attaching the lace pieces: Attach the piped lace pieces to the upper scribed line with dots of royal icing, positioning them gently with either a fine paintbrush or your fingers.

12 Making the flowers and leaves: Make the flowers according to the steps outlined below, and then leave them to dry.

13 Binding the flowers: Bind the bouquets together with green floristry tape. Place some around the sides of the cake and one in the centre.

14 Adding the ribbon: Attach an ivory-coloured ribbon around the edge of the cake board.

MAKING THE BELLBINE

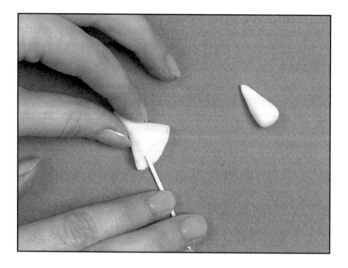

1 Forming the cone shape: Roll out some white flower paste into a cone shape. Insert a cocktail stick into the cone and roll it around in order to form the funnel shape. Leave this to dry on a piece of sponge.

2 Marking the funnel: Mark the dividing lines of the funnel with a cocktail stick and then use a ball tool to frill the edges of the funnel. Do not worry if the marks are not clear – they will show up once they have been petal dusted.

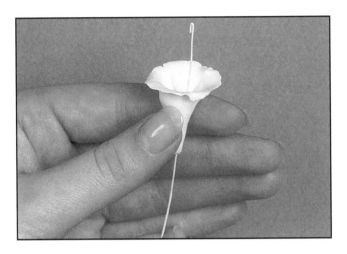

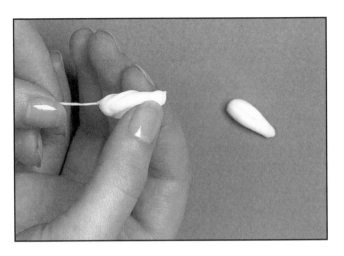

3 Inserting the wire: Dip the end of some hooked wire into egg white and thread through the funnel, straight end first, so that the hook rests in the throat of the flower.

4 Making the bud: Form another cone of flower paste and score lines on it with a cocktail stick. Dip straight piece of wire into egg white, thread through the cone and twist.

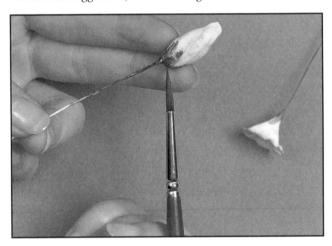

5 Adding petal dust: Dust the petals with a mixture of pink petal dusts, deepening the colour at the base. Dust the throat of the flower and highlight the veins of the petal.

6 Adding a calyx: Paint a calyx on the base of the flower and bud with green paste food colours. Extend the colouring down along the wire.

---

helpline

MAKING THE POSY

Using the template provided, cut some leaves from dark green, thinly rolled flower paste. Wire them in the usual way and leave them to dry by sticking them upright into a piece of foam. When they are dry, dust them with a selection of green petal dusts. Make a selection of bellbine buds and flowers, as shown above.

Starting with a bud at the left-hand end, tape a half-open flower next to it. Then tape an open flower and a leaf to each side. Bend the heads to the required angle with tweezers. Add a few more open flowers.

Then, working from the right, make another small spray, starting with a half-open flower, then adding an open flower and a leaf.

Join the two sprays together so that the wires cross each other. Clip away the excess wire from each end of the spray and bind the two stems together with tape.

Adjust the flower leaves of the spray so that no wires show. You can use tweezers to make a perfect arrangement. Store the sprays carefully and place them on the cake at the last minute in order to prevent any breakage or damage.

BUILDING THE SIDE DESIGN

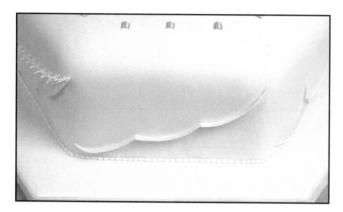

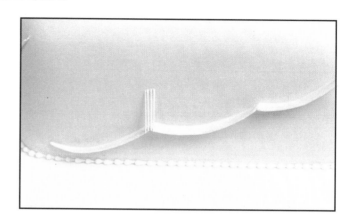

1 Piping the bridge: Using a no. 1 or 2 piping tube and fresh ivory-coloured royal icing, pipe a bridge on each side of the hexagon. Paint it with runny pink royal icing.

2 Piping the extension work: Using a no. 0 piping tube, pipe the extension work, keeping the lines as straight as possible and tucking the ends in under the bridge.

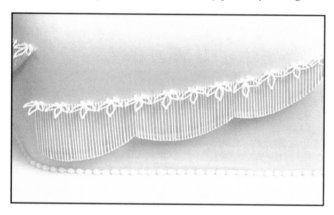

3 Attaching the lace pieces: Attach the piped lace pieces along the top line with tiny dots of royal icing. Use your fingers or a fine paintbrush to do this.

4 Completing the design: Add sprays of bellbine at intervals around the side of the cake so that they sit comfortably under the extension work.

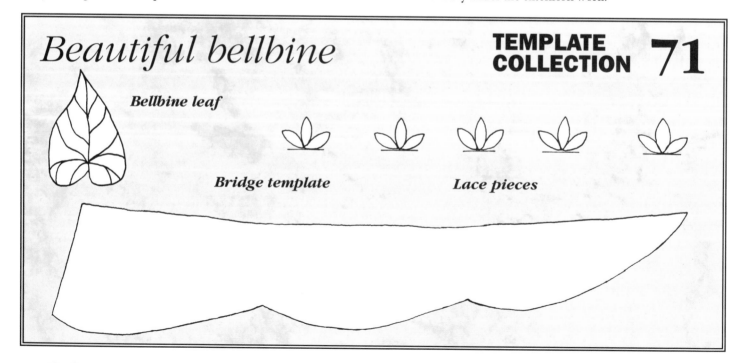

Beautiful bellbine

TEMPLATE COLLECTION 71

Bellbine leaf

Bridge template

Lace pieces

Happy Hogmanay

Celebrate the New Year Scottish style with this Hogmanay cake featuring tartan, thistles and lucky heather.

Whether you have Scottish friends or relatives, or just feel like joining in the Scottish atmosphere that prevails over the New Year celebrations, make our Happy Hogmanay cake to mark the occasion. It's decorated with classic Scottish symbols – tartan, thistles and heather.

We baked our cake in a scalloped oval tin, but you could use an oval tin and cut the scallops yourself. Make a rich fruit cake well in advance, so that you have plenty of time to give it liberal doses of whisky before coating it with marzipan and covering with white sugarpaste.

BALANCING THE COLOURS
This cake is one where the cake board plays an important part. Covering it with tartan fabric is a way of introducing a strong tartan motif that would be too overpowering on the cake itself. We have used a red tartan in fine wool that moulds itself easily round the scalloped shape of the board. If you have genuine Scottish connections, you will of course want to pick the right tartan for your family. The thistles in the posy need to be an authentic colour for the flower, but they could be more mauve than the violet-blue we have used.

You might also want to vary the colour used for the sugarpaste covering. For example, a yellow and black tartan could be complemented by pale lemon sugarpaste; or one that is basically green could be teamed with ivory sugarpaste.

We have used strips of the tartan fabric that covers the cake board to make the bows. But you may prefer to use a matching tartan ribbon. The finishing touch, the greenery round the edge of the cake board, can be provided with any kind of evergreen foliage, or even sprays of real heather.

USING TRADITIONAL FLOWERS
Two flowers associated with Scotland appear on the cake. The national emblem, the thistle, is piped on the sides and made into a posy on top. The white heather that grows on the moors is also included in the posy. If you don't want to make it, buy a spray from a florist's shop.

STEP-BY-STEP GUIDE

1 Preparing the cake: Brush the cake with apricot glaze and then coat it with a layer of marzipan. Allow to dry.

2 Covering the cake: Brush the surface with clear alcohol and then cover it with white sugarpaste. Leave it to dry.

3 Cutting tartan fabric: Use the cake board as a template to cut a piece of tartan fabric to cover it. Follow the scallops carefully, but have the fabric about 4cm (1½in) larger all round.

4 Covering the board: Lay the board (right side up) centrally on the fabric, matching scallop to scallop. Turn the surplus over and stick it to the board.

5 Positioning the cake: Place the covered cake on the board, making sure that the scallops match up exactly.

6 Piping a shell border: Using a no. 43 rope tube and white royal icing,

decorate the join between the cake and the board with a shell border.

7 Piping the thistles: Using a no. 1 tube and white royal icing, pipe thistles on the side of the cake at the point of each scallop.

8 Making the bows: Cut 5mm (¼in) strips from the remaining tartan fabric (or use ribbon). Make four small bows, cutting the loose ends at an angle.

9 Attaching the bows: Attach the bows to the side of the cake, in the indents of the scallops, with dabs of white royal icing. (You may prefer to do this after completing the decoration.)

10 Tracing the inscription: Using the template provided, trace the 'Happy Hogmanay' inscription on to the top of the cake. Position it off-centre in order to leave enough room for the posy of thistles.

11 Piping the inscription: Use a no. 1 tube and mid-blue royal icing to pipe on the inscription.

12 Making the thistles: Make up four thistles from violet-coloured sewing cotton and floristry wire (see below).

13 Making the leaves: Use the template provided to make four wired leaves from deep green flower paste.

14 Making the heather sprigs: Pipe green royal icing on to three lengths of wire to make the tiny, spiky heather leaves. When they are dry, pipe tiny white circles to represent the flowers.

15 Assembling the posy: Push the wires into a flattened ball of sugarpaste. Fill any gaps in the posy with small loops of tartan fabric.

16 Attaching the posy: Attach the posy to the cake top with royal icing.

MAKING THE THISTLES

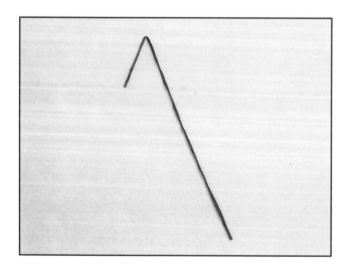

1 Hooking the wires: Cut four suitable lengths of 28g covered floristry wire for the stalks of the thistles. Then bend about 1cm (½in) of the wire back at the top in order to form a hook.

2 Winding the cotton: Wind approximately 2m (2yd) of violet-blue sewing cotton around your forefinger – but not too tightly. Pass the hooked end of a wire through to pull the loops off. Twist wire round itself to secure cotton.

3 Cutting through the loops: Using small sharp scissors, cut through the top of all the loops of cotton and allow the threads to fan out to form the flower head.

4 Finishing the flower heads: Apply green floristry tape to the base of the cotton. Wrap it round tightly and then tape down the stem. Neaten the top of each flower.

5 Making calyxes: Make balls of deep green flower paste. Use a sharpened dowel to form into cup shapes. Slip over stems and attach to base of flower with egg white.

6 Finishing off: Using a no. 0 piping tube and green royal icing, pipe upward-pointing spikes all around the green flower paste cups.

Inscription template

Happy Hogmanay

PROFESSIONAL SECRETS

Making heather and thistle leaves

- To create the tiny, spiky heather leaves, take some 28g floristry wire and cut it into pieces about 6cm (2½in) long.

- Wrap some smaller wire pieces around the central stem.

- Colour some royal icing dark green. Using a no. 0 tube, pipe the icing on to the wire, to create a spiky effect.

- When the icing is dry, pipe on some tiny white circles to represent the flowers.

- Colour some flower paste deep green for the thistle leaves. Roll the flower paste out thinly, creating a central ridge.

- Cut out several leaves, using a scalpel or sharp knife.

- Insert a length of 28g green-covered floristry wire into the base of each leaf.

- Vein the leaves with a suitable leaf veiner.

- Using a large soft brush, finish the leaves with green and brown petal dust.

ADDING THE DECORATIONS

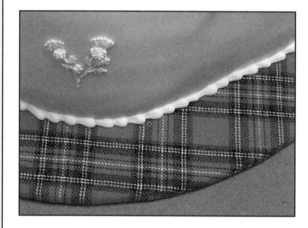

1 Piping the shells: Position the cake centrally on the cake board. Using a no. 43 rope tube and white royal icing, pipe a border of shells around the base of the cake in order to cover the join between the cake and the cake board.

2 Piping the inscription: Use the template provided to copy the 'Happy Hogmanay' inscription. Scribe the inscription on to the top of the cake, placing it off-centre to leave plenty of room for the thistle posy. Pipe over the outline using a no. 1 piping tube and blue royal icing.

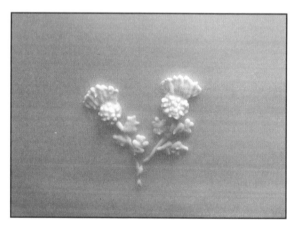

3 Piping the thistles: Using a no. 1 tube and white royal icing, pressure pipe four pairs of thistles on the side of the cake. Position them halfway down, at the point of each scallop.

4 Making the bows: Take the fabric left over from covering the cake board and cut out strips about 5mm (¼in) wide. Tie the strips into four small bows, and trim the loose ends at a 45° angle. Attach the bows to the cake with dabs of white royal icing, placing them at the indents between each scallop.

Crowning glory

The crown on top of this cake is the perfect platform for displaying a special floral arrangement.

HAVE TO HAND

Ingredients: 25cm (10in) round rich fruit cake • 12.5 cm wide x 4cm deep (5 x 1¹/₂in) round rich fruit cake • apricot glaze • 875g marzipan • 875g sugarpaste • clear alcohol • royal icing • flower paste • egg white • cornflour • selection of roses and pulled flowers • cream and ivory paste food colourings.

Equipment: 30cm (12in) round cake board • nos. 1 and 43 piping tubes • roller • scriber • greaseproof paper • tilting turntable • glass-headed pins • scalpel • satin ribbon with picot edge • sharp knife • fine, soft paintbrush • straight frill cutter • cocktail stick.

Main skills: making shaped cakes • attaching frills • piping embroidery • making sugar flowers.

DIFFICULTY	TIME	SUITABILITY
✓ ✓ ✓	⊠ ⊠ ⊠	🍾

This elegant, rounded wedding cake is ideal for a small wedding party. Its colour scheme is subtle and understated, being mainly ivory with peachy pinks and green appearing in the floral decoration.

DECORATING THE CROWN

The crown of the cake is topped with a crescent-shaped floral spray – a mixture of roses and small pulled flowers, interspersed with rose leaves and ribbon loops. You can choose any flowers to sit on the crown – perhaps something to match the bride's bouquet.

The crown itself is baked as a separate cake and is a useful feature on a single-tier cake, since it can serve the same purpose as an extra tier and be saved for the christening of the first baby.

SHAPING THE CAKE

The main cake is baked in a deep, round tin, and the sides are then shaped to form an even, gradual slope all the way round. If you prefer, you could bake the cake in a large pudding basin, in order to gain the same rounded effect.

The cake is covered with marzipan and ivory sugarpaste in the usual way, and piped embroidery is applied to the sides. The sides of the cake are sloped, so it is advisable to pin the template to the cake first, then mark it out with a scriber, to be sure of achieving an even effect all the way round. The embroidery is the only decoration on the larger cake, giving it a very restrained effect and drawing attention to the crown.

MAKING THE FRILL

The frill, inspired by a traditional wedding garter, is cut with a straight frill cutter. As each strip is applied, take care to ensure that the joins are as neat and unobtrusive as possible.

The clever effect of the double frill is actually created by applying lengths of a single frill to both the bottom of the crown and also to the top where it peeps over the edge. The join is then hidden with a picot-edged, satin ribbon.

STEP-BY-STEP GUIDE

1 Shaping the cake: Using a sharp knife, shape the larger fruit cake by cutting away the top edges so that the sides are rounded into a gentle slope.

2 Using a shaped basin: Alternatively, if you have a heat-proof bowl similar to the shape you want, you can bake the cake in this.

3 Marzipanning the cake: Cover both the large cake and the smaller crown cake with marzipan and then brush them both with clear alcohol.

4 Covering with sugarpaste: Cover both cakes with ivory-coloured sugarpaste and leave them to dry.

5 Covering the board: Cover the cake board with the same ivory-coloured sugarpaste and leave it to dry.

6 Attaching the cake: Use a few dabs of royal icing to secure the large covered cake to the board. Place the cake and the board on a tilting turntable.

7 Piping a row of shells: Using ivory royal icing and a no. 43 rope tube, pipe a line of shells around the base of the cake to hide the join.

8 Tracing the side design: Trace the side pattern from the template on to greaseproof paper.

9 Positioning the template: Place the paper template very carefully on the curved surface of the cake and secure it in position with two glass-headed pins.

10 Scribing the pattern: Scribe the pattern on to the side of the cake. You will find this easier to do if you use a tilting turntable.

11 Piping the embroidery: Keeping the cake on the turntable and, using a no. 1 tube and ivory royal icing, pipe the embroidered pattern around the sides, following the scribed lines. Set aside and leave to dry.

12 Attaching the crown: Position the small, circular covered cake on top of the large cake and attach it with a few dabs of royal icing.

13 Making the frills: Make the two frilled sections according to the steps outlined below.

14 Attaching the frill: Attach the frills by brushing egg white around the side of the small covered cake.

15 Attaching the ribbon: Hide the join around the middle of the small cake with an ivory-coloured, picot-edged, satin ribbon.

16 Attaching the flowers: Use royal icing to attach the flowers to the top of the crown.

CREATING THE CROWN

1 Attaching the crown: Position the crown centrally on the cake and attach it with royal icing. Any unevenness around the lower edge will be disguised by the frill.

2 Preparing the frill: Mix equal quantities of ivory sugarpaste and ivory flower paste, kneading well together. Roll the paste out thinly on a board dusted with cornflour.

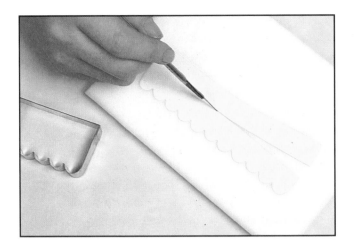

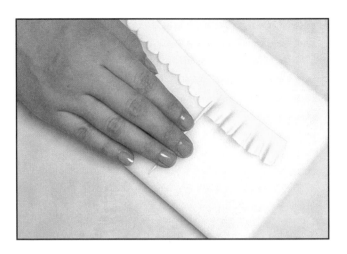

3 Cutting the frills: Use a straight frill cutter to cut lengths of frill. Trim away half the depth on the straight edge with a scalpel.

4 Frilling the edges: Roll a cocktail stick across each scallop of the frill to create the raised, frilled effect. Work quickly to prevent the paste from drying out.

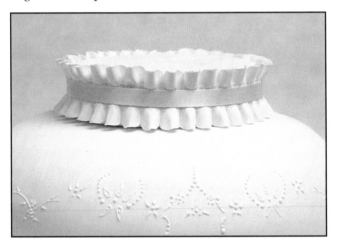

5 Attaching the frill: Curve frilled sections around the bottom of the crown and attach. Attach frill around the top of the crown in the same way. Add ribbon to hide the join.

6 Adding flowers: Position flowers on top of the crown. Pipe a crescent of royal icing on top to hold the flowers in place.

helpline ATTACHING THE FRILLS

The double frill is attached to the cake section by section – cut each frill to the length that you feel comfortable working with. It is very important that you maintain the shape of the frill as it sits around the cake. Look carefully at it before you begin – it is not shaped like a Garrett frill.

Each frill section should join the next without disrupting the shape of the frill in any way. Make sure that the joins are placed on an inward curve, altering the edge of the frill where appropriate.

A continuous band of egg white should be placed around the crown of the cake. Don't put egg white on the frill itself – it will show up as a shiny area. The way the frill is shaped means that the paste is only attached to the cake at certain points.

The best paste to use for this type of frill is a sugarpaste and flower paste mix. Flower paste used on its own would dry out too quickly and become too brittle to work with, while sugarpaste used on its own would be too soft to hold the stiff folds of the frill.

The ribbon that is attached afterwards to hide the join should complement the frill – we have chosen ivory, but another pastel shade would look just as pretty.

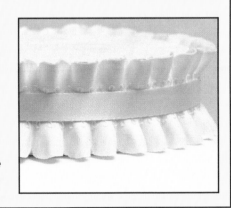

Embroidery template

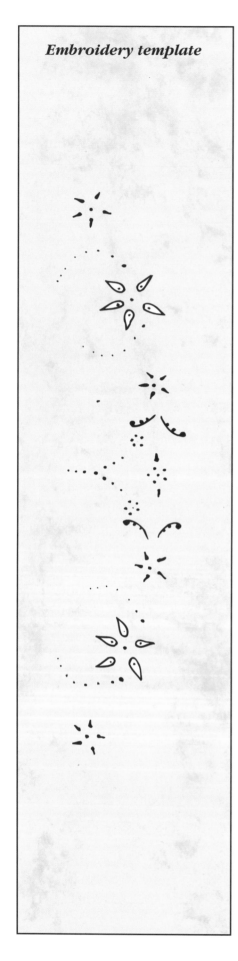

CREATING THE SIDE DESIGN

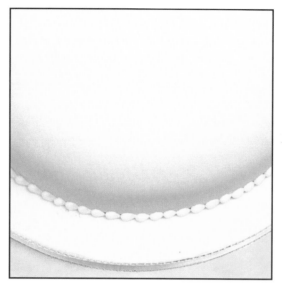

1 Piping a row of shells: Once the sugarpaste coating on the cake has dried, colour a small quantity of royal icing with cream paste food colouring in order to match the ivory sugarpaste. Then, using a no. 43 rope tube, pipe a row of shells around the base of the cake where it meets the board.

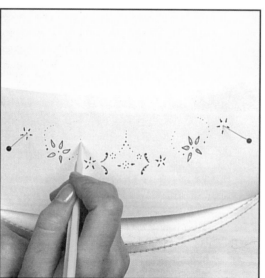

2 Scribing the design: Using the template provided, scribe the design on to the side of the cake. You may find it easier if you pin it in place – and it will certainly be easier on a tilting turntable. Remember that the pattern should be continuous. Continue to scribe until the pattern has been marked continuously around the cake.

3 Piping the design: Using a no. 1 piping tube and ivory-coloured royal icing, pipe over the scribed lines. If you make a mistake, lift it off with a fine, soft paintbrush. If you prefer, you could colour the icing a very pale pink in order to complement the colour of the roses on the top of the cake.

Fantasy frills

This hexagonal cake provides a wonderful opportunity for decorating all six sides with such a wealth of frills that very little extra decoration is needed.

HAVE TO HAND

Ingredients: 23cm (9in) hexagonal rich fruit cake • apricot glaze • 1kg marzipan • clear spirit • 750g sugarpaste • cream and apricot food colours • royal icing.

Equipment: 30cm (12in) round cake board • scriber • greaseproof paper • absorbent kitchen paper • tilting turntable • Garrett frill cutter • cocktail stick • nos. 1 and 2 piping tubes • pins • 1m (1yd) cream satin ribbon.

Main skill: fitting sugarpaste frills.

DIFFICULTY   TIME   SUITABILITY

Frills added to the sides of a cake draw the eye immediately. A double frill adds even more emphasis, while an inverted double frill adds an unusual, ruffled and very striking decorative effect.

The technique needs to be handled with some care if the frill is not to be too overwhelming. The balance has been achieved perfectly in this hexagonal cake, where a double frill and an inverted double frill provide an attractive frame for some simple, piped flowers on all six sides.

CREATING INVERTED FRILLS

An inverted double frill, where the frilled edges point upwards instead of hanging down, is produced in exactly the same way as a normal frill, but has to

be attached with the cake turned upside down. It is best to work on a tilting turntable, so you have a really good view of the sides. If you don't have one, see the Helpline on page 35. Position the cake on the cake board before starting work, as you will not be able to touch the sides after the frills are in position. Before inverting the cake, protect the top against possible damage or marks by spreading absorbent kitchen paper on top of the turntable.

Work around the cake, attaching the frills with piped royal icing along a previously scribed line close to the top edge. Because the cake has been inverted, the top edge now seems like the base of the cake. Make sure that all the frills are dry and secure before you return the cake to its normal position.

COMPLETING DECORATION

The two frills that make up the other half of the frilled framework can then be applied to all six sides of the cake.

When the frills are complete, use the template and a scriber to mark out a design to go in between them. Pipe the same design on each side, using shades of royal icing which complement those chosen for the sugarpaste frills.

If the sides of the cake are elaborately decorated, then the top needs very little adornment. Simply add an inscription – piped in the colour of the deeper frill – and perhaps a simple spray of flowers in toning colours.

A simple but beautiful cake such as this one would be ideal for a formal birthday celebration, an anniversary, or even a small wedding.

STEP-BY-STEP GUIDE

1 Preparing the cake: Glaze the cake with boiled apricot jam and cover with marzipan. Allow to dry overnight.

2 Coating the cake: Brush the cake with clear spirit and then coat it with cream-coloured sugarpaste. Leave until the sugarpaste is thoroughly dry.

3 Attaching the cake to the board: Coat the board with cream-coloured sugarpaste. Attach the cake to the board and, using a no. 2 tube, pipe shells around the base to hide the join.

4 Inverting the cake: Cover the turntable with absorbent kitchen paper. Then carefully invert the cake and the board on to the turntable.

5 Marking the frill positions: Cut the template provided from greaseproof paper. Pin it in position, on one of the sides of the cake. Mark all round the template with a scriber.

6 Creating the apricot frills: Colour some sugarpaste apricot. Cut out a frill with a Garrett frill cutter, frill the edges with a toothpick, cut open at one side and straighten the frill out. For a narrower frill, trim the straight edge.

7 Attaching the frills: Use a no. 1 tube to pipe a line of royal icing along the scribed line, and then attach the frill. Repeat the process for all six sides.

8 Creating the cream frills: Colour some sugarpaste cream, then roll it out and cut and frill as before.

9 Attaching the frills: Using a no. 1 tube, pipe a line of royal icing on the inner edge of an apricot frill and attach the first cream frill. Continue until all the frills are attached; leave until dry.

10 Repositioning the cake: Remove the cake from the turntable and replace it the right way up.

11 Completing the frills: Make and attach a double frill along the lower scribed edge on each side of the cake.

12 Marking the central decorations: Using a scriber, mark the position of the central floral decoration on all six sides.

13 Decorating the frill edges: Using a no. 1 piping tube and cream royal icing, pipe evenly spaced dots around the inner edges of the frills.

14 Adding the central decoration: Using apricot royal icing and a no. 1 tube, pipe in the central floral decoration. Add cream leaves, and pipe tiny cream flowers around the central ones.

15 Completing the cake: Decorate the top with a spray of apricot and cream roses or other flowers. Attach the ribbon to the cake board.

MAKING THE FRILLS

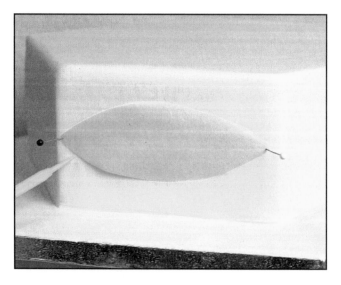

1 Marking frill positions: Position the template provided centrally on one side of the cake, pinning it lightly to secure it. Mark round the edge with a scriber.

2 Cutting out the first frill: Colour some sugarpaste deep apricot and roll it out. Cut a frill with a Garrett frill cutter. Cut the circle, straighten it, and trim the straight edge.

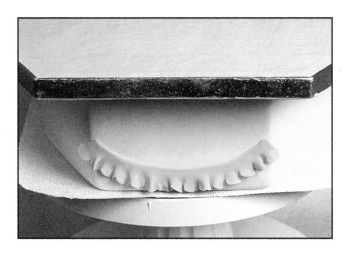

3 Attaching apricot frills: Lightly frill edges with a cocktail stick and cut open at one side. Invert cake on to turntable. Attach frill to scribed line with piped royal icing.

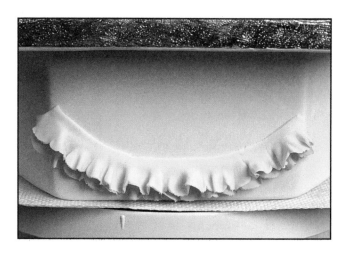

4 Adding cream frills: Make a frill exactly as before from cream sugarpaste. With the cake still inverted, attach frill along the inner edge of first frill with piped royal icing.

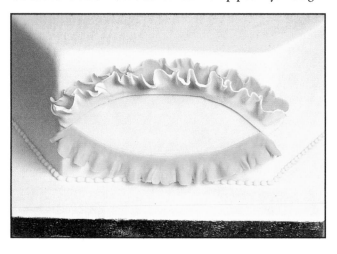

5 Adding second apricot frill: Make another apricot frill as before. Carefully return cake to upright position and pipe a line of royal icing over lower scribed line. Attach frill.

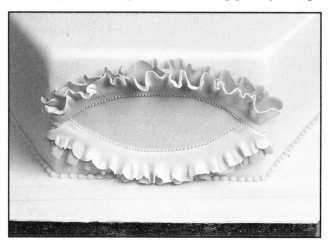

6 Adding second cream frill: Make another cream frill exactly as before. Attach to the apricot frill with a line of royal icing, ensuring a neat finish where the edges meet.

helpline WORKING INVERTED FRILLS

Inverted frills look very impressive, and it takes a little extra care to produce them as the cake must be worked on upside-down and left in this position until the sugarpaste has dried thoroughly.

Ideally, work with the cake on a tilting turntable. Start by securing the cake extra firmly to the cake board so that there is absolutely no risk of it coming loose. Having the cake board in position first makes it much easier to handle the cake, especially when all the frills have been worked and you cannot touch the sides.

Put a couple of sheets of absorbent kitchen paper on the turntable top to protect the surface of the cake from being damaged. Pick the cake and cake board up carefully and then invert it on to the turntable. Work all 12 inverted frills and then leave them to dry before turning the cake the right way up in order to work the remaining 12 frills.

An ordinary turntable is not really suitable for working inverted frills,

as you must have the cake tilted in order to see the sides clearly. Unless you can work out a really secure way of propping it up from below, it's better to use an alternative technique.

Secure the cake firmly to the cake board as before. Place a second cake board on the work surface, on top of a dampened tea towel to prevent it slipping, and prop it up securely. A pair of plastic door wedges is ideal; failing this, use whatever comes to hand. Cover the propped-up board with sheets of absorbent kitchen paper and carefully invert cake plus cake board on to it. Work the frills as before and leave them to dry thoroughly before turning the cake the right way up again.

If you have some thin sheet foam to hand, you can use this instead of absorbent kitchen paper to protect the cake top from being damaged. Cut the foam sheet down to the approximate size of the turntable or cake board before putting it in position.

DESIGN TOUCH

You can vary the colours of the frills and alter the nature of the central frill decoration in a variety of ways to produce a different effect.

For a more subtle effect, you could make up both layers of the frill in cream sugarpaste and then simply brush the frilled, cut edge with coloured petal dust, matching this to the colour of the central, piped flower.

Instead of piping a central flower design, you could add lines of ribbon-insertion work, parallel to the inner edges of the frill. Another idea would be to use the frills as a framework for a run-out plaque on which you can work a floral motif in bas-relief. Alternatively, work a simple broderie anglaise decoration in the six areas between the frills. These sections could also be worked on with an embossing stamp to emboss a pattern into the sugarpaste. Finish by lightly tinting it with petal dust. (In both the last two cases, work the decoration on freshly applied sugarpaste. Do this before applying the frill, outlining the central area with the template and scriber.)

If you decorate the cake top with a posy of sugar flowers, you might like to repeat them in the central motifs, piping a different flower in each panel.

PIPING THE CENTRAL DESIGN

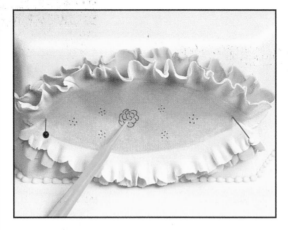

1 Marking out the side design: Pin the template provided very carefully into position at the centre of the frills. Then, using a scriber, mark the central flower of the piped design. Take care when removing the template so that it can be reused on the remaining five sides.

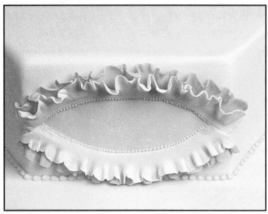

2 Piping an edging on to the frill: Using cream royal icing and a no. 1 piping tube, pipe a line of evenly spaced dots around the inside edges of both the upper and lower frills to neaten them.

3 Piping the design: Using a no. 1 piping tube and deep apricot-coloured royal icing, pipe on the central flower. Then add the leaves, using a no. 1 piping tube and cream royal icing.

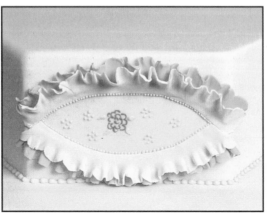

4 Completing the decoration: Using a no. 1 piping tube and cream-coloured royal icing, pipe a series of dots to create the tiny flowers that surround the central, apricot flower.

With love from Ted

This delightful cake, featuring an old-fashioned Teddy bear surrounded by broderie-anglaise frills and ribbon inserts, will suit many different occasions.

HAVE TO HAND

Ingredients: 20cm (8in) round fruit cake • 900g marzipan • apricot glaze • clear spirit • 1kg sugarpaste • food colourings.

Equipment: 28cm (11in) round cake board • Garrett frill cutter • acetate • five-petal eyelet cutter • rose and leaf embossers • dividers • cocktail stick • nos. 1 and 2 piping tubes • fine paintbrush • ribbon insertion tool • 1.25m (1½yd) red ribbon • 1m (1yd) white ribbon.

Main skills: embossing • ribbon insertion • making a runout • piping.

DIFFICULTY	TIME	SUITABILITY

The plain, classic effect of the flat frills, combined with the simple teddy-bear decoration, make this a cake with a number of uses. As well as being a child's birthday cake, it could be made as a get-well cake, a grown-up's birthday cake, a welcome-home cake – or for almost any informal occasion.

The teddy is modelled on an old-fashioned bear, not a modern one, which gives him an old-world charm. This is emphasised by the surrounding broderie-anglaise frills and ribbon-insertion decoration.

The cake features dramatic use of colour, as the inscription, the ribbon inserts and the teddy bear's bunch of roses are all bright red. But as each element is quite small, there is no risk of the colour being overpowering. You could, of course, vary the colour to suit your occasion, but keep to fairly strong shades to get the same effect.

BUILDING UP THE DESIGN
The cake is decorated in a series of distinct stages, so you can spread the work over several days. First, pipe a snail's trail around the base. Then mark the positions for the ribbon insertions while the sugarpaste is still soft. Create and emboss the deep frill and attach it to the cake. Carefully paint in the embossed red roses and green leaves, using a fine, pointed paintbrush. Add the narrow frill and leave to dry for a few days.

Meanwhile, run out the teddy on to acetate. When dry, paint in his facial features and make his posy of roses. Add the eyelet and frill-edge piping and the ribbon inserts. Pipe on the inscription. Attach the run-out teddy and posy to the cake. (If you want to keep the teddy, you could attach him to a sugarpaste plaque first.) Finish off with red and white ribbons around the cake and the cake board.

FRILLING ALTERNATIVES
If you would like to make the flat frill stand out, put a rope of sugarpaste around the top of the cake before attaching it. Place the rope about 5mm (¼in) down from the top of the cake. When applying the frill, make sure its top edges cover the rope.

Alternatively, cover the top of the cake with a sugarpaste drape measuring 4cm (1½in) wider than the diameter of the cake and attach a frill to this.

STEP-BY-STEP GUIDE

1 Preparing the cake: Cover the cake with apricot glaze, then apply a layer of marzipan. Leave to dry.

2 Covering the cake: Brush the marzipan with clear spirit. Cover the cake with white sugarpaste. Do not leave to dry at this stage.

3 Covering the cake board: Cover the cake board with white sugarpaste separately from the cake.

4 Piping a snail's trail: Set the cake in position on the cake board. Then, using a no. 2 tube and white royal icing, pipe a snail's trail all around the join.

5 Preparing for the ribbon insertion: Mark positions for the ribbon insertion around the top of the cake, close to the outside, using a ribbon insertion tool. Leave for a day or two until the sugarpaste is dry.

6 Creating the deep frill: Cut out the deep, flat frill from white sugarpaste, Use an eyelet cutter on alternate scallops; emboss the remaining ones with a rose embosser. Attach to the cake.

7 Creating the narrow frill: Cut out a narrow frill and attach it over the deep one with white royal icing.

8 Decorating the narrow frill: Using a cocktail stick, pierce holes in the centre of each scallop.

9 Painting the decoration: Using red and green paste food colours mixed with clear spirit, paint in the rose and leaf details on the deep frill.

10 Adding piping: Using a no. 1 tube and white royal icing, pipe a snail's trail around the top edge of the cake. Also pipe round all the eyelets and the scalloped edge of the deep frill.

11 Inserting ribbon: Insert the ribbon into the slots on top of the cake.

12 Flooding the teddy bear: Flood the shape of the teddy bear in cream-coloured royal icing.

13 Painting the teddy bear: Use brown, black and peach paste food colourings to paint in the fur and features. Attach the bear to the cake.

14 Creating the roses: Make a posy of tiny roses from red flower paste, and attach them to the bear with royal icing.

15 Piping the inscription: Using the template provided as a scribing guide and a no. 1 tube, pipe on the inscription with first white, then red, royal icing.

16 Adding ribbons: Attach the red ribbon to the base of the cake and the white ribbon to the edge of the board.

CREATING THE FLAT FRILLS

1 Cutting the wide frill: Using template provided or a frill cutter, roll out some white sugarpaste and cut a length of frill. Use the eyelet cutter in alternate scallops. Emboss a rose and two leaves in the remaining scallops.

2 Attaching the wide frill: Using a no. 1 tube, pipe a line of white royal icing on the side of the cake around the top edge, and then carefully attach the frill. Work quickly, before the frill begins to set.

3 Adding the narrow frill: Cut this frill with a Garrett frill cutter, trimming it down to size with a scalpel. Attach it on top of the wide frill with a line of royal icing.

4 Decorating the narrow frill: Insert a cocktail stick into the centre of each scallop on the narrow frill. Paint the roses and leaves with red and green paste food colouring.

5 Adding white piping and ribbon: Pipe a snail's trail around top edge of cake. Pipe round the eyelets and lower edge of deep frill. When dry, add the ribbon inserts.

6 Adding the inscription and teddy: Using the template as a guide, pipe the inscription in white, then red royal icing with a no. 1 tube. Position the teddy and roses.

helpline   ADDING DECORATIVE TOUCHES

As the decorative touches on this cake are carried out in strong colours, they need to be done very neatly to look professional.

Paint the embossed roses and leaves on the deep frill with red and green paste food colouring mixed with clear spirit. Use a very fine, pointed paintbrush. Give them an illusion of depth by diluting the colouring with more spirit to create paler areas.

You could use petal dust instead, but it is more difficult to keep the colour in exactly the areas required.

We painted the roses and leaves after adding the narrow top frill, but you may find it

more convenient to reverse the procedure.

Remember not to let the sugarpaste covering dry out before making the incisions for the ribbon inserts. If it is not still soft when these are made, it can easily crack.

When working the inscription, pipe it in white royal icing first, then overpipe in red once the first layer is dry. This means that any mistakes made in red can be lifted off without the colour staining the cake top.

Continue the red theme with teddy's posy of roses and a band of narrow red ribbon set just above the snail's trail that has been piped around the base of the cake.

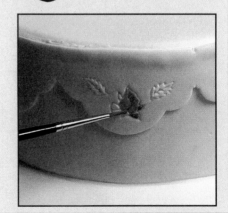

- The teddy bear can be handled in a number of different ways. Choose the one that you feel most comfortable with.

- We have run him out on to acetate. This has the advantage that if anything should go wrong at the painting stage, then you can simply start again.

- However, if the teddy bear is run out on to acetate, you must use a cranked palette knife to transfer him to the cake top.

- If you want to keep the teddy bear after the cake has been eaten, place him on a sugarpaste plaque first, then on the cake.

- If you run the teddy out on to a sugarpaste plaque, attach the roses before positioning the plaque on the cake.

- If you run the teddy out on to acetate, you will probably find it easier to attach him to the cake first, then put the posy of roses in place afterwards.

- When painting the teddy, take care to capture his old-fashioned character. First, get the colour of the fur exactly right. It should be a soft yellow-brown.

- Use dark brown colour to draw a line upwards from the eyes to the ears to indicate the stitching of the head seams. Also use dark brown for the undersides of the teddy bear's paws.

- Outline the black eyes in deep peach to simulate the shiny, old-fashioned, glass eyes.

CREATING THE TEDDY BEAR

1 Flooding the teddy shape: Trace the outline from the template on to greaseproof paper, then tape a piece of acetate over the top. Flood the teddy bear shape in dark cream royal icing. Leave to dry thoroughly.

2 Starting to paint the teddy: Using two shades of brown paste food colours mixed with clear spirit, paint in the teddy bear's fur, paws and ears. Use the darker brown to colour the bottom of all four paws and to shade the insides of the ears.

3 Adding the teddy bear's features: Using black paste food colour and a fine, pointed brush, paint in the nose, mouth and eyes. Then use deep peach paste food colouring to encircle the eyes. Lift the teddy bear carefully off the acetate and attach him to the cake top with dabs of royal icing.

4 Adding the posy of roses: Form some red flower paste into tiny balls. Flatten these between sheets of acetate to form petals. Combine the petals into rose shapes and add green rose leaves. Attach the posy to the teddy bear with royal icing.

Drape with frills

This frilled drape sits prettily on the cake top and is balanced by a bouquet of trailing ivy and small blossoms.

HAVE TO HAND

Ingredients: 18cm (7in) round rich fruit cake • apricot glaze • 875g marzipan • 875g sugarpaste • clear spirit • peach food colouring • royal icing • selection of wired paste flowers and pulled blossoms.

Equipment: 30cm (10in) round cake board • no. 1 piping tube • narrow satin ribbon • tracing paper • large tweezers • cocktail stick • compass • pencil • card • scissors • green floristry tape • Garrett frill cutter • floristry ribbon • green floristry wire.

Main skills: positioning and attaching drapes and frills • making and wiring flowers.

DIFFICULTY	TIME	SUITABILITY

This elegant cake has an unusual frilled drape on the top, set off by a beautiful spray of mixed pulled flowers and blossoms. The drape, which has the appearance of a frilled tablecloth, stands away from the cake, an effect achieved by covering the top and sides of the cake in a particular way to create a hard edge.

The cake is first covered with marzipan. Then the side (not the top) is sugarpasted to create the right effect. The drape falls in folds to the back and sides of the cake, and is lifted to the front.

ATTACHING THE FRILLS

The double frill is cut in sections with a Garrett frill cutter. The white frill sits on top with the peach frill just peeping out underneath. The edge of the drape rises at the front of the cake, exposing more of the colour of the lower frill. Finish the edge of each frill with a piped snail's trail and add some tube embroidery around the edges of the drape. This decoration should be kept simple as the double frill and the spray of flowers have quite a dramatic impact.

MAKING THE BOUQUET

When making the spray to decorate the top of the cake, you will find that it helps if you first draw out the required finished shape of the spray, in the correct size, on a piece of tracing paper. You can then lay this over the top of the cake in order to check the effect. You can also use it as a working guide as you bind in your flowers, to keep the correct proportions of the spray. Once you begin to experiment with the wiring and placement of bouquets, you will find that there are many ways of presenting blooms, so making each of your cakes rather special.

Because the cake has a light and delicate feel to it, it is preferable to use pastel-coloured ribbons and blossoms so that you do not detract from the fluid movement of the drape and bouquet.

This cake would suit any formal occasion – a birthday, wedding anniversary or small wedding. In the case of the latter, the colours of the frill could be tied in to the bride's dress, while the spray of flowers could be copied from the bridal bouquet.

STEP-BY-STEP GUIDE

1 Covering the cake: Brush the cake with apricot glaze and coat it with marzipan. Leave it to dry.

2 Covering with sugarpaste: Brush marzipan with clear spirit. Roll out white sugarpaste and coat sides of cake. Cover the board with white sugarpaste.

3 Positioning the cake: Position the cake centrally on the board and secure it with dabs of royal icing.

4 Piping a snail's trail: Using a no. 1 tube and white royal icing, pipe a snail's trail around the base of the cake where it meets the board.

5 Attaching the ribbon: Attach a length of narrow, peach, satin ribbon around the cake just above the snail's trail and secure it with royal icing.

6 Cutting the drape: Make a circular template with a diameter of 23cm (9in). Roll out some white sugarpaste and use the template to cut a circle from the sugarpaste. Do not distort the drape when you lift it.

7 Attaching the drape: Moisten the marzipan on cake top. Attach the drape, allowing 2.5cm (1in) to overlap the front. The rest should fall in folds to the back and sides. Leave to dry for 2 or 3 days.

8 Making the peach-coloured frills: Cut circular sections of frill from peach-coloured sugarpaste with a Garrett frill cutter. Cut them open and then frill the edges with a cocktail stick.

9 Attaching the frill: Attach frill to edge of drape with royal icing. If you have difficulty handling the length of frill, cut it into smaller sections. Always handle the frill and drape very gently.

10 Making the white frill: Make a white frill and attach it to the cake in the same way as the peach. The peach frill should peep from beneath the white frill and the white frill must cover the join between the peach frill and the drape.

11 Piping a snail's trail: Using a no. 1 piping tube and white royal icing, pipe a snail's trail where the white frill meets the drape .

12 Piping tube embroidery: Use a no. 1 tube and white royal icing to pipe tube embroidery around the drape. Leave a gap where the bouquet will be attached.

13. Making the bouquet: Make up the floral arrangement for the cake top. Include yellow mini irises, ivy leaves, pink blossoms, purple pulled flowers, daisies and roses. Attach to cake top by placing the stem in a bulb of sugarpaste.

14. Adding ribbon loops: Hide the sugarpaste and stem by adding peach ribbon loops.

ATTACHING THE FRILLS

1 Piping a snail's trail: Cover the cake with marzipan and then the side only with sugarpaste. Position centrally on the board. Pipe a snail's trail around the base.

2 Trimming with ribbon: When the piping is dry, attach a length of ribbon above the piping. This must be done now, before the drape is attached to the cake.

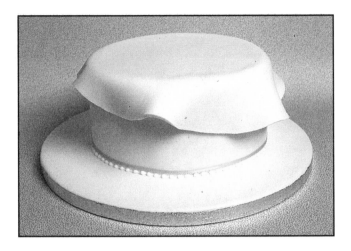

3 Adding the drape: Cut the drape from sugarpaste. Dampen marzipan on cake top and position drape over cake so that most of the drape falls to the back. Leave to dry.

4 Attaching first frill: Roll some peach sugarpaste and cut sections with a Garrett frill cutter. Cut open, frill edges with a cocktail stick and attach to edge of drape.

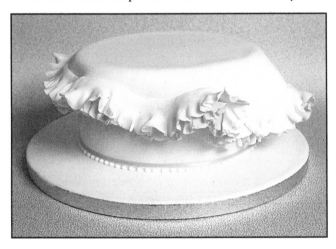

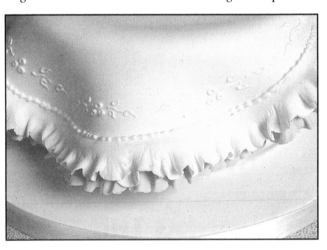

5 Adding the top frill: Roll out some white sugarpaste and cut more frills. Apply over the peach frill so that it exposes the bottom edge and covers the top edge.

6 Final decoration: Pipe another snail's trail on the top edge of the frill where it joins the drape. Pipe tube embroidery above the snail's trail at regular intervals.

Alternatives

SHAPING FLORAL ARRANGEMENTS

We have used a teardrop shape as a pattern for our floral arrangement, but you can change this depending on the shape of your cake and the position your bouquet is going to occupy on the cake top.

Try wiring bouquets into a circular shape, or base the outline on a letter. Try a 'C' shape, for example, or an 'S' curve. A 'V'-shaped arrangement can look very attractive on a square cake. You do not have to wire everything on to the same

stem – you could make a number of smaller sprays and then wire them into the appropriate shape. Use your outline as a guide and make sure you know where the bouquet will sit on the cake.

If the cake is for a wedding, you can present a miniature replica of the bride's bouquet, changing the colour scheme to suit. The arrangement can then be saved and given to someone very special, perhaps the bride's grandmother.

Keep a selection of paste flowers to hand, but if you still feel unsure of yourself, you can practise wiring with fabric flowers. You can even make an arrangement which features both paste and fabric flowers.

Fill in any smaller gaps with tiny fabric flowers rather than paste flowers, since the latter can be very time-consuming to make. You may have to replace the stems of the fabric flowers first because they are often thick and unwieldy.

ASSEMBLING THE BOUQUET

1 Beginning the bouquet: Draw an outline of the required finished shape on tracing paper. Wire together some ivy leaves with small leaves at the top. Add purple flowers and yellow mini irises. Bind with floristry tape.

2 Adding more blossoms: Add some daisies and some pale pink blossoms further down the bouquet but sitting centrally. Place a rose and rose leaf to one side of the bouquet, keeping an eye on the overall shape.

3 Making a second spray: Bind in another rose and rose leaf and place them to the opposite side of the other rose, making sure that you keep a balanced effect. Make another small spray of yellow and blue flowers.

4 Finishing the bouquet: Bind together the two bouquets of flowers. Use tweezers to arrange each flower so that it sits in the right position and to ensure that the shape follows the outlined tracing.

helpline — WIRING FLORAL ARRANGEMENTS

One of the most important things to consider about the above floral arrangement is its shape. It should build to a point and drape delicately over the front of the cake. The movement of the floral arrangement is quite fluid and emphasises the drape itself.

The flowers should balance the longer length of the drape at the back of the cake; therefore, ivy is a particularly good choice for this kind of hanging arrangement since it leads the trailing effect over the edge of the cake. There are many other types of hanging plants which you could also consider when making such a bouquet.

The ivy leaves are twisted together and bound with green floristry wire. This then serves as the central stem to which all the other flowers are wired. Each flower is wired individually, covered with green floristry tape and then bound tightly into the central bouquet. Make sure that the wiring is neat, tidy and not too bulky, otherwise it will be hard to manipulate and will look ugly when placed on the cake.

An outline of the bouquet is particularly important since it guides you as you wire the flowers. Remember to control the height of the arrangement as well as the width and

length. A graduated effect can look very pretty – in this case the arrangement gains height as it bends over the side of the cake.

Use a large pair of tweezers to shape and bend the flower heads until you are satisfied with the arrangement.

The flowers can then be attached to the cake in a number of different ways. Here, the stem is placed in a ball of sugarpaste which is attached to the cake. Ribbon loops are then added to emphasise the colours of the flowers and to hide the base of the stem. Ribbons not only look extremely pretty, but they can also hide a multitude of sins!

Golden-wedding cake

A golden wedding calls for a really special cake, and this stunning and elegant two-tier creation would be absolutely perfect.

HAVE TO HAND

Ingredients: 25 x 30cm (10 x 12in) oval fruit cake • 10cm (4in) round fruit cake • apricot glaze • 1.5kg marzipan • 2kg sugarpaste • flower paste • royal icing • egg white • green, red and gold paste food colourings • gold lustre petal dust.

Equipment: dowelling • rose-petal cutters • white floristry tape • dried gypsophila • 30 x 35cm (12 x 14in) cake board • 15cm (6in) round cake card • sharp knife • greaseproof paper • pins • insertion tool • Garrett frill cutter • cocktail stick • nos. 0, 1 and 2 piping tubes • paintbrush • 1m (1yd) white ribbon • 1m (1yd) gold ribbon.

Main skills: ribbon insertion • flooding runouts • shaping cakes.

DIFFICULTY	TIME	SUITABILITY

This large oval cake, coated in ivory sugarpaste, then frilled, and decorated with a spray of roses, carnations, ivy and gypsophila, features a bell as a separate tier. The tier is positioned off-centre on top of the cake and is supported by tiny pillars made from dowelling which has been trimmed with twists of the gold ribbon used in the ribbon insertion throughout the cake. The golden theme is continued with the run-out number '50' which adorns the bell.

The ribbon-insertion points on the cake and bell must be marked while the sugarpaste is still soft, otherwise the surface of the cake could be damaged. It is a good idea at this stage to decide on the position of the posy pick, as it is easier to carve out the paste while it is still soft. Once it has set hard, you run the risk of cracking the surface. A posy pick is essential, as wired flowers must not be placed directly into the cake.

IMAGINATIVE ALTERNATIVES

If you don't have a cake tin which is the right size and shape for baking the bell, you can use a large baked-bean tin or fruit tin which has been thoroughly washed and dried. The bell shape can be carved once the cake has cooled.

You can vary the flowers in the spray to suit the season, or to match flowers that you know the recipients like. Since it is a golden wedding cake you may prefer to add golden flowers. Remember that the spray must appear balanced from where it is placed on the bell.

An alternative way of presenting the run-out numbers on the bell would be to put them on to a decorated plaque. This could then be detached before the cake is cut and kept as a memento.

Remember that gold paint is inedible and all items painted with it should be removed before the cake is eaten.

STEP-BY-STEP GUIDE

1 Preparing the cake: Brush large cake with apricot glaze and coat with a layer of marzipan. Then brush with clear alcohol and cover with ivory sugarpaste. Cover cake board with white sugarpaste.

2 Marking ribbon-insertion points: Use the template to mark the ribbon-insertion points on top of cake with a pin. Cut slits at the marked points.

3 Making the cake frill: Mix equal amounts of sugarpaste and flower paste. Roll out and cut sections of frill with a Garrett frill cutter. Frill edges and attach frill to cake, looping it up at centre front.

4 Decorating the frill: Using a no. 2 tube and white royal icing, pipe a snail's trail around the top of the frill. Dust edges with gold lustre petal dust.

5 Adding ribbon: Insert lengths of gold ribbon into slits. Pipe triangles of dots between each insertion with a no. 0 piping tube.

6 Writing the inscription: Using the template, scribe the inscription. Using a no. 1 tube, pipe inscription in white royal icing, then paint in gold.

7 Making the flower spray: Use cutters to make several red roses and pale pink carnations. Wire them together with ivy and dried gypsophila.

8 Positioning the posy: Place the posy at the front of the cake, securing it in a small ball of sugarpaste.

9 Making the pillars: Cut three lengths of dowelling and sharpen one end of each.

10 Positioning the pillars: Use the template to mark insertion points, then prepare these points by gouging them gently with a scalpel. Then, push the pillars in right through to the base of the cake. Cover the protruding sections of the pillars with white floristry tape and decorate them with gold ribbon.

11 Making the bell: Carve the small cake into a bell shape. Cover it with marzipan and sugarpaste and set it on a sugarpaste-covered cake card. While the paste is still soft, carve out a section where the posy pick will be positioned.

12 Making ribbon insertions and frill: Mark the ribbon-insertion points on the bell. Make a narrow Garrett frill, open it out and attach it to the bell. Finish the top with a snail's trail.

13 Decorating the bell: Dust edges of frill with gold lustre dust. Insert gold ribbon into the slits and pipe a triangle of dots in between each insertion. Run out number '50' in white royal icing and paint it with gold food colouring. Attach it with royal icing. Put bell on pillars.

14 Attaching posy: Insert posy pick and flowers into the top of the bell.

15 Finishing off: Trim the cake board with white ribbon.

ASSEMBLING THE CAKE

1 Marking ribbon insertion: Prepare the cake and use the template and a pin to mark ribbon-insertion points in the sugarpaste on the top. Remove the template and cut insertion slits with a scalpel, sharp knife or insertion tool.

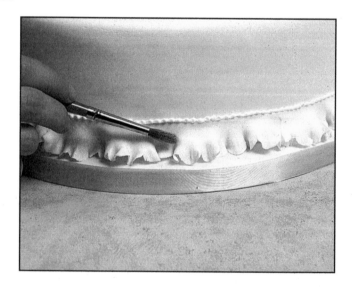

2 Making frill: Cut sections of frill from flower paste and sugarpaste with a Garrett cutter. Frill edges and attach to cake with egg white. Loop frill up at centre front. Pipe snail's trail to cover join. Dust edges with gold lustre petal dust.

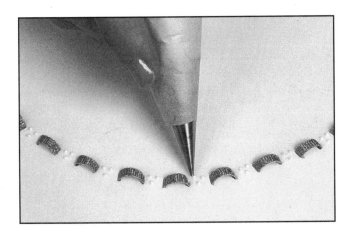

3 Ribbon insertion: When the sugarpaste is dry, insert short lengths of narrow gold ribbon into the positions marked. Using a no. 1 tube and white royal icing, pipe a triangular design of dots in between the lengths of ribbon.

4 Attaching flowers: Use template to scribe inscription. Pipe it in white, then paint over it in gold. Make a spray of pink carnations and red roses, ivy and gypsophila. Position at front beneath frill, securing in a small ball of sugarpaste.

5 Making pillars: Cut three equal lengths of dowelling, sharpening one end of each. Cover with white floristry tape and wrap in gold ribbon. Use the template to mark insertion points, then push the pillars all the way through the cake.

6 Positioning the bell: Carefully place the finished bell on top of the cake, setting the cake card squarely on the pillars. Line up the run-out number '50' so that it is parallel to the inscription.

Alternatives
OTHER WEDDING ANNIVERSARY CAKES

The design of the golden-wedding anniversary cake can be adapted to suit other anniversaries by simply changing the numerals and the colours of the decorations and flower posies.

For example, for a 25th wedding anniversary, change all the gold items to silver – a silver number '25' encircled with silver ribbon insertions on the bell; silver ribbon insertions and inscription on the cake top; and silver lustre petal dust (also inedible) on the edges of the frills.

The sprays could also be changed to the couple's favourite flower, and combined with silver leaves and dried gypsophila.

For a ruby wedding anniversary – the 40th – the deep-red roses on the original cake would be ideal. Or you could use other red flowers – such as anemones, orchids, poppies or poinsettias. Change the ribbon to red and paint the number '40' with red food colouring. Dust the frills with red petal dust.

For a pearl wedding anniversary – the 30th – keep to a silver theme, but incorporate pearls in the flower sprays; you could also form the number in pearls.

Several other anniversaries provide good opportunities for the cake decorator by virtue of their colour: for example, the 14th, which is ivory; the 35th (coral); and the 55th (emerald). Use ivory and pale coral for the sugarpaste covering (though emerald is best kept for details). The 13th wedding anniversary is dedicated to lace, and would provide a good opportunity for elaborate lace decorations instead of frills.

MAKING THE BELL

1 Creating the bell shape: Bake a fruit cake in a 10cm (4in) round tin. If you don't have such a small tin, you could make do with a large baked-bean or fruit tin. Use a large, sharp knife to carve the cake into a bell shape.

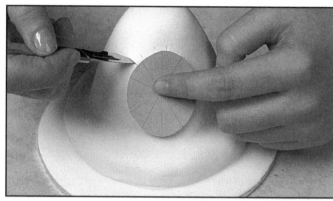

2 Covering the bell: Brush the bell with apricot glaze and coat with marzipan and sugarpaste. Set it on a cake card covered in white sugarpaste. Use the template to mark ribbon-insertion points with a ribbon-insertion tool or scalpel.

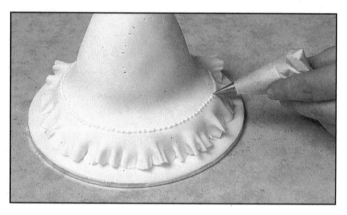

3 Creating the frill: Mix equal amounts of sugarpaste and flower paste together. Cut a narrow Garret frill. Frill its edge, open it out and attach to edge of bell. Using a no. 2 tube and white royal icing, pipe a snail's trail round the top of the frill.

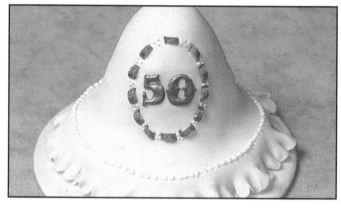

4 Adding decoration: Dust frill edges with gold lustre. Insert gold ribbon into marked points. Pipe dots in between. Run out '50' in white royal icing, dry and paint with gold food colouring. Fix to centre of ribbon insertion with royal icing.

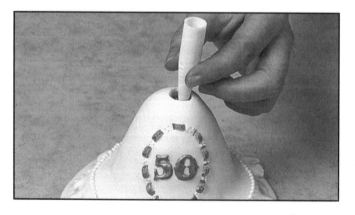

5 Inserting the posy pick: Decide on a position for the posy pick, then carve out an area of sugarpaste to the same diameter. Do not try to insert the pick without doing this, or the sugarpaste will crack. Push it in so top is level with icing.

6 Adding the spray of roses: Using cutters, make several red roses and pale pink carnations and wire them together with ivy and dried gypsophila to make an appropriately shaped spray. Insert wires into the posy pick.

Mildly marbled

*Simple and restrained, this delicately marbled cake – complete with
a run-out plaque – is suitable for a wide range of occasions.*

HAVE TO HAND

Ingredients: 25 x 20cm (10 x 8in)
oval fruit cake • apricot glaze •
marzipan • 1.25kg sugarpaste • clear
spirit • green, peach and pink paste
food colours • royal icing.

Equipment: 35 x 30cm (14 x 12in)
oval cake board • tracing paper •
waxed paper • nos. 1, 2 and 3 piping
tubes • fine paintbrush • scriber •
narrow and broad pink and white
ribbons • cocktail stick.

Main skills: marbling sugarpaste •
handling run-out plaques.

DIFFICULTY   TIME   SUITABILITY

✓✓   ⊠⊠   🍾

Much of the impact of this cake is derived from the subtle, swirled effect of the marbled sugarpaste used to coat both the cake and the board. The decoration is kept very simple so that it doesn't detract from the effect of the marbling; it consists merely of ribbon trims on the side of the cake and an inscribed run-out plaque on the top. The colours in the marbling dictate the tones of pink used for the ribbon decoration.

CHOOSING COLOURS
Three colours of sugarpaste were used to create the marbling: white, pale pink and peach, with an added streak of deep pink paste food colour. The finished result is actually a subtle blend of pinks,

with the veining in a deeper shade. Make sure that you continue to knead the sugarpaste until you have just the right effect. If you do not work with it for long enough, the colours will not appear delicate; but if you work it for too long, it may appear muddy.

PLEASING PLAQUES
The oval plaque, which echoes the shape of the cake, is run out with little eyelet holes all around. A narrow pink ribbon is then threaded through the holes. The inscription is first lightly scribed on to the plaque, then piped in white and overpiped in pink royal icing. A decorative trail of green foliage is used to highlight and embellish the first and last letter of the inscription, adding a

tiny touch of complementary colour. The ribbon theme used on the sides of the cake is echoed here in the tiny pink and white double bow used to trim the plaque. The plaque is set off-centre for interest and positioned at an angle, using a roll of sugarpaste as a support.

A simple but striking cake such as this would be suitable for a variety of occasions, from the birth of a new baby or a christening through to birthday and wedding anniversary celebrations. As the plaque is placed off-centre, there is room for additional decoration on the top – a baby in a cradle, for example, or a spray of carnations. It is also a simple cake to make – one which would be ideal if you were asked to produce something at short notice.

STEP-BY-STEP GUIDE

1 Marzipanning the cake: Brush the surface of the cake with apricot glaze and coat it with a layer of marzipan.

2 Marbling the sugarpaste: Mix equal quantities of white, pale pink and peach sugarpaste together. Add a streak of deep pink paste food colouring until you have the required marbled effect.

3 Covering the cake: Brush the marzipan with clear spirit. Roll out the sugarpaste and cover the cake and board in one go.

4 Piping a snail's trail: Using a no. 3 tube and white royal icing, pipe a snail's trail around the base of the cake.

5 Trimming the board: When the sugarpaste is completely dry, trim the edge of the board with ribbon.

6 Adding side ribbon: Trim the sides of the cake above the snail's trail with two lengths of narrow pink and white ribbon.

7 Tracing the template: Following the instructions below, trace the template on to greaseproof paper.

8 Outlining the plaque: Using white royal icing and a no. 1 piping tube, pipe the outline of the plaque and the eyelet holes.

9 Flooding the plaque: Using run consistency icing, flood the plaque and tidy it with a fine paintbrush. Leave it to dry for 24 hours.

10 Decorating the plaque: Pipe a picot edge around the plaque with a no. 1 tube and pink royal icing. Leave to dry.

11 Threading the ribbon: Carefully remove the plaque from the wax paper and thread narrow ribbon through the eyelet holes.

12 Piping the inscription: Scribe an inscription on to the plaque. Pipe over this using white royal icing and a no. 2 tube. Leave it to dry, then overpipe it in pink with a no. 1 tube.

13 Adding a decorative design: Using green royal icing, add a decorative design, representing foliage, over the first and last letters.

14 Adding ribbon trim: Make a tiny double bow from narrow pink and white ribbons. Position it on the plaque and attach with royal icing.

15 Positioning the plaque: Make a pink sausage shape from sugarpaste as a support for the plaque. Position it slightly off-centre on the top of the cake.

16 Securing the plaque: Place the plaque at a slight angle, leaning it against the support, and attach it with a dab of royal icing.

MAKING THE PLAQUE

1 Outlining the plaque: Trace the template and place it on a flat surface. Tape a piece of wax paper securely over it. Use pink royal icing and a no. 1 tube to pipe the outlines.

2 Flooding the outline: Using white royal icing, flood the plaque, avoiding the eyelet holes. Use a fine paintbrush to tidy the icing and leave it to dry overnight.

3 Piping a picot edge: Using pink royal icing and a no. 1 piping tube, pipe a picot edge around the outside edge of the plaque.

4 Piping the inscription: Scribe the lettering on to the centre of the plaque and then pipe it with white royal icing and a no. 2 tube. Overpipe in pink with a no. 1 tube.

5 Adding decoration: Using a no. 1 tube and green royal icing, embellish the initial letter and the tail of the last letter with trails of greenery.

6 Ribbon insertion: Gently remove the plaque from the wax paper and carefully thread the ribbon through the eyelets. Secure the loose ends at the back with royal icing.

helpline ~~~~~~~~~~~~~~~~ **THREADING RIBBON**

Run-out plaques are very delicate and must be handled carefully. If you find it easier, you can support the plaque on foam and thread the ribbon from that position, touching the plaque as little as possible. In this way you are unlikely to damage the picot edge.

Make sure that the plaque is entirely dry before you begin inserting the ribbon. At the very least, it should have been left overnight. The width of the ribbon is also an important consideration. The eyelet holes on this cake are 5mm (¹/₄in) wide. The ribbon must be slightly narrower than this and easy to manipulate. If the ribbon is too thick, it will be hard to thread.

When you thread the ribbon, secure one end of it at the back of the plaque with royal icing. Gently thread it around the plaque, not too tight and not too loose. You will find it easier to thread the ribbon through the holes if you place a piece of sticky tape over the loose end in order to stiffen it.

Secure the other end at the back of the plaque. When you place the plaque on the cake, the back will not be visible, but it should nevertheless be tidily finished.

ASSEMBLING THE CAKE

1 Piping around the base: Using a no. 3 piping tube and white royal icing, pipe a snail's trail around the base of the cake in order to hide the join between the cake and the board. Leave to dry.

2 Making the plaque support: Roll some pink sugarpaste into a sausage shape and flatten it on one side to give it a triangular shape. Position it on the top of the cake to support the plaque.

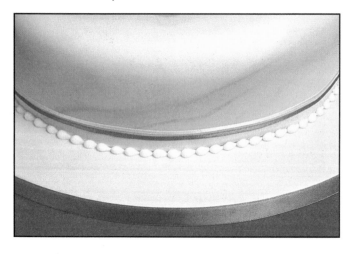

3 Adding ribbon: Trim the cake board with a broad pink ribbon. Use a narrow ribbon in a matching shade to trim the side of the cake just above the piped snail's trail. Finish with a narrow white ribbon running parallel to the narrow pink one.

4 Decorating the plaque: Make a tiny double bow from narrow pink and white ribbons. Fix it at an angle to the edge of the plaque with a dab of royal icing. Attach the plaque to the sugarpaste with royal icing and support it until it is dry.

Alternatives
MAKING PLAQUES

We have provided a template for the plaque on top of the marbled cake, but you could easily make your own if you wanted a different size or shape.

You can flood all shapes and sizes if you have outlined them first, but remember that some shapes are more conducive to the ribbon-insertion technique than others.

The eyelet holes have to be part of the template. They must also correspond to the overall size of the plaque and to the width of the ribbon. Remember to pipe around the eyelet holes so that they do not close up.

You may prefer to make a sugarpaste plaque, either by using a sugarpaste cutter or by making a template. In this case, the

eyelets would have to be made with an instrument such as a ribbon-insertion tool or a scalpel. Leave the plaque for at least 48 hours before inserting the ribbon. In this way you could make a matching marbled plaque or, if you have any marbled sugarpaste left over, use it to make a plaque for another cake.

A time for celebration

A challenge for the experienced cake decorator, this christening cake features an unusual, dropped-loop border and bootees decorated with cornelli work.

HAVE TO HAND

Ingredients: 21cm (8½in) round fruit cake • 1kg marzipan • clear spirit • 1.25kg sugarpaste • pastillage • royal icing • pale blue, peach and cream paste food colourings.
Equipment: 32cm (13in) round wooden board • greaseproof paper • 1m (1yd) each narrow and wide satin ribbons • scriber • nos. 0 and 1 piping tubes • tilting turntable.
Main skills: shaping cakes • line piping • cornelli work.

DIFFICULTY	TIME	SUITABILITY
✓ ✓ ✓	☒ ☒ ☒	🍾

The dropped-loop extension work that decorates the side of this unusually shaped christening cake is quite difficult and time-consuming to create, so we have restricted it to one section at the front. But you could always carry it out on two or more sides of a round or square cake.

The dropped-loop border supports are vertical rather than horizontal, which is unusual in extension work. To begin the design, divide the circumference of the cake, or section to be decorated, evenly. To do this, fold a strip of paper into sections, making sure that the gaps between the divisions are no more than 3cm (1¼in) wide.

The cake is baked as a round, rich fruit cake, and then the sides are cut away to make a feature of the front for the dropped-loop border. The finished effect is unusual, intricate and striking.

A tilting turntable is vital for this work. Tilt it towards you so that the strands or loops fall slightly away from the cake as you work.

PIPING THE LOOPS

The piped loops are graduated. The first one falls from the top of the first triangular support to the base of the second one. The next starts a little way in along the top section and stops above the first loop on the second support, with even spacing between each.

When working with the second colour of icing, work in the opposite direction in the usual way – that is, work upwards, from the base of the first triangular support to the top of the second support. This is an unusual method, but it means that you are less likely to break any of the previously piped loops.

MAKING THE BOOTEES

The delightful, delicate bootees are made from modelling paste – a mixture of flower paste and sugarpaste – to give them flexibility. The paste is coloured peach or pale blue, as appropriate. The soles are made of pastillage, the uppers being rolled around the sole and joined with a seam at the back. They are then overpiped with cream cornelli work.

A tiny blue or peach-coloured button piped in royal icing adds a finishing touch. The bootees are mounted on a pastillage plaque adorned with the name of the baby piped in a toning colour.

STEP-BY-STEP GUIDE

1 Shaping the cake: Using the template provided, shape the round fruit cake with a sharp knife, cutting curves at each side.

2 Covering the cake and board: Brush the cake with apricot glaze and coat it with marzipan. Cover cake and board separately with ivory sugarpaste.

3 Positioning the cake: Place the cake on the cake board and fasten a narrow, cream satin ribbon around the base of the cake to hide the join.

4 Marking out sections: Measure the front side of the cake and divide it into four equal sections, allowing a half-section space at either end. Mark vertical positions with a scriber.

5 Cutting the triangles: Roll out some pastillage and cut four triangles using the template provided. Leave them to dry for 24 hours, turning them once.

6 Attaching triangles: Fix triangles to the marked positions, with wider area at base, using vertical lines of royal icing.

7 Piping blue loops: Place the cake on a turntable tilted towards you. Using pale blue royal icing and a no. 0 tube, pipe the first section of dropped loops. Pipe remaining sections in the same way.

8 Piping peach loops: Change to peach royal icing and pipe overlapping dropped loops in the first section, working from base of first support to top of second support. Complete the first section, then the two remaining sections.

9 Adding decoration: Using a no. 0 tube, pipe blue and peach dots on top of each dropped loop in alternating colours.

10 Starting the bootees: Cut out four pastillage soles and leave them to dry overnight. Cut four uppers out of modelling paste.

11 Making up the bootees: Fix the soles to the uppers with royal icing, then leave them to dry.

12 Decorating the bootees: Use cream royal icing and a no. 0 or 1 tube to overpipe the bootees with cornelli work.

13 Mounting the bootees: Make a pastillage plaque and secure the bootees to it with royal icing. Use a no. 0 or 1 tube to pipe the name in royal icing, then overpipe in the appropriate colour.

14 Making the sprays: Make up some carnations, roses, pink and blue pulled flowers and some blossom sprays. Assemble into two sprays, including some dried gypsophila and ribbon loops.

15 Assembling the cake: Fix the plaque to the top of the cake with royal icing. Secure the sprays on each side with royal icing. Trim the cake board with the wide white satin ribbon.

CREATING THE DROPPED LOOP BORDER

1 Making triangles: Roll out pastillage thinly on a wooden board. Use the template to cut out four triangles. Lift surplus away – but do not move the triangles. Leave to dry for 24 hours, turning gently once to avoid distortion.

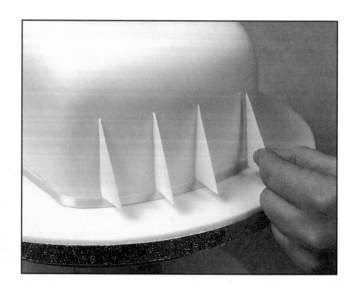

2 Positioning triangles: Trim cake base with narrow ribbon. Work out even spacing for four triangles, leaving a space at start and finish. Mark positions with scriber. Attach triangles with lines of royal icing, resting bases on ribbon.

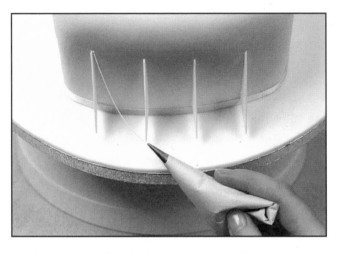

3 Piping first loop: Set cake on turntable. Using a no. 0 piping tube and pale blue royal icing, pipe a line from the top of the first triangle to the base of the second triangle.

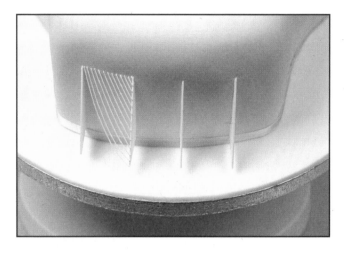

4 Continuing loops: Finish first section, dropping loops down at regular intervals from top. Then pipe loops upwards from the base of triangles. Pipe last two sections.

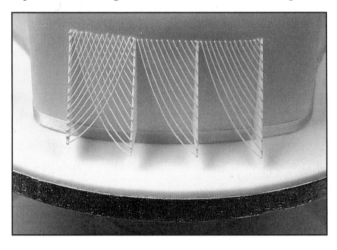

5 Finishing loops: Using peach icing, start at base of first triangle support and work up to top of second, over top of blue icing. Complete, forming curved 'V's at lower edge.

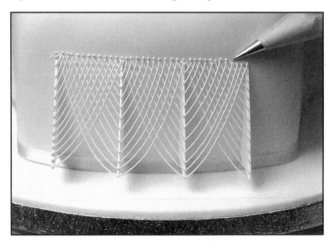

6 Adding dots: Pipe dots of alternate colour on top of the dropped loops, using peach and blue royal icing and the no. 0 piping tube.

helpline

ACHIEVING PERFECT RESULTS

To achieve a perfect finish to the cake, there are a few basic points you must take into account. When you cut the fruit cake into the required shape, there will almost certainly be small holes left in the cut areas. These must be filled with small marzipan plugs before the marzipan coating is applied.

When covering the cake, take care not to stretch the sugarpaste as you smooth it over the angled sections at the front and sides of the cake.

Make the soles of the bootees from pastillage, but mould the uppers from flower paste. This is more pliable and easier to work with.

The bootees are decorated with cornelli work. Use a small piping tube – such as a no. 0. If you use too large a tube, the decoration will look clumsy.

It is important that the pastillage plaques are neither too large nor too small. They should have a large enough surface area to hold the bootees and the inscription, but there should not be too much undecorated space. If you wish, you can colour the pastillage with paste food colouring or lightly brush it with petal dust. If you use petal dust, make sure that you apply it before the plaque is attached to the cake.

The extension work is very delicate and must not be rushed. Ensure that the triangular pieces are straight and attached securely before you start the dropped loops.

Finally, if the cake has to be transported once it has been made, pack the decorative elements separately in a small cake box, protected with tissue paper, and secure them in place with royal icing once the cake has reached its final destination.

MAKING THE BOOTEES

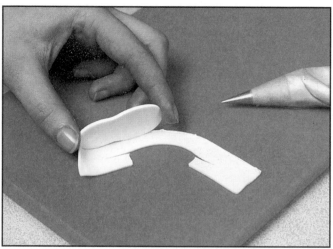

1 Cutting out the soles and uppers: Using the template provided, cut out a sole for each bootee from white pastillage. Leave them to dry overnight. Cut the uppers from modelling paste coloured pastel blue.

2 Joining the soles and uppers together: Coat the edge of the sole with royal icing. Roll the straight edge of the bootee around the sole, positioning the join in the upper at the centre back of the bootee.

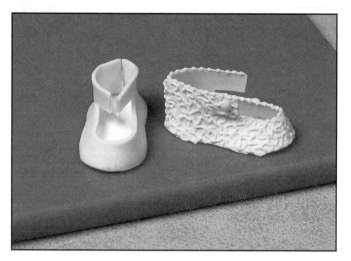

3 Decorating the bootees: Join centre back seam of upper with royal icing. Leave bootees to dry. Using a no. 0 tube and cream royal icing, pipe cornelli work all over the bootees. Pipe tiny shells round top edge. Add coloured button.

4 Positioning the bootees: Place the bootees on a pastillage plaque at a slight angle to each other. Using a no. 1 tube and cream royal icing, pipe on the baby's name. Then overpipe in blue or peach, as appropriate.

Alternatives

TULLE BOOTEES

The bootees on this christening cake are very small; if you would like a larger pair, cut them out of tulle and pipe the cornelli work on to this. The tulle can be white, with white cornelli work, or you could use pastel shades – such as pink, blue or lemon. Use the template as a pattern for the soles and uppers, but enlarged to about twice the size. Cut out from sugar paste or flower paste. Turn one sole over to make a pair. Place each sole on some wax paper and stand them on pieces of foam sponge. Attach the straight edge of the uppers to the soles with royal icing, sticking pins into the foam all around the edge to support the tulle until the icing dries. Carefully remove the pins by twisting them gently. Then pipe cornelli work as before, using a no. 0 tube. Finish by piping a line of tiny shells around the base of each bootee. Decorate with a tiny button.

Spring celebration

Yellow smocking and flowers make this fresh and pretty cake ideal for celebrating Easter – or simply the arrival of spring.

HAVE TO HAND

Ingredients: 18cm (7in) round fruit cake • apricot glaze • 750g marzipan • 600g yellow sugarpaste • 100g white sugarpaste • royal icing • flower paste • lemon, yellow, orange, purple and green paste food colourings • selection of petal dusts.

Equipment: greaseproof paper • scriber • 25cm (10in) round cake board • smocking roller • tweezers • cocktail stick • straight scalloped cutter • nos. 0, 1 and 2 piping tubes • scalpel • frill cutter • foam sponge • fine paintbrush • ball tool • 1m (1yd) broad white satin ribbon.

Main skills: smocking • brush embroidery • making flowers.

DIFFICULTY   TIME   SUITABILITY

Yellow is a colour special to Easter, associated with spring flowers such as daffodils and crocuses, fluffy Easter chicks and the first beams of spring sunshine. So this pretty cake, elaborately decorated in shades of lemon, deep yellow and orange, is ideal for an Easter or spring celebration.

EXERCISING YOUR SKILLS
The first step is to cover both the cake and the board in one go with lemon-yellow sugarpaste. The sides are then covered with a layer of white sugarpaste,

scalloped at the top and curving into a drape shape at the centre front. This is decorated with smocking in deep yellow; the same colour outlines the scallops at the top. A snail's trail in lemon yellow covers the angle between cake and board, and a dainty white frill trims the bottom edge of the smocking.

The cake top is covered with a fantasy flower design in green and purple brush embroidery, embellished with large yellow flowers cut from flower paste. Two smaller flowers, backed by painted leaves, peep out from the frame that has been created by the raised edges of the draped frill.

If you prefer, you could make different flowers to decorate the top and side of the cake. But keep to yellow or

yellow and white spring flowers – summer flowers would be inappropriate.

WORKING THE SMOCKING
When applying the white sugarpaste to the side of the cake, work on one section at a time – do not try to apply all the paste in one go. Roll out and cut one or two sections and attach them to the cake. Using tweezers, mark the smocking points quickly, before the paste hardens.

When piping the diamonds, start at the top and work diagonally down to the next mark. Then pause briefly before continuing. There is no need to break the line of piping, but you must make contact with the marked points to create the diamond effect. Do not try to pipe a diagonal line in a single movement.

STEP-BY-STEP GUIDE

1 Marzipanning the cake: Brush the surface of the cake with apricot glaze and then coat it with a layer of marzipan.

2 Covering cake and board: Put the cake on the cake board and cover both with lemon-yellow sugarpaste.

3 Marking central shape: Use the template provided to cut the shape from greaseproof paper. Position it on the cake and mark the design with a scriber.

4 Shaping the sugarpaste: Roll out some white sugarpaste with a smocking roller and shape both ends of two sections using the template provided. Then use a scalloped cutter to shape the top edges, and the template to reduce the sections to the correct depth.

5 Marking smocking points: Attach the sugarpaste sections round the cake one at a time and mark the smocking points with tweezers. Work

quickly, before the sugarpaste begins to harden. Mark one section at a time – do not try to apply all the paste in one go.

6 Starting smocking: Using a no. 0 tube and deep yellow royal icing, pipe the diamond effect from point to point.

7 Finishing smocking: Use the no. 0 tube to pipe horizontal 'stitches' where the diamonds join, and a line of yellow dots to emphasise the scalloped top edge.

8 Piping snail's trail: Using yellow royal icing and a no. 2 tube, pipe a snail's trail around the base of the cake.

9 Positioning frill: Cut a frill from white sugarpaste and attach it to the lower edge of the smocking. Using a no. 2 tube and white royal icing, pipe a shell border over the join.

10 Starting brush embroidery: Use the template provided to scribe the

flower design on to the top of the cake. Paint the stems and leaves in green paste colour mixed with clear spirit.

11 Finishing the embroidery: Pipe around the flowers and calyxes with white royal icing and a no. 2 tube. Use a brush dipped in some green or purple colouring to pull the icing into the centre of each flower.

12 Making the yellow flowers: Make up two large yellow flowers for the cake top and two miniature ones for the side front.

13 Completing the decoration: Attach the two large flowers to the top of the cake. Paint small green leaves in the space framed by the frill. Attach the small yellow flowers to the top.

14 Trimming the cake board: Finish the edge of the cake board by attaching a broad, white satin ribbon.

SMOCKING THE SIDES

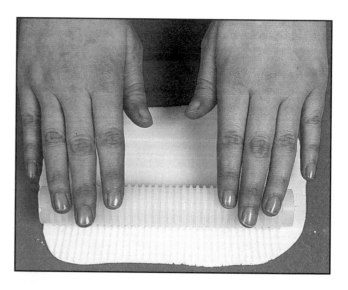

1 Scribing the central shape: Cut the template from a strip of greaseproof paper. Place it around the cake, aligning it with the top edge. Mark the central shaping with a scriber.

2 Rolling out the sugarpaste: Roll out some white sugarpaste. Then use a smocking roller to mark the lines of ribbing that will form the smocked pattern on the side of the cake.

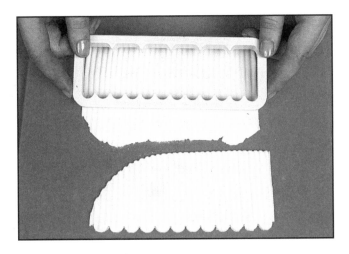

3 Shaping sugarpaste: Use the template to shape the ends of two sections of paste. Use a scalloped cutter to shape upper edges. Use template to cut sections to correct depth.

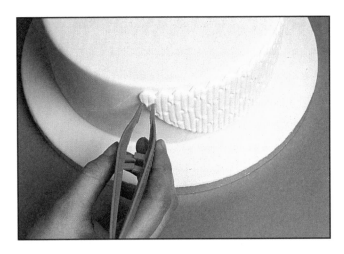

4 Marking the smocking: Moisten the back of one section of paste and attach to the cake. Mark the smocking points with tweezers. Work quickly before paste hardens.

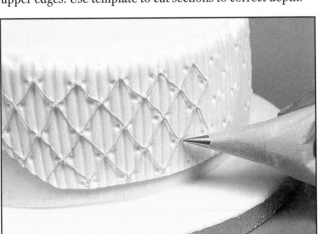

5 Piping diamonds: Attach second section and mark smocking. Cover rest of cake with straight sections. Using a no. 0 tube and deep yellow royal icing, pipe diamond effect.

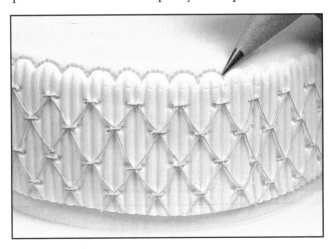

6 Completing piping: Using the same tube and colour, pipe horizontal cross-stitch effect at each join of diamonds. Pipe dots all round scalloped edge where it joins the cake.

helpline   MAKING FLOWERS

Use the template to cut seven petals for each of the two large flowers from white flower paste. Shape each petal into a curve, working on the underside with a ball tool. Leave them to dry on a piece of sponge.

When the petals are dry, dust them with yellow petal dust and paint a central vein on each petal with orange paste food colour mixed with clear spirit. Assemble the petals on top of the cake, overlapping them and securing them with dabs of royal icing. Using orange royal icing and a no. 1 tube, pipe dots in the centre to represent stamens.

For the two small flowers on the side of the cake, use the template provided to cut each one out in a single piece of flower paste. Curve the individual petals with a ball tool. Dust them with yellow petal dust and paint in the veins with orange food colouring mixed with clear spirit as before. Pipe orange dots in the centre of each flower.

Paint the leaves separately on the side of the cake with green food colouring mixed with clear spirit.

Attach the flowers to the cake with dabs of royal icing.

COMPLETING THE DECORATION

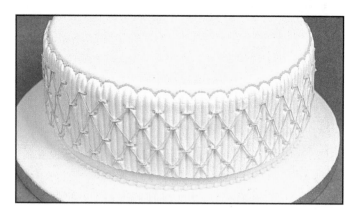

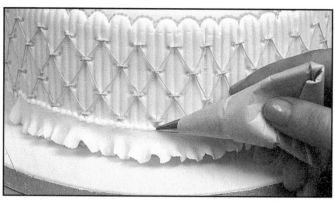

1 Piping a snail's trail: Use a no. 2 tube and lemon-yellow royal icing to pipe a snail's trail around the base of the cake. (This will be partially obscured by the frill, so don't worry too much about any imperfections.)

2 Adding the frill: Cut a frill 1cm (½in) deep from white sugarpaste. Frill its edge with a cocktail stick and apply it to the lower edge of the smocked paste. Finish top of frill with a shell border piped with a no. 2 tube and white royal icing.

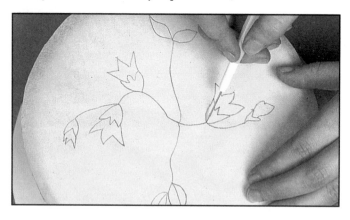

3 Transferring the flower design: Copy the template provided for the purple flowers and leaf design on to greaseproof paper. Centre the paper on the top of the cake and scribe the design on to the sugarpaste.

4 Painting the flower design: Paint the stems and leaves of the scribed flowers in green paste colour mixed with clear spirit. Use a fine paintbrush to create fine stems and serrated-edged leaves.

5 Finishing the brush embroidery: Use white royal icing and a no. 2 tube to pipe the outline of the flowers and calyxes. Pull the icing into centre of each with a brush dipped in a green or purple colouring. Make two yellow flowers (see Helpline, page 64) and attach them to the cake.

6 Finishing the side decoration: Trim the cake board with the broad white satin ribbon. Use the template provided to cut out two small flower-paste flowers (see Helpline, page 64). Paint leaves on to the side of the cake. Attach the flowers with dabs of royal icing.

Two hearts entwined

Celebrate the union of two hearts and two countries

with this charming double heart design.

HAVE TO HAND

Ingredients: *18cm (7in) heart shape fruit cake • 23cm (9in) heart shape fruit cake • apricot glaze • 2kg marzipan • 2.5kg sugarpaste • royal icing • flower paste • clear spirit • green paste food colouring • green, pink, yellow and brown petal dusts • selection of campion and gentian flowers • stamens.*

Equipment: *43cm (17in) heart-shaped cake board • scriber • greaseproof paper • medium-sized soft paintbrush • scriber • no. 1 piping tube • 1m (1yd) silver ribbon.*

Main skills: *working with sugarpaste • making paste flowers.*

DIFFICULTY	TIME	SUITABILITY

Cake decorators are often asked to bake or help with wedding and engagement cakes, so you need to have a good stock of ideas to ensure that you can produce something suitable for all occasions. This delightful fruit cake was designed and decorated to symbolise the union of an English bride and a French groom.

HEART BAKE
The cake depicts interlocking hearts set on a heart shaped board. The larger heart is trimmed using a template, so that the smaller heart will interlock with it. The cakes must not be coated too thickly with marzipan and sugarpaste, or you will have difficulty fitting them together. The board is covered with moss-green sugarpaste as a fitting background to the floral theme.

FLORAL TRIBUTE
The floral decoration at the front of the cake consists of strikingly coloured flowers – red campion and blue gentians set in a ball of spaghnum moss. This is easily made from a flattened ball of green sugarpaste with green royal icing of quite a soft consistency randomly piped over the top. Tiny piped flowers are placed around the base of the cake and small yellow and white daisies are piped around the edge of the top design.

PLACING THE INSCRIPTION
Positioning the inscription on a cake such as this can be a problem, particularly if you want to use a fairly long word, such as 'Congratulations'. We have overcome this by positioning the greeting down one side of the cake, following the gentle curve of the heart, then piping the names horizontally across the cake.

Do not be tempted to add more decorations to the top of the cake, or the end result will be too fussy. The shape of the cakes is so attractive that you do not need to overload it. The pretty painted side design and the floral spray which nestles between the two hearts are really all that are needed.

STEP-BY-STEP GUIDE

1 Shaping the cakes: When the cakes have cooled, use the template provided to cut away a section of the larger cake.

2 Covering the cakes: Cover both cakes with marzipan and sugarpaste. Be sparing with the paste so that you do not distort the shape of the cake. Leave to dry thoroughly.

3 Covering the board: Cover the board with moss-green sugarpaste. Position the larger cake off-centre and slide the other in next to it.

4 Brushing with petal dust: Using moss-green petal dust, dust around the base of each cake to give the impression of grass.

5 Painting in the small flowers: Use petal dust and clear spirit to paint in the stems and leaves of the small flowers around the base of the cake.

6 Beginning the pink flowers: Paint in the stems of the pink flowers with clear alcohol mixed with green and brown petal dusts.

7 Adding the petals: Use royal icing and a no. 1 tube to add the petals in pink and the centres in yellow.

8 Adding the blue flowers: Paint in the stems of the blue flowers with petal dust and clear alcohol. Then pipe in the petals and centres as before.

9 Adding the white daisies: Make the white daisies by using a no. 1 tube to pipe a sequence of small white dots around the edges of both cakes and across the join.

10 Adding the yellow daisies: Alternate each white daisy with a yellow one, piped in the same way. There should be a double row where the two hearts meet.

11 Adding the inscription: Scribe the inscription on to the top of the cake and then run it out directly.

12 Preparing the campion: Use the template to make the campion from pink flower paste. Add leaves and a calyx. Wire into a spray and leave to dry.

13 Making the gentian: Use the template provided to make the gentian from blue flower paste.

14 Making the moss: Place a ball of green sugarpaste in front of the cake board and pipe green squiggles over it with a no. 1 piping tube.

15 Adding the flowers: Place the flowers into the support, positioning the campions to the back of the arrangement and the gentians to the front.

16 Adding ribbon: Add a silver ribbon around the cake board.

BUILDING THE DESIGN

1 Shaping the cakes: Cool the cakes and use the template provided to shape the larger of the two hearts, cutting away a section so that the two cakes can be joined.

2 Covering the cakes: Brush the cakes with apricot glaze, coat them with marzipan and leave to dry. Brush with clear spirit and coat with sugarpaste – but not too thickly.

3 Covering the board: Coat the board with moss-green sugarpaste. Position the larger heart off-centre on the board and slide the smaller heart into position beside it.

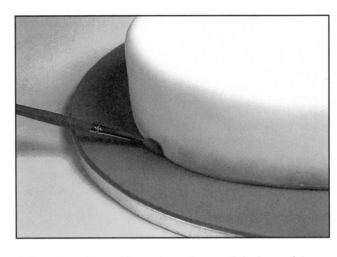

4 Dusting the sides: Dust all around the base of the cake with a medium-sized soft paintbrush and moss-green petal dust. Take the dusting a little way up the side.

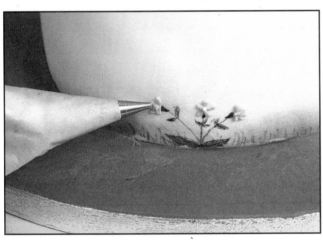

5 Piping flowers: Paint in stems and leaves of pink flowers with green and brown petal dusts and clear spirit. Pipe in daisies with pink royal icing. Add white centres.

6 Completing piping: Paint in the stems and leaves of the blue flowers with green and brown petal dusts mixed with clear spirit. Pipe in blue flowers and add white centres.

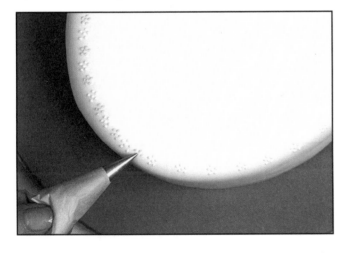

7 Piping daisies: Use white royal icing and a no. 1 tube to pipe dotted white daisies around cake edges. Space evenly, allowing room for yellow daisies piped in the same way.

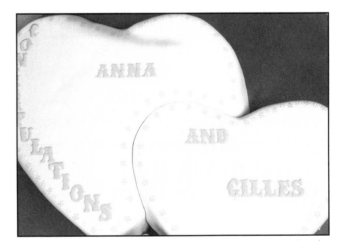

8 Piping lettering: Using yellow royal icing, run out the lettering directly on to the top surface of the cake. Lightly scribe the position of the letters first as a guide.

FLORAL ARRANGEMENT

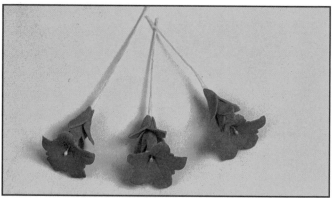

1 Making the campion: Using the template provided, make the campion from pink flower paste. Paint the calyx deep red. Form into a small spray of flowers, including a partly opened bud and two or three tight buds. Bind in several leaves.

2 Making the gentian flowers: Using the template provided, make gentians from blue flower paste. Add a single white stamen. Brush the petals with deep blue petal dust. Mould two or three green leaves and the base of the calyx.

3 Making the moss: Put a ball of green sugarpaste on the front of the board. Flatten it slightly and pipe random squiggles over its surface with dark green royal icing and a no. 1 tube. This is to represent a ball of moss.

4 Arranging the flowers: Working while the icing is still soft, push the flowers into the support, placing the larger campion to the back of the arrangement and the smaller gentians to the front.

Alternatives

CHOOSING A MOTIF

If you are baking a cake to celebrate the wedding or engagement between two people of different countries, there are many different design alternatives which you could choose as decorative touches.

Try a thistle and a rose to symbolise the union between a Scot and an English man or woman. The *fleur de lys* has long been associated with France, the shamrock with Ireland and the maple leaf with Canada.

Asia produces wonderfully exotic flowers such as orchids and jasmine. Think of the African violets, or bougainvillea, which is also associated with Africa, and the pretty blossom associated with Japan.

But it is not just flowers that can represent a country. A dragon conjures up images of China (whose marital celebration colour is red), and there is no mistaking the home of the kangaroo! Also, a cake board covered in a tartan fabric would be perfect if the recipient was of Scottish origin.

Whatever you choose to represent a country, there are many opportunities for colour. Consider the national flags involved. You can make arrangements in the appropriate colours, to symbolise the flag of a particular country.

Remember that designing a cake of this kind, with several emblems involved, needs to be thoroughly planned so that the designs, colours and spacing all come together in an attractive whole.

It is worth taking time to think through your designs. A cake which welcomes someone into your community in such a way will be worth a thousand words when they see how much time you have taken to bake a very special celebration cake.

Bright Ideas

Dressing-table cake

This glamorous dressing-table cake will delight ladies and little girls alike.

HAVE TO HAND

Ingredients: *two 20 x 15cm (8 x 6in) oval sponges • buttercream • jam • 1.5kg sugarpaste • green, blue, apricot, hydrangea, lilac, turquoise and peach paste food colourings • gold liquid food colouring • pastillage or gum paste.*

Equipment: *no. 1 piping tube • 33cm (13in) round cake board • crimpers • piece of sponge • cocktail stick • miniature strung beads • rolling pin • Garret frill cutter • foil • stick adhesive • clay gun • scalpel • fine paintbrush.*

Main skills: *working with sugarpaste • shaping a sponge cake.*

DIFFICULTY	TIME	SUITABILITY
✓ ✓		

This pretty dressing-table cake recalls an era of femininity and glamour, and will delight those who like to dress up and have fun. It is suitable for women of all ages, and is just as likely to be appreciated by a five-year-old as a ninety-five-year old.

COVERING THE CAKE

The cake is made from two sponges, moulded into a kidney shape. It is then covered with peach-coloured sugarpaste and a soft, apricot-coloured drape surrounds the entire table. This takes time, but it's worth doing to get just the right effect.

Once the pleated sections are in place, with no joins showing, they should not be moved in case they crack. They are then overlaid with a darker peach frill which is cut with a Garrett frill cutter and made in about six sections. On the top stands a three-way mirror made from pastillage (or gum) paste. This paste rolls very thinly and dries quickly to a hard finish. Silver foil is then stuck on the paste using stick adhesive. The frames of the mirror are made from gold-painted sugarpaste and so should be removed from the cake before it is eaten.

FINISHING TOUCHES

A range of feminine accessories comprise the little finishing touches which give the cake so much charm. On the dressing table sit a flower-paste hairbrush with matching mirror, a box of tissues, and a necklace. There is also a pair of slippers, which sit on the cake board.

The board is covered with sugarpaste and sponged with runny royal icing to give the effect of a bedroom carpet. The look of the dressing table can be altered to suit the recipient – some girls are not as tidy as others!

PROFESSIONAL SECRETS

Making the accessories

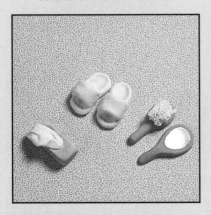

• Use coloured flower paste to make the items for the dressing table. A tissue box, a hairbrush, a mirror and a pair of slippers are shown here.

• You can, of course, add more personal items – for example, a teddy bear, some favourite pieces of jewellery, perfume, a dish or ornament or some cosmetics. It all depends on the recipient.

• Use turquoise sugarpaste to make the hairbrush and the three mirrors. Cover the glass surface of the mirrors with tin foil. Make the bristles of the hairbrush with white sugarpaste and a clay gun.

• Mould a rectangle of lilac sugarpaste to form the tissue box, and drape a white tissue made out of sugarpaste over the top of it.

• To make the pearl necklace, buy some tiny strung beads by the metre. You will get them either from the haberdashery counter in a large department store, or from good cake-decorating suppliers.

STEP-BY-STEP GUIDE

Preparing the cake board: *Coat board with a thin layer of white sugarpaste. Crimp the edges. Colour some runny royal icing with green and hydrangea food colours. Sponge the board randomly, and leave it to dry.*

1

Shaping the cake: *When the cake is cold, sandwich the two sponges together with jam and buttercream. Cut it into the required kidney shape with a sharp knife, using the template provided.*

2

Coating the cake: *Colour some sugarpaste pale peach. Spread some jam all over the cake and then coat it with sugarpaste. Position the cake centrally towards the back of the cake board.*

3

Making the lower frill: *Combine sugarpaste and flower paste and colour a deep peach. Roll into 6-8 strips, 8cm (3in) long and 10–15cm (4–6in) wide. Attach to the cake with royal icing. Pleat the top edge in sections. Continue around the cake, overlapping sections to hide the joins.*

4

Making the top frill: *Combine sugarpaste and flower paste and colour a deeper peach. Roll out thinly and cut frills with a Garrett frill cutter. Frill the edges with a cocktail stick and attach to the cake with royal icing. Fold the outside edges over to make the joins neater.*

5

Making the mirror frames: *Mix a small quantity of soft sugarpaste, place in a clay gun fitted with a suitable top to produce the frame, and extrude three ropes of paste. Using a no. 1 tube, pipe small dots of royal icing around each foil-covered mirror and attach a rope of paste.*

8

Painting the frames: *Using a medium-sized paintbrush and gold food colouring, paint the frames. Wipe away any colouring that spills on to the mirrored surface at once. Leave to dry. Remember: gold-coated objects are inedible and must be removed before the cake is eaten.*

9

Covering the join: *Colour a small quantity of royal icing a darker peach than the top frill. Use a no. 1 piping tube to pipe a tiny row of shells to hide the join between the top frill and the cake. If you wish, you could use a contrasting colour, such as moss green, for the shells.*

6

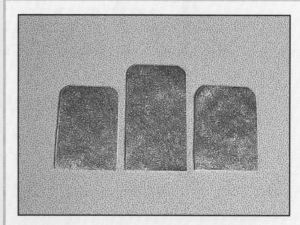

Making the mirrors: *Using the templates provided and a scalpel or sharp, pointed knife, cut one large and two small shapes for the mirrors from pastillage. Using the same templates, cut pieces of foil and attach them to the mirrors with a non-toxic adhesive.*

7

Attaching the mirrors: *Position the mirrors on the cake and attach them with royal icing. Use balls of sugarpaste to support the mirrors until the icing is dry. (If the cake is to be moved, retain the sugarpaste supports until it has reached its final destination).*

10

Decorating the dressing table: *Make the objects for the dressing table from coloured sugarpaste and arrange them on top of the cake (see Professional Secrets). The type of objects you make for the dressing table should reflect the recipient of the cake.*

11

Artist's palette

A colourful and original cake, sure to please art lovers everywhere!

HAVE TO HAND

Ingredients: *23cm (9in) round fruit cake • apricot glaze • 1 kg marzipan • flower paste • 1.5kg sugarpaste • royal icing • red, yellow, blue, green, brown, black and violet food paste colourings • liquid silver colouring • petal dusts in shades of brown • a few strands of uncooked spaghetti.*
Equipment: *nos. 1, 2 and 4 piping tubes • 33cm (13in) round cake board • greaseproof paper • small knife • scalpel • cocktail sticks • sugarpaste roller • soft brush • paintbrush.*
Main skills: *moulding sugarpaste • making paste decorations • using colour.*

DIFFICULTY	TIME	SUITABILITY

One of the pleasures of cake decorating is that you can design cakes which reflect the interests and personalities of specific friends and relations. It is this kind of thoughtfulness and imagination which makes receiving a cake a special and memorable affair.

The cake shown here is designed with artists and art lovers in mind, and it would be ideal for someone who works in an artistic field, or who has outside hobbies and interests which relate to the world of art.

BEGINNING THE DESIGN

The top of the cake consists of a raised artist's palette, shaped from marzipan using a template, and then covered with champagne-coloured sugarpaste. The tubes of paint and the paintbrushes are made from an equal mixture of sugarpaste and flower paste, and are moulded and attached to the cake when it is dry.

Much of the success of the cake lies in the accurate and confident moulding of these sugarpaste artifacts. The càke is then brought to life with wonderful splashes of colour on the palette.

WORKING WITH COLOUR

With so many bright, strong colours displayed on the cake, you must be very careful not to spill any colour or petal dust. The surface of the cake is light and would be ruined by smudges of petal dust and drops of paint in the wrong place. Follow our instructions for keeping the colours separate and everyone will proclaim that your cake really is a masterpiece!

PROFESSIONAL SECRETS

Planning your cake

• Before you begin to decorate your cake, make a rough timetable for yourself so that your work is as efficient and streamlined as possible.

• In this case, we made all the component parts for the cake in advance and assembled them some days later.

• When you have sugarpasted the cake as outlined in step 2, leave it to dry for two days. Make sure it is covered to avoid dust falling on it. Sugarpaste attracts dust if left uncovered.

• Next, begin to make the tubes of paint. This is a fiddly job as you have to cut and attach the labels once each tube has been moulded. There are quite a few to make, and so you may want to make just one or two at a time.

• When the tubes are finished, leave them to dry on a cake board in a warm, dust-free place. The little dabs of colour piped on to the tip of the tubes can be done once the tubes are in position on the cake.

• You will need to make two or three brushes, and these should be left to harden for at least a couple of days before the 'hair' is piped on.

• Only when everything is thoroughly dry should you assemble the cake, attaching the brushes and tubes of paint with royal icing.

STEP-BY-STEP GUIDE

Marzipanning the cake: *Cover the cake with marzipan. Trace the template provided on to greaseproof paper and cut out the palette from marzipan. Position the palette, off-centre, on top of the cake.*

1

Covering with sugarpaste: *Cover the cake with sugarpaste, starting at the top and moulding the sugarpaste around the palette. Pipe a row of bulbs with a no. 4 tube and light-brown royal icing.*

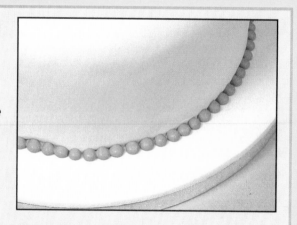

2

Petal dusting the palette: *Mask the cake with the greaseproof paper, making sure that everything is covered except the palette. Stop up the centre. Dust the palette with a mixture of brown petal dusts.*

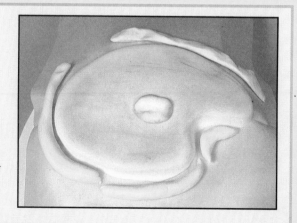

3

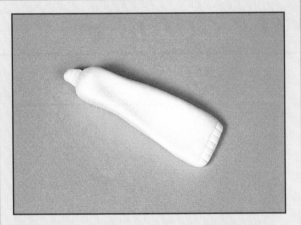

Moulding the tubes: *Mould the paint tubes from a mixture of sugarpaste and flower paste. Create a squeezed effect for some, and a fuller effect for others. Use a small, fairly blunt knife to serrate the base and to mark the thread on the end of the tubes. Make seven tubes in all.*

4

Adding the bands of colour: *Choose colours for your paints and make a note of them. Roll out sugarpaste bands in each chosen colour. Add a narrow black strip to the centre and roll gently into the main colour. Cut to size and add to tube of paint. Paint top and bottom in silver.*

5

Adding the paint: *Mix seven different colours of royal icing which correspond with the coloured bands on the tubes of paint. We have used yellow, red, green, blue, violet, black and brown. Use a different cocktail stick each time to place splashes of colour around the palette.*

8

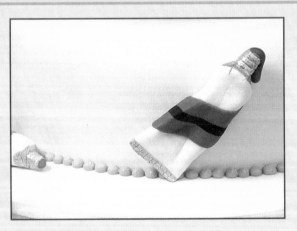

Attaching the tubes: *Attach the tubes of paint to the cake with royal icing. Place some on the top, some on the side, and some on the board itself. Use the coloured royal icing and the cocktail sticks to give the effect of paint oozing out from the tubes.*

9

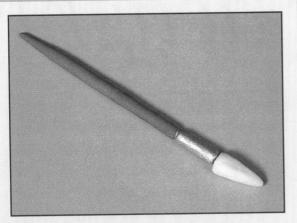

Making the brushes: *Roll out some brown sugarpaste. Take a piece of uncooked spaghetti, place it on the rolled sugarpaste, and roll the paste around the spaghetti. Add a white cone of sugarpaste to the top of the brush, and make indentations for the silver band.*

6

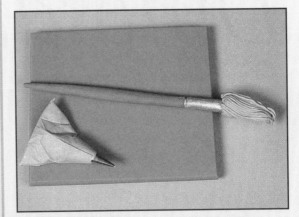

Adding the bristles: *Using a mixture of yellow and brown royal icing and a no. 2 piping tube, pipe in the bristles. The sugarpaste cone underneath will give a tapered look to the brush. Use a real paintbrush to neaten your work. Paint the metal band in silver.*

7

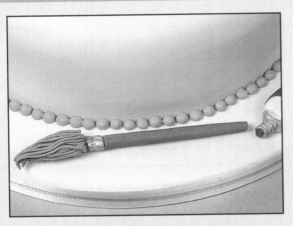

Attaching the brushes: *Using dots of royal icing, attach the paintbrushes to the cake. We have positioned two on top of the cake and one on the board. These, and the tubes of paint, must be removed before the cake is eaten, since silver food colouring is inedible.*

10

Piping the inscription: *Pipe the inscription of your choice freehand, using a no. 1 piping tube and white royal icing. Overpipe this in dark brown royal icing. The inscription should sit to the side of the palette and not be squashed in any way.*

11

Dinosaur delight

Mark a big occasion in your child's life with this exciting dinosaur cake.

Starting school is a big event in a child's life, and one way of marking such an occasion is with a special cake. The cake could equally well be made to celebrate other events, such as passing an exam or learning to ride a bicycle. Dinosaurs are very popular with children, so these decorations are bound to be a success. They are made with edible rice paper, so expect some competition between friends and siblings as to who is going to eat what!

The base is a sponge cake, sandwiched with buttercream and jam, which most children seem to prefer to fruit cake. Both the cake and the board are covered with pale green sugarpaste, which provides an ideal background for the dinosaurs and the decorative grassland.

MAKING THE DINOSAURS

The fierce-looking beasts are all cut out of rice paper, then coloured with petal dust and food-colouring pens. The head of a large and ferocious

Tyrannosaurus rex peers out through the foliage in a specially recessed corner cut into the cake. Smaller dinosaurs run through the grassland along the sides of the cake, while the top is decorated with three familiar dinosaur figures – a *Triceratops*, an *Allosaurus* and a *Stegosauru*s.

FINISHING TOUCHES

A bright red ribbon around the cake board sets off the scene and ties in well with the lettering on the top. The rice-paper figures could be made well in advance, and then stored carefully until they are needed.

For a party with several small children, you will find that they will all want their own dinosaur, so make plenty of extra rice-paper models so that everyone can have one to take home with them.

PROFESSIONAL SECRETS

Working with rice paper

- Rice paper is a thin, edible, semi-transparent sheet made from rice flour, commonly used as a base for baking sticky confections such as macaroons. The paper is smooth on one side and textured on the other. For baking purposes, you can use it either side up, but for making the dinosaurs, have it smooth side up as it is easier to apply colour to this surface.

- Keep water or other liquids away from the rice paper as they will dissolve it. You can lightly dampen the paper to make it stick to the strips supporting the taller figures – the large *Tyrannosaurus* head for the recess, the standing *Allosaurus*, and the *Stegosaurus*.

- When colouring rice-paper figures with petal dust, try to keep the dust away from the tabs used to attach the figures to the cake, otherwise the colour may transfer to the surface of the cake when you position them, and so spoil the sugarpaste.

- Cut out rice figures very carefully, as the paper is quite brittle and easily damaged.

- Stabilise the tall figures with a supporting strip of rice paper about 2.5cm (1in) long by 1cm (½in) wide. Fold the top end down and attach it to the back of the figure. Fold the lower end up and attach it to the flap by damping it very lightly.

STEP-BY-STEP GUIDE

Shaping the cake:
Sandwich the cakes together. Cut away one corner of the cake with a 9cm (3½in) pastry cutter. Sugarpaste the cake and board and leave to dry. Edge the board with red ribbon.

1

Making short grass:
Use the template to cut lengths of short grass from rice paper. Cut enough to go all round the cake, excluding the recess. Colour smooth side with petal dust. Attach with piping gel.

2

Making tall grass:
Using the template, cut a section of tall grass and colour it a deeper green with extra petal dust. Add the details with a food colouring pen. Use clear piping gel to attach it to the recess in the cake.

3

Making the small dinosaurs: *Using the template, cut out two small, running dinosaurs to go on to two sides of the cake. Colour them, using green petal dust and food colouring pens. Position them centrally behind strips of grass on either side of the recessed section.*

4

Making the *Tyrannosaurus* head: *Cut out the large head and colour it with petal dust and food colouring pens. Bend the flap back and cut a support.*
Attach it to back of dinosaur and flap. Use clear piping gel to secure the head in the recess.

5

Making the *Allosaurus*: *Use the template to trace the standing Allosaurus on to rice paper. Colour with petal dust and food colouring pens, before cutting out carefully. Use a strip of rice paper to help support the figure, as before. Apply gel to the tab and attach to the cake top.*

8

Making the *Triceratops*: *Trace the horned Triceratops from the template, colour it with petal dust, and add details with food colouring pens. Trace and colour small clumps of grass in the same way. Cut out carefully, apply gel to the tabs, and secure them to the cake top.*

9

Hiding the *Tyrannosaurus*: Cut another piece of tall grass and colour it green as before. Trim away the lower edge of the grass so that it comes half-way up the head. Using piping gel, stick each end of the grass to each side of the recessed area so that it bows slightly.

6

Making the *Stegosaurus*: Use the template to trace the Stegosaurus on to rice paper. Using the photograph as a guide, colour the beast in with petal dust and food colouring pens. Cut it out carefully and make a supporting tab as before. Attach to the cake top with piping gel.

7

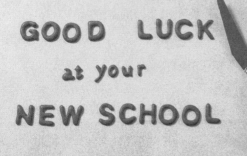

Running out the lettering: Use masking tape to secure a sheet of acetate film over the top of the lettering template. Prepare some run-out consistency royal icing and colour it red. Outline the lettering with a no. 1 piping tube, allow it to dry, then flood in the letters.

10

Applying the lettering: When the letters are dry, carefully remove them from the acetate with a palette knife. Using the template as a guide, mark the position of the letters with a scriber on top of the cake. Attach the letters with dabs of royal icing.

11

Autumn basket

Transform a simple cake with a profusion of colourful flowers, berries and foliage.

This flower basket may look very complicated, but it is, in fact, a very simple cake, topped with an elaborate and striking floral decoration. The flowers and foliage used here are all autumnal – pine cones and pale yellow late roses have been highlighted by brilliant splashes of colour, provided by hawthorn berries, Carnathus thistles, and the deep mauve of Michaelmas daisies. It would be a particularly suitable cake for an autumn birthday party or other celebration, perhaps even for a harvest festival.

The cake itself is formed from two circular sponges, sandwiched with jam and buttercream, and covered with a layer of brown sugarpaste.

PIPING THE BASKETWORK
First, pipe the vertical lines in brown royal icing, ensuring you have an odd number evenly spaced around the cake. Then pipe short, broad, horizontal lines, using a tube with a flattened tip. In the top row, pipe from one vertical, over the top of the second, stopping short of the third. Repeat all the way round. Start the second row one vertical along from the first row, so the piped lines alternate and appear to lie either across, or behind, the verticals, producing a woven effect.

Rolls of brown sugarpaste are used to make the rim of the basket, but flower paste is used for the handle, as a stronger finish is needed. All the flowers, berries and leaves are made out of flower paste. The pine cones are made out of brown sugarpaste, and the scales are piped in brown royal icing, using the same tube used to create the basketwork effect.

FLATTENING A TUBE
Use a hammer to flatten the end of a no. 3 piping tube to produce the broad lines required for the basket-work effect.

PROFESSIONAL SECRETS

Making the thistles

• The orange thistles on the cake are called Carnathus. The fluffy centres are made from two colours of sewing cotton.

• To make these flowers, you will need green flower paste, bright orange cotton thread, bright yellow cotton thread, and 28g covered floristry wire.

• Prepare a length of 28g covered floristry wire, and form a hook at one end.

• Working with both colours of cotton together, wind the two strands around your first two fingers, but not too tightly. Continue looping until you have a sizeable amount.

• Thread the wire in beneath your fingers and catch the cotton in the hook, pulling the loops off. Wind the cotton around just above the hook a few times to secure it.

• Cut through the top of the loops to form the fluffy centre of the thistle flower.

• Cut a calyx from green flower paste. Thread it on to the wire and push it up around the cotton.

• Build up the calyx by adding several small leaves around it, sticking them on with egg white.

• Cut some longer, thinner leaves from flower paste, and thread these on to the wire to form a loose arrangement.

STEP-BY-STEP GUIDE

Piping basketwork:
Using a flattened no. 3 tube for horizontal lines and a no. 2 tube for verticals, pipe basketwork in brown royal icing on cake sides. Roll two long, thin, brown sugarpaste sausages for the rims.

1

Making the handle: *Roll two long, thin, sausages of brown flower paste; twist together. Curve into shape and pinch them together at ends. Form two small rings to support the handle. Leave to dry overnight.*

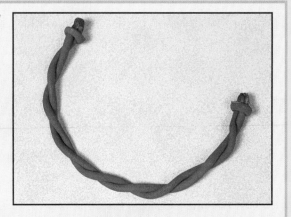

2

Attaching the handle: *Position the handle over the cake and gently push its ends into the sugarpaste until the rings are resting on the surface of the cake, supporting the weight of the handle.*

3

Making daisies: *Colour some flower paste deep mauve and, using a large daisy cutter, cut out several flower shapes. Attach them to 26g floristry wire, closing up the petals slightly on some flowers. Dust the centres with black petal dust, and pipe tiny yellow dots around them.*

4

Making pine cones: *Form some brown sugarpaste into a cone; support on a cocktail stick. Starting at top of cone and working down, pipe rows of scales upwards with flattened no. 3 tube, revolving the cone as you go. Dust with petal dust and support on balls of sugarpaste.*

5

Making full roses: *Work in the same way as when making the half roses, but carry on building up several more layers with large petals, fanning them out as you work. There is no need to add a calyx – simply push the wire of the finished flower into a ball of sugarpaste.*

8

Making rose leaves: *Colour flower paste mid-green, roll it out thinly, and cut out the leaves using a rose-leaf cutter or the template provided. Thread on to 26g covered wire and shape the edges with a ball tool. Leave to dry, supported by a piece of sponge.*

9

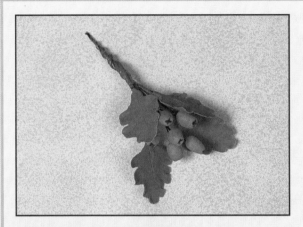

Making hawthorn clusters: *Mould orange-red flower paste into oval berry shapes and thread on to 28g covered wire. Indent tops and paint a cross with brown food colour. Use a leaf cutter for leaves and frill edges with a cocktail stick. Wire clusters of berries and leaves together.*

6

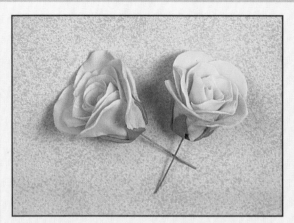

Making half roses: *Colour some flower paste pale yellow. Cut several small petals with a rose-petal cutter, form a central cone around a length of 26g wire, and build up the petals in layers, adding larger petals last. Keep roses fairly tight and add a green flower-paste calyx.*

7

Making the thistles: *Make the fluffy centres of the Carnathus thistles from sewing cotton, and the calyx and small leaves from green flower paste. Cut smaller, thinner leaves from flower paste and wire these up with the flowers.*

10

Assembling the cake: *Secure the wires of all the flowers in balls of brown sugarpaste. Reserving a half rose for the side, arrange the flowers, pine cones, berries and foliage in a pleasing arrangement on top of the cake. Adjust the position of the wires with tweezers.*

11

Little fat hen

Our plump hen looks so realistic that you can almost hear her clucking softly as she sits on her eggs!

HAVE TO HAND

Ingredients: three 20 x 15cm (8 x 6in) oval sponge cakes • jam • buttercream • apricot glaze • 1kg marzipan • 1.25kg sugarpaste • red, yellow, brown and black paste food colourings • egg white.

Equipment: large – at least 30 x 20cm (12 x 8in) – oval cake board • non-stick rolling pin • plastic film • scalpel • clay gun.

Main skills: making shaped cakes • moulding sugarpaste shapes • colouring sugarpaste.

DIFFICULTY   TIME   SUITABILITY

Our little fat hen would make a delightful birthday cake for someone in almost any age group, from a small child to a grandparent. Alternatively, she would make a splendid Easter cake – or even a theme cake for a hen party!

The cake is made from three oval sponge cakes joined together and shaped to make a lovely plump bird. Cover them with marzipan first, then coat them with terracotta-coloured sugarpaste. The lovely ruffled feathers are made by flattening tiny balls of sugarpaste into an oval shape, then layering them from the tail forwards, and attaching them with egg white. You will need to be patient and build up the feathers gradually for the best results.

This terracotta-coloured hen is modelled on a Rhode Island Red, but you could make any kind of hen you like – either a real variety, such as a Leghorn or Buff Orpington, or hens featured in children's story books.

MAKING THE NEST

This fat hen rests on realistic yellow feet, again made from sugarpaste. Her striking red comb and wattle are also moulded out of sugarpaste. The light brown straw for her nest is created by extruding sugarpaste from a clay gun. If you don't have one of these tools, then you could adapt some drinking straws instead.

For an Easter cake, tuck some hard-boiled bantams' eggs, or small chocolate eggs, into the straw.

MAKING FEATHERS
Flatten several small balls of sugarpaste between two layers of plastic film – this will peel away quickly and easily.

DESIGN TOUCH

This hen, made in a lovely warm terracotta colour, is very similar to a Rhode Island Red. This is not a particularly common kind of hen, however, and you might prefer to represent a more familiar breed, especially if the cake is for a child. This is easily done simply by changing the colour of the sugarpaste.

For a speckled hen, for example, use sugarpaste marbled in grey and black. Alternatively, use grey sugarpaste, and brush black petal dust over the edges of the feathers on the finished hen.

Check an encyclopedia or other library reference book for details of other varieties of hen. Two of the most attractive are the Buff Orpington – which is easy to create by making golden-yellow feathers and white feet – and the Leghorn, which is virtually pure white apart from the yellow feet.

A black hen would also be realistic, or you could let your imagination run riot and produce a hen with feathers coloured to your own specifications.

Alternatively, if you decide to use a hen featured in a child's favourite story-book, just model your version on the illustrations in the book you have chosen.

STEP-BY-STEP GUIDE

Shaping the sponges: *Sandwich two oval sponges together with jam and buttercream. Cut the third sponge to shape, standing upright, to form the hen's head and breast. Coat with apricot glaze.*

1

Coating with marzipan: *Roll out the marzipan and use it to cover the cake, being careful to mould it closely to the shape of the hen as you work. Build it up slightly at the back to form the tail.*

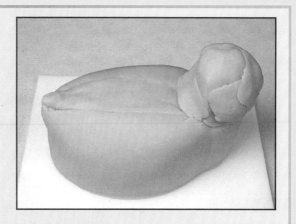

2

Covering with sugarpaste: *Colour a large quantity of sugarpaste terracotta. Roll a portion out on to a work surface dusted with icing sugar. Mould firmly over cake, hands dusted with icing-sugar.*

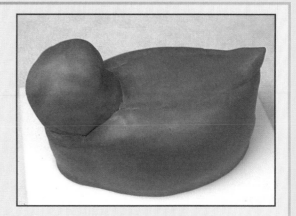

3

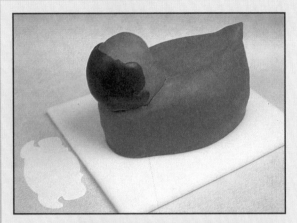

Starting the face: *Use the template provided to cut out the 'mask' that covers the entire front of the hen's head. Colour a small quantity of sugarpaste deep brown. Then, cut out the 'mask' and attach it to the front of the head with dabs of royal icing.*

4

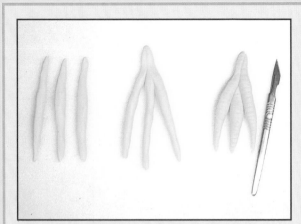

Making the feet: *Colour some sugarpaste yellow, then roll out six thin, tapered sausages. Pinch three together at one end, then splay them out at the other end. Using a scalpel, mark horizontal lines all over each foot to indicate the scales.*

5

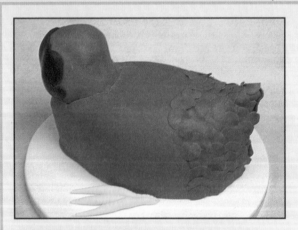

Attaching the feathers: *Use egg white to attach the feathers to the body. Start at the tail end and work forwards, stopping well short of the wing areas. Use the template provided to cut out the wings. Scribe the wing shape on each side of the hen's body.*

8

Making the wings: *Roll out some terracotta-coloured sugarpaste and use the template to cut out two wings. Attach them to the hen's body with small dabs of royal icing. Continue adding feathers to the body, overlapping them neatly at the back, underneath the tail.*

9

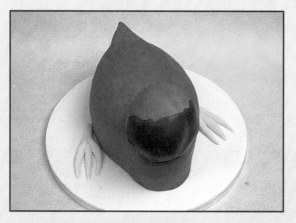

Assembling the hen: *Cover a large oval cake board with ivory-coloured sugarpaste, and leave it to dry. Position the hen centrally on the board and place the feet on either side of her body. Attach the body and the feet to the board with small dabs of royal icing.*

6

Making the feathers: *Form terracotta-coloured sugarpaste into tiny balls, place them between two layers of plastic film, and flatten each one into a disc with your thumb. Peel the film away, and continue until you have enough; you will need a large number to cover the hen all over.*

7

Making the face: *Add feathers to wings. Cut a comb, wattle and cheek patches from red sugarpaste. Mould a yellow beak and attach it with a cocktail stick. Make eyes from small discs of white sugarpaste, topped with black. Paint on black claws.*

10

Making the straw: *Colour some sugarpaste light brown, and use a clay gun to extrude long lengths of this to make the straw. Pile the straw up around the base of the cake on all sides of the hen to make the nest. For an Easter cake, tuck in a few real or imitation eggs.*

11

Robins in the snow

This cheerful Christmas cake, with a family of robins having fun in the snow, is sure to put everyone in the Christmas spirit.

HAVE TO HAND

Ingredients: *20 x 15cm (8 x 6in) oval fruit cake • apricot glaze• 1kg marzipan • 1.25kg sugarpaste • petal dust • paste food colourings • caster sugar • royal icing • length of uncooked spaghetti • pastillage paste.*

Equipment: *oval cake board • 26g covered floristry wire • floristry tape • scriber • piping bag • tweezers.*

Main skills: *colouring and moulding sugarpaste • making sugarpaste figures • texturing cake boards.*

DIFFICULTY   TIME   SUITABILITY

I f there are children in your family, you may decide to decorate your Christmas cake in a way which will particularly appeal to them. Even if you have already made the family Christmas cake, you might still like to make another smaller cake. In this way you can make one cake with lots of brandy for the grown-ups, and another for the children – without brandy! You can even make this as a sponge cake if they would prefer it.

CHRISTMAS FESTIVITIES

The above cake, featuring a family of robins having fun in the snow, is a perfect choice. It is humorous and also provides a refreshing change

from the more traditional styles of Christmas cake decoration.

The cake is first baked in an oval tin and a wedge shape is then cut out at the front to form a slide. The cake is covered in the usual way with white sugarpaste and marzipan. Snowdrifts are built up with stiff royal icing and sprinkled with caster sugar to add the sparkle of freshly fallen snow. Choose quite a large cake board so that you have plenty of room to attach the figures to the scene.

The robins are made in different sizes, and their beaks give them different expressions. These are made either from a solid triangle or a folded diamond shape.

The finished cake is a great conversation piece for the tea table – but you'll probably have to defend your little robins from children's eager fingers! Since all the decorations, apart from the sledge, are made with sugarpaste, the children can eat them as a special treat – but do make sure you remove the spaghetti legs first.

A TASTY ALTERNATIVE
If your children do not like sugarpaste, make the yule log from a flaky chocolate bar so that they can still have a treat from the cake top.

PROFESSIONAL SECRETS

Assembling the cake

• Many of the final touches to the figures are added while the cake is being assembled. You will need royal icing to secure all the details in place.

• Attach the white snow robin to the base of the cake and position the sledge. Place the baby robin lying down in the snow with his beak open.

• Pipe in the eyes of the robins with tiny dots of royal icing. When they are dry, colour the centres with a food-colouring pen.

• Make the snowballs for the top of the cake by rolling little sugarpaste balls. Dip them into stiff royal icing and cover them with icing sugar. Pile them at the foot of the mother robin. Place one on her wing.

• If you want to add a little Christmas tree, make a cone of green sugarpaste and snip at it with scissors to give the impression of leaves. You can add caster sugar to it to give the impression of fallen snow. You could also place some colourful little sugarpaste presents around the base of the cake.

STEP-BY-STEP GUIDE

Shaping the fruit cake: *Using a sharp knife, carefully sculpt one side of the fruit cake so that it resembles the shape of a down-hill slope or slide. Use the template as a guide.*

1

Coating with sugarpaste: *Cover with marzipan, retaining the shape of the slope. Coat cake and board with white sugarpaste. Make the snowdrift with stiff royal icing sprinkled with caster sugar.*

2

Making the robins: *Roll a dark brown sugarpaste ball for the robin's body and a smaller one for the head. Make two flat cones for the wings, a red circle for the breast, and a beak. Assemble with royal icing.*

3

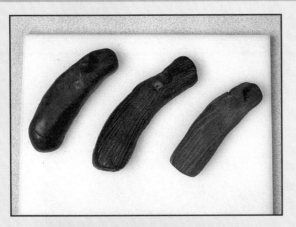

Making the log: *Roll a large sausage of dark brown sugarpaste, squaring off the edge, flattening the base and curving it slightly. Make the side branch by pinching a piece of sugarpaste near the top. Scribe bark markings and brush with brown and cream petal dust.*

4

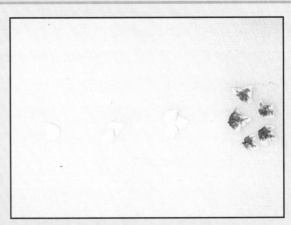

Making the ivy: *Cut a 'V' shape in the top of a piping bag. Use white royal icing to pipe the leaves. Leave them to dry and then paint dark green markings at the centre of each leaf with paste food colour and clear alcohol. Attach them to the cake with dots of royal icing.*

5

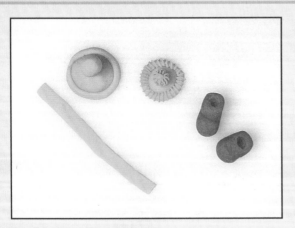

Making the hat and scarf: *Roll a thin strip of sugarpaste for the scarf and assemble it before it begins to dry. Make a woolly hat from an indented half-sphere shape. Top with a tiny ball and add a brim. Pipe ribbing. Form boots from cylinders of paste and indent top with scriber.*

8

Making the snowdrift: *Add a lump of sugarpaste to the base of the slide. Coat it with royal icing and dust it with caster sugar. Cut two 2.5cm (1in) pieces of uncooked spaghetti and insert them into snowdrift. Add a pair of boots and an open beak peeping out of the snowdrift.*

9

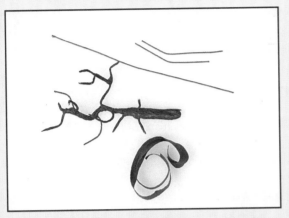

Making the tree: *Take a 7.5cm (3in) length of covered floristry wire and bind some smaller pieces of wire along its length to form the branches. Make up some more pieces of wire into small, forked branches and bind these on too. Bend them into shape with tweezers.*

6

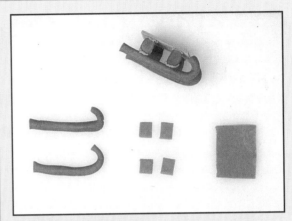

Making the sledge: *Make a postage stamp-sized rectangle out of mid-brown-coloured pastillage, plus four tiny squares and two walking stick-shaped runners. Allow to dry, then assemble with royal icing, supporting the sledge base on the squares which sit on top of the runners.*

7

Making the snow robin: *Make a snow robin in the same way as an ordinary robin, but using white sugarpaste. Use black sugarpaste for the eyes, and add a turquoise scarf and hat. Make some sugarpaste snowballs dipped in royal icing and caster sugar.*

10

Attaching the birds: *Attach the log to the cake and sit the father robin on it. Attach his spaghetti legs and boots. Stand the mother robin at the edge of the cake. Stand the tree in sugarpaste. Pile up 'snow' around its base and dust the branches. Add a trail of ivy to the log.*

11

Clamped-car calamity

Take the sting out of the disaster of having a car clamped by commemorating the event with a special cake.

HAVE TO HAND

Ingredients: *two 20cm (8in) round sponge cakes • jam • buttercream • apricot glaze • 1kg marzipan • 2kg sugarpaste • 150g pastillage paste • royal icing • yellow, grey, black, red and silver food colourings • brown food-colouring pen • petal dusts*

Equipment: *large rectangular cake board • scriber • rolling pin • ball tool • no. 2 piping tube • pieces of foam sponge.*

Main skills: *making shaped cakes • moulding sugarpaste • line piping.*

DIFFICULTY	TIME	SUITABILITY
✓ ✓	⊠ ⊠	🍒 🍾

This delightful canary-yellow car squats by the kerb on a city street – parked on double yellow lines. Turn the cake round and you will see that the car has acquired not only a parking ticket but also the ultimate disaster, a wheel clamp.

If you have a friend or relative who has suffered from having their car clamped recently, this cake would make a fun reminder of their trauma! It would also be the perfect birthday cake for anyone with a love of cars.

The car itself is created quite straightforwardly by sculpting two round sponge cakes. These are then covered, first with marzipan and then with sugarpaste. The window and bonnet details are added with sugarpaste, highlighted with piped white royal icing. Pastillage is used to create the very effective chrome accessories: bumpers, headlights, hub caps and bonnet handle. The details (such as the spokes of the hub caps) are first piped on, then each piece is painted with silver food colouring. As this is non-edible, take care to remove the silver-painted items before cutting the cake.

ADDING FINISHING TOUCHES

Pastillage is also used to create the clamp, numberplates and parking ticket, as it can be rolled very thinly and dries hard. The car rests at the kerbside of an all-too-typical city street, liberally potholed. The gutter is littered with autumn leaves and rubbish. We made a squashed cola can, but beer cans, crisp packets and cigarette butts would also be fun.

VARYING THE DESIGN

Your car doesn't have to be yellow; black (with white windows) or bright red would look particularly good with the silver bumpers and accessories. You could also add an appropriate inscription to the sun visor, or personalised numberplates.

You could of course make a different model of car altogether. For a conventional saloon, carve the sponges into a more angular shape and leave out the wheel arches.

PROFESSIONAL SECRETS

Making the street

- To add extra interest to the cake, decorate the cake board to suggest a typical city street, complete with autumn leaves and a crumpled tin can lying around in the gutter.

- Start building up the street scene by putting small lumps of sugarpaste round the long edges of the cake board. Then coat the whole thing with grey sugarpaste. Make the potholes by texturing the surface with the handle of a rolling pin.

- Make the kerb from a long strip of grey sugarpaste, marked with a scalpel to suggest individual stone blocks. Shade the blocks with darker grey petal dust.

- Form the double yellow lines from two strips of thinly rolled yellow sugarpaste.

- Make the drain from a rectangle of black sugarpaste, overlaid with strips of dark grey to form the grating.

- To make the cola can, use a small cylinder of red sugarpaste, then squash it in the middle to give the crumpled effect. Pipe the lettering in white and paint the ends silver.

- Finally, roll out some yellow sugarpaste thinly and cut out a number of leaf shapes. Shape them with a ball tool to give a dry, withered look, then give them their autumn colours by brushing them liberally with red, orange and brown petal dust.

STEP-BY-STEP GUIDE

Shaping the sponges:
Halve horizontally and sandwich with jam and buttercream. Then halve vertically and sandwich together, flat sides down. Cut an L-shape for windscreen; angle downwards for bonnet.

1

Preparing the board:
Coat the cake board with grey sugarpaste. Mark the potholes and add the kerb, double yellow lines, drain, cola can and fallen leaves (as described in Professional Secrets).

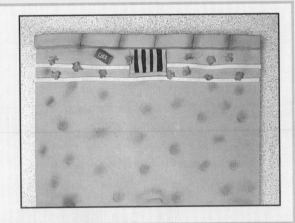

2

Covering the cake:
Coat the cake with apricot glaze. Roll out the marzipan and cover the cake, moulding it firmly around the shape. Dry overnight, then cover with yellow sugarpaste. Place on prepared cake board.

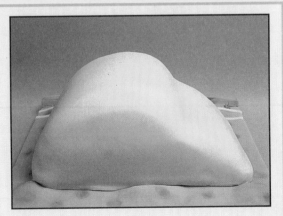

3

Making the wheels and the running boards: Using the templates provided, cut out two running boards from thinly rolled black sugarpaste, and then four wheels from thickly rolled black sugarpaste. Attach the running boards and the wheels with dabs of royal icing.

4

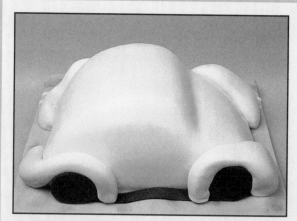

Making the wheel arches: Roll out four fat sausages of yellow sugarpaste, flaring out the front ends on two of them to match the template. Attach the shaped arches over the two front wheels, and the plain ones over the two back wheels.

5

Piping the details: Using white royal icing and a no. 2 piping tube, pipe around each window and pipe the outlines for the doors. Pipe a door handle on each front door and a line down the centre of the bonnet. Also pipe two windscreen wipers at an angle across the windscreen.

8

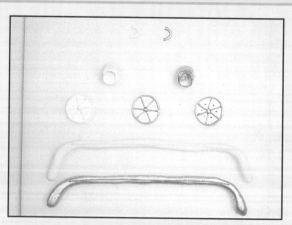

Making accessories: Use two rolls of pastillage to form bumpers, and make two headlamps and a bonnet handle. Cut four hub caps from thinly rolled pastillage. Pipe details with white royal icing. Paint everything silver. Add black dots between hub cap spokes.

9

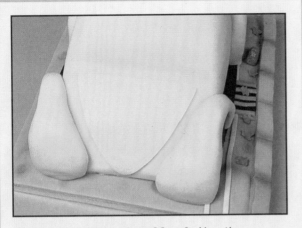

Making the bonnet and boot: *Use the templates to cut out the bonnet and boot lid from yellow sugarpaste. Attach them to the car. Scribe a line around the bonnet, parallel to the outside edge. Mark blocks of short parallel lines on the top of the boot lid as air vents.*

6

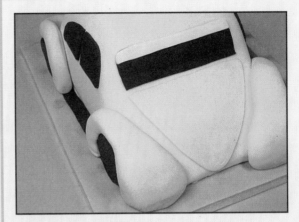

Making the windows: *Using the templates provided, cut out four side windows, a windscreen and one rear window from black sugarpaste. Cut a strip for the sun visor out of white sugarpaste. Attach them all with a line of royal icing piped around their back edges.*

7

Attaching the accessories: *Use dabs of white royal icing to attach the hub caps to the centres of the wheels, and to hold the headlights and boot handle in place. Attach the bumpers, supporting them with pieces of foam sponge until they are completely dry.*

10

Adding final details: *Colour some pastillage yellow, roll it out thinly and use the template to make the wheel clamp. Mark lines with food-colouring pen; attach with royal icing. Cut a tiny pastillage parking ticket, add black lettering and attach. Do the same for the numberplates.*

11

Time for bed

Bedtime is more fun with this cake made in the shape of a bed complete with sleepy teddies!

HAVE TO HAND

Ingredients: *sponge baked in a 26 x 36cm (10 x 14in) swiss-roll tin • jam • buttercream • 1.25kg sugarpaste • royal icing • black, brown, beige, pink, lilac and blue paste food colours • cream, brown and beige petal dusts • pastillage.*

Equipment: *30cm (12in) square, scalloped cake board • roller • foam • straight frill cutter • scalpel • black food-colouring pen • lace cutter • paintbrushes • no. 1 piping tube.*

Main skills: *working with sugarpaste.*

DIFFICULTY	TIME	SUITABILITY

B edtime's here and Big Teddy is ready for bed. His own toy teddy is already tucked in under the crisp white sheets and cosy patchwork quilt, and Big Teddy is about to climb in to bed himself. This cake, beautifully executed in subtle pastel shades, would be a great success at a small child's birthday party, and it would also be suitable for other age groups. It would, for example, be perfect for anyone recuperating from an illness.

MAKING THE BED

The bed is made from a sponge cake baked in a swiss-roll tin which is then cut into quarters and sandwiched together. It is covered with sugarpaste in the usual way, then covered with a pale blue, sugarpaste quilt. A plump, white, sugarpaste pillow sits at the head of the bed. The frills on the bed are also made from sugarpaste, which means that – apart from the foot and head of the bed, which are pastillage – the whole cake is edible. Triangles of pastel-coloured sugarpaste are used to decorate the quilt, although it would be easy to modify this design if you wanted to.

The cake board is prepared first. It is coated with sugarpaste, left to dry, and then sponged with soft, pastel shades of royal icing. The headboard and footboard are made from brown-coloured pastillage paste, and are then dusted with a mixture of brown petal dusts in order to create the wood-grain effect.

SUGAR TEDDIES

The heads and paws of both teddies are coloured in creamy beige-coloured sugarpaste. Since it is hidden beneath the quilt, the body of the toy teddy can be formed from white sugarpaste, but Big Teddy's body is made from lilac sugarpaste to represent his sleepsuit. The features of both bears are created using a black food-colouring pen to form the mouth, and black sugarpaste to form the nose and eyes.

If the cake is for someone other than a child, you can put cocktail sticks inside the larger teddy to support his limbs and head, but remember that these represent a choking hazard, so they must be removed before you serve the cake.

DESIGN TOUCH

You can take the original idea of the teddies-in-bed cake and change it in order to produce a cake which becomes very personal to the recipient.

For example, if the recipient is a great collector of soft toys, then you could fill the bed full of soft teddies, so that there is hardly enough room for Big Teddy to climb in.

Change the quilt cover to resemble a favourite cover of the recipient – perhaps flowery, or with a bright geometric design. Add in little extras, such as an open book face down on the bed, or a pair of slippers beside the bed.

You could also include a bedside table with an alarm clock, and perhaps a glass of milk and a plate of biscuits.

For a cake for a little boy, change the colour scheme and make up the bedding and quilt in a mixture of bright, primary colours. Make Big Teddy's sleepsuit brightly coloured, and use stronger colours of royal icing to sponge the cake board.

For a humorous anniversary cake, make a male and female teddy – perhaps one with mini curlers in her hair, the other wearing a pair of stripy pajamas.

Covering the cake board: *Coat the scalloped cake board with white sugarpaste, trimming the edges carefully, and then sponge it with royal icing in shades of pink, blue and lilac.*

1

Assembling the sponge: *Cut the sponge into four 13 x 18cm (5 x 7in) sections. Sandwich them together with jam and buttercream. Cover with white sugarpaste and place the cake centrally on the board.*

2

Making the frills: *Roll out some pink sugarpaste and use a straight frill cutter to cut lengths of frill. Frill the edges with a cocktail stick. Moisten the back and attach frill to the long sides of the bed.*

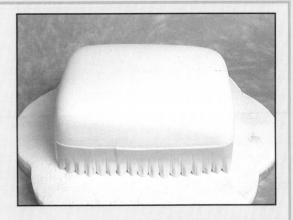

3

STEP-BY-STEP GUIDE

Making the pillow: *Form the pillow out of a ball of white sugarpaste, moulding it into shape and making an indentation for the small teddy's head. Position the pillow at the head of the bed, securing it with a dab of royal icing.*

4

Making the toy teddy: *Make the toy teddy's head from beige-coloured sugarpaste. Add ears and a pale muzzle. The eyes and nose are black sugarpaste, and a food-colouring pen is used for the mouth. Mould body out of white sugarpaste.*

5

Making the big teddy: *Make a teddy's head as before, but larger. Pipe in the whites of the eyes. Form the sleepsuit from lilac sugarpaste. Mould the paws and feet from beige sugarpaste and attach them with dabs of royal icing.*

8

Making head and footboards: *Colour some pastillage beige and roll it out thinly. Using the templates, cut out a headboard and footboard. Dust them with a mixture of cream, beige and dark brown petal dusts to simulate wood grain.*

9

Cutting the quilt: *Roll out a rectangle of pale blue sugarpaste, 23 x 15cm (9 x 6in). Cut the shorter edges with a lace cutter. Moisten the back with water and smooth it in position over the teddy, folding back the top right corner.*

6

Decorating the quilt: *Cut a strip of white sugarpaste 23 x 3cm (9 x 1¼in). Moisten the back and attach to the top edge of the quilt. Cut triangles from pink, white and blue sugarpaste and attach to the quilt with dabs of royal icing.*

7

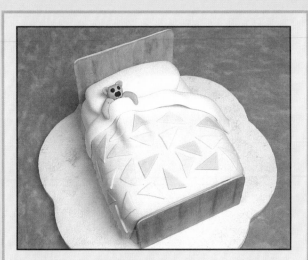

Completing the bed: *Make the arms for the toy teddy from beige-coloured sugarpaste and place them over the sheet, attaching them with royal icing. Attach the head and footboard to the ends of the bed with dabs of royal icing.*

10

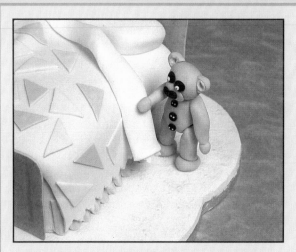

Assembling the big teddy: *Use royal icing to assemble the teddy. Position him beside the bed as if to climb in, securing the paw to the sheet with a dab of royal icing. Support him with a piece of foam until completely dry.*

11

Bees around the honey pot

This pretty pot is so full of honey that it's spilling out and attracting a buzz of busy bees!

Our delightful honey pot is made from a sponge cake baked in a pudding bowl, which gives it the authentic shape. The up-turned cake is covered with marzipan, and extra rings of marzipan create the effect of the moulded sides. A stopper-type lid is then added, and a coating of deep creamy-brown sugarpaste gives the cake the look of a traditional, glazed, stoneware honey pot.

This cake would make a great novelty birthday cake for any age group. It would be particularly suitable for a lover of honey, or even a fan of Pooh Bear! For a children's party, you could add honey sandwiches and honey biscuits.

MAKING THE BUSY BEES
The bees are made out of balls of black and yellow sugarpaste, some of which are flattened into discs to form the body, with a cone for the 'tail' and

a black ball for the head. The striped bodies are created by joining discs in alternate colours. A little black sting is then added to the tail.

The bees' antennae are simply made out of flower stamens which are poked into the bee's head, and the eyes are piped with white and terracotta royal icing. Pastillage paste is used to create the wings, which are brushed with lustre petal dust to give them a shine. They are attached at an angle with royal icing and supported with pieces of foam sponge until they are dry. A black food-colouring pen is used to draw in the veined markings on both sides of the wings.

MAKING HONEY AND HONEY POT
The blobs of honey are made out of royal icing coloured bright yellow and run out in various sizes on to a piece of acetate or greaseproof paper. When they are completely dry, some are stuck on to the sides of the honey

pot to look like honey dripping down, while others are combined to resemble pools of honey on the cake board. The final touch is a sugarpaste label bearing the word 'Honey'.

MAKING THE WINGS
The wings of the bees can also be made from rice paper rather than pastillage.

PROFESSIONAL SECRETS

Adding a taste of honey

• If you want to add the flavour of honey to the cake, there are several recipes for sponges which use honey instead of, or in combination with, sugar.

• However, because the cake is baked in a pudding bowl instead of a standard tin, you are likely to have difficulty in making the recipe work satisfactorily.

• A better idea would be to flavour the buttercream, used to sandwich the sponge layers together, with honey. You should use a clover or heather honey, as they have a more distinctive taste than ordinary honey.

• To make enough honey-flavoured buttercream to sandwich the honey-pot sponge together, use 360g sifted icing sugar, 150g softened butter and one tablespoon of clear honey.

• Put the butter in a bowl and beat it until it is pale and fluffy. Gradually add the icing sugar, mixing it in thoroughly as you go. Finally beat in the honey. Use just enough to flavour the buttercream and leave it thick enough to spread.

• If the cake is made for a children's party, you could continue the honey theme by serving honey sandwiches. But be sure to make them with thick, not runny honey, otherwise the resulting mess could be appalling!

Marzipan coating: *Split the sponge into several horizontal layers and sandwich them together with jam and buttercream. Cover with apricot glaze and coat with marzipan. Make a lid out of marzipan.*

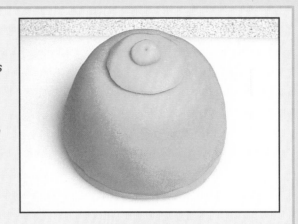

1

Shaping the honey pot: *Roll out several thin sausages of marzipan. Attach them at intervals around the pot, using water or clear spirit, to create the moulded shape of a traditional honey pot.*

2

Coating the cake board: *Cover the cake board with ivory sugarpaste. Dust it with a mixture of cream and brown petal dusts, forming a pattern of lines to achieve a wood-grain effect.*

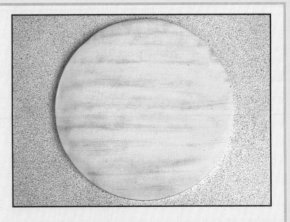

3

STEP-BY-STEP GUIDE

Covering the honey pot with sugarpaste:
Colour some sugarpaste a deep creamy brown and roll it out. Brush the marzipan with clear spirit. Cover the honey pot with the sugarpaste, moulding it carefully over the rings created with the marzipan.

4

Making the label: Roll pale yellow sugarpaste very thinly and use template to cut two labels. Roll some more sugarpaste into a thin sausage and use it to write 'Honey' on one label. Wet back of second label, lay over writing and press gently in place until 'Honey' can be clearly read.

5

Assembling bees: Join yellow and black discs with dabs of royal icing. Insert sting into end of cone. Attach head to front at a slightly higher level. Roll out pastillage and, using templates, cut out wings. Draw veins on both sides and brush with lustre petal dust. Attach at an angle.

8

Making the honey: Colour some royal icing bright yellow and use it to run out 16-20 pools of honey in various sizes on a sheet of acetate. Leave them to dry overnight before easing them carefully away from the sheet with a cranked palette knife.

9

Attaching the label: *Brush the honey pot with dark brown petal dust, concentrating the shading underneath the rings. Attach the label halfway up the front of the pot with white royal icing. Support the label on a piece of foam sponge until it is completely dry.*

6

Forming bees: *Colour some sugarpaste black and some creamy yellow. Form two small discs and a cone of yellow, and two discs and one ball of black. With a no. 1 tube, pipe two white eyes on black ball and add antennae made of flower stamens. Mould sting from black sugarpaste.*

7

Finishing the pot: *Roll a long, thin sausage of creamy-brown sugarpaste and form into rim for pot. Attach with royal icing. Attach blobs of honey to give effect of it spilling out around the pot and on the board. Use a no. 2 tube to pipe more honey below rim with yellow royal icing.*

10

Positioning the bees: *Using a no. 1 tube and terracotta royal icing, pipe centres of the bees' eyes and decorate label with flowers. Using royal icing, attach two bees to top of the pot, one to cake board and one to the side. Support bees on the side with foam sponge until dry.*

11

Back to the Sixties

A novelty cake with a difference, featuring Sixties-style furniture and flooring.

This is a cake for when you want to produce something really different. It is based on furnishing ideas from the 1960s, which frequently used bold and contrasting colour schemes. One of its most striking features is the black and white flooring effect on the cake top, which produces a different perspective according to the angle from which it is viewed.

The cake itself has an unusual, asymmetrical shape – these were also very fashionable at the time – being a square with one corner removed. All the colours used are extremely dramatic – black and white for the cake board and cake covering, and strong colours, such as red and blue, for the furniture.

The strong lines of the cake are set off by the plain blue ribbon tied around its base, and the contrasting black cake board.

MAKING THE DESIGNER FURNITURE

The bizarrely shaped furniture and its brilliant colours also set the pieces firmly in the right era. The amazing 'red lips' velvet sofa – shades of Mick Jagger! – and the small, blue, moulded armchair are both made from coloured sugarpaste.

Pastillage paste, being much harder and stronger than sugarpaste, is used to create the box shelving unit – another innovative feature of the time – and the unusually shaped legs of the glass-topped coffee table.

The top of the coffee table is great fun to make. Looking exactly like the asymmetrical table-tops made out of coloured glass that were popular at the time, it is actually made from a

boiled sweet. The sweet is baked in the oven so that it melts and spreads into a flat, free-form shape with a clear, jewel-like sparkle. It's a good idea to bake several to be sure of getting one that is a suitable shape – no two turn out exactly alike!

USING THE SIXTIES CAKE

Guaranteed to be a major talking point at any party, this brilliantly original cake would be suitable for almost any adult birthday celebration – anything from a coming-of-age party to a 50th birthday.

It would also make a particularly appropriate anniversary cake for a couple who were teenagers and got married in that era – the 'groovy', swinging Sixties – bringing back a host of memories. But be warned: once they start talking about those years, there'll be no stopping them!

DESIGN TOUCH

The recipient of the cake may have some much-loved piece of furniture that you would like to reproduce instead of the designs shown here.

Alternatively, you could look through furniture design books of the Sixties and choose some suitable pieces. Designs of the period were mostly either very angular, or very soft and squashy. These are easy to reproduce if you use sugarpaste for more rounded items, such as sofas and bean-bag chairs. Colour is also a very strong indicator of the period, so follow the colours of any item carefully. Look out for orange, bright red, purple and bitter chocolate. When you make the 'glass' coffee-table top, it is worth baking a few extra boiled sweets in case you accidentally crack your chosen piece, or it does not come out as expected. Each boiled sweet will melt into a different asymmetrical shape. Some will set with air bubbles trapped inside, which may or may not be to your liking. Try out lots of different colours, then choose the one which works best (or alternatively, the one which clashes the most) with your chosen set of furniture.

Shaping the cake:
Bake a deep, square fruit cake. Using the template provided, cut off one corner. For an even finish, make sure you remove an equal amount from the whole depth of the cake.

1

Covering the cake and board: *Brush cake with apricot glaze, coat with marzipan and leave to dry overnight. Brush with spirit and coat with white sugarpaste. Cover the cake board in black sugarpaste; assemble.*

2

Creating the floor:
Using the template provided, lightly scribe the lines for the tile markings on to the top of the cake. Then, draw over the scribed lines with a black food-colouring pen and ruler.

3

STEP-BY-STEP GUIDE

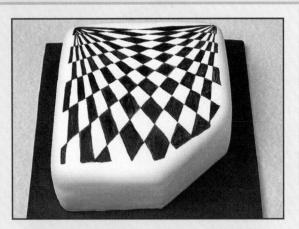

Colouring the tiles: *Using a fine paintbrush and black petal dust mixed with clear spirit, carefully paint in alternate tiles throughout the whole cake top design. Be careful to keep the tile shapes neat, and not to let any petal dust blow on to the white sugarpaste.*

4

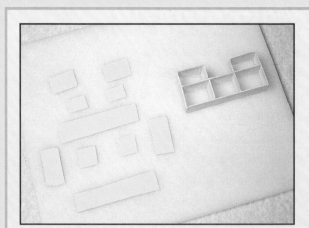

Making the shelves: *Roll out some yellow pastillage and use the templates provided to cut out the shelf sections. Leave overnight. When dry, use royal icing to assemble sections into a box-shelving unit. Support vertical pieces with foam sponge until they are dry.*

5

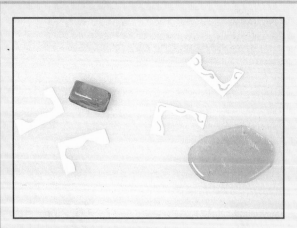

Making the coffee table top: *Place a couple of boiled sweets on a piece of baking parchment. Bake at 150°C/300°F/Gas Mark 2 for 8-10 minutes. Leave to cool. Meanwhile, use the template to make the legs from white pastillage. Decorate with piped, yellow swirls.*

8

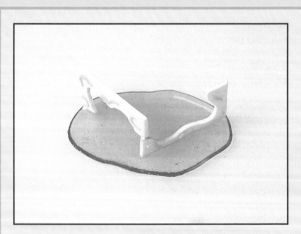

Assembling the coffee table: *Put the prepared pastillage coffee table legs together with royal icing and position them as shown on the underside of the table top. Support them with a piece of foam sponge until they are completely dry.*

9

Making the 'red lips' sofa: *Divide the red sugarpaste into two pieces. Mould them into the upper and lower lip shapes, using the template provided. Then assemble the two lip shapes to form the sofa, using royal icing to hold them firmly together.*

6

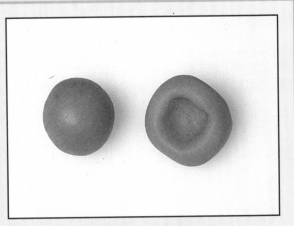

Making the moulded chair: *Roll out some blue sugarpaste into a small ball. Indent the top of the ball deeply with your thumb in order to create the seat. Position the indentation slightly off centre, so that the back of the chair is higher than the front.*

7

Adding ribbon to the cake: *Fix a length of broad blue satin ribbon around the base of the cake. Secure it at the back with a dab of royal icing. (If you want to make the cake look even more dramatic, you could use a red ribbon instead, to pick up the colour of the 'lips' sofa.)*

10

Arranging the furniture: *Trim the edge of the cake board with a length of black satin ribbon. Arrange the furniture as shown, or however you prefer, on the top of the cake. When you are happy with the relative positions, secure each piece with dabs of royal icing.*

11

Cosy cottage

Create a fairy-tale cottage with flowers around the door, a thatched roof, and a cat waiting to be let in.

HAVE TO HAND

Ingredients: two 25 x 35cm (10 x 14in) sponge cakes, baked in swiss-roll tins • jam • 1kg marzipan • clear spirit • 1.2kg sugarpaste • buttercream • 50g flower paste • 500g royal icing • orange, brown, green, cream, yellow, pink and black paste food colours • brown, cream, black and green petal dusts.
Equipment: 30cm (12in) square cake board • sharp knife • palette knife • no. 1 piping tube • cocktail stick • piece of foam sponge • medium and fine paintbrushes • small and medium sized plunger cutters.
Main skills: moulding sponge cake • working with sugarpaste • using colour.

DIFFICULTY	TIME	SUITABILITY
✓ ✓	⊠ ⊠	🍒 🍾

Have you ever dreamed of a whitewashed, thatched cottage in the country, with roses around the door, a well-kept, flower-strewn lawn and a cat waiting to greet you at the door? Well, now is your chance to own one – even if it is just in edible form!

This wonderful country cottage would be the ideal birthday cake for any city-dweller with a yearning for the countryside, and would also make a charming retirement cake.

MOULDING THE COTTAGE

The cottage is moulded from two sponge cakes baked in swiss-roll tins. It is cut to shape, then sandwiched with jam and buttercream and coated with marzipan and sugarpaste.

The thatched roof is created by spreading royal icing thickly over the marzipan, then texturing it with a cocktail stick or sharp knife. Royal icing is also used to sponge the walls of the cottage, giving them a rough appearance, and to sponge the green lawn, giving the effect of grass.

The pretty flowers and foliage that decorate the house and garden are all made from flower paste, apart from some piped leaves in the flower pots. The cat is pressure piped with black royal icing. The rest of the details are painted on to the house with petal dust and clear spirit.

DESIGN ALTERNATIVES

The basic cottage shape is very simple to make and you could have fun creating different designs or copying a real cottage for someone lucky enough to own one. The walls can be covered in sugarpaste of a different colour – pink, perhaps – and then sponged with royal icing in the same tone.

Alternatively, stonework walls can be created by painting in the outlines of stones with soft grey or golden brown petal dust. The roof thatch could be darker, or you could even create a tiled roof, applying tiles of appropriately coloured sugarpaste instead of royal icing. Take ideas from books, magazines and photographs – or from real life.

The one drawback of this lovely cake is that the recipient may become such a proud owner that he or she will find that they can't bear to eat it!

PROFESSIONAL SECRETS

Making the flowers and pussy cat

- Flowers – Colour flower paste in three shades of pink and cut out the flowers for the lawn and around the door with small and medium-sized plunger cutters.

- Ivy leaves – Colour flower paste deep and mid-green and use the template to cut out the leaves.

- Tulips – Flatten some small balls of flower paste in the three pink colours to form thin petal shapes. Roll up to make tulips.

- Leaves – Use template provided to cut these out of deep green flower paste. Use scalpel to mark fine veins on ivy and tulip leaves.

- Pots – Mould these from terracotta-coloured sugarpaste. Fill them with soft brown icing, then add plunger blossoms with piped centres. Use a greaseproof-paper bag with a hole cut in one corner to pipe the leaves directly on to the pots.

- Cat – This is pressure piped from black royal icing. The face details are piped: white royal icing for muzzle and eyes; pink for the nose; and black for the pupils.

Shaping the cottage: Cut cakes into quarters. Stack six pieces and sandwich with jam and buttercream. Stand two on the end of the stack to form chimney breast. Shape roof to a point and carve a chimney.

1

Coating with marzipan: Spread jam over the cake and cover it with marzipan. Work in sections, covering the walls and the roof separately. Then coat the chimney breast. Leave to dry overnight.

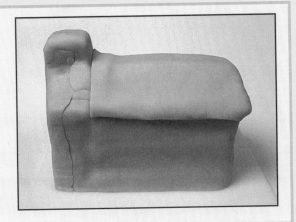

2

Covering the cake: Brush cake with clear spirit. Coat walls and chimney breast with ivory sugarpaste. Leave roof exposed. Cover board with green sugarpaste and place cake to rear of board.

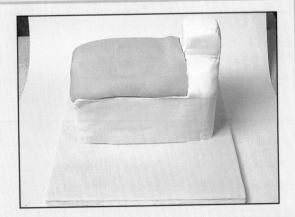

3

STEP-BY-STEP GUIDE

Creating the roof: *Make up a quantity of royal icing to normal piping consistency and spread it over the marzipan roof with a palette knife. At this stage, just spread it thickly and don't worry about achieving a smooth finish. The rough finish is part of the effect.*

4

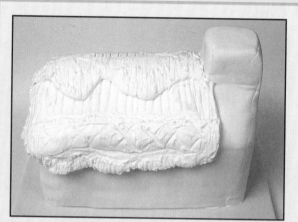

Texturing the roof: *Add another scalloped layer of royal icing to the top of the roof to suggest layers of overlapping thatch. Texture the thatch with a cocktail stick or a scalpel, marking vertical lines and diamonds. Leave it to dry overnight.*

5

Adding the windows: *Using the template provided, scribe the windows, then dust the frames with brown petal dust. Use a fine paintbrush and black petal dust mixed with clear spirit to paint in diamond shapes to represent old-fashioned, leaded windows.*

8

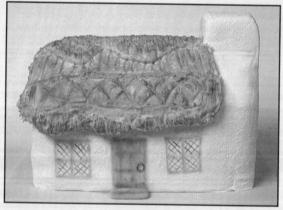

Texturing the walls: *Using a small piece of sponge and cream-coloured royal icing, sponge the walls to give them a rough-cast, textured look. Work carefully around the windows and below the thatched roof, covering over any joins in the sugarpaste surface.*

9

Colouring the thatch: *Mix some brown and orange paste food colours with some royal icing. Paint the thatch with a paintbrush, adding a small amount of water if necessary. Take your time over this so that you gain the most realistic effect possible.*

6

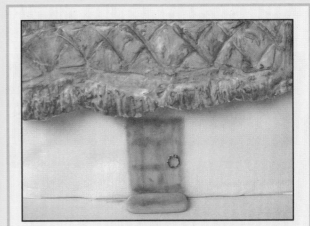

Adding the door: *Using the template, scribe the outline of the door. Dust it with brown and cream petal dust to create the effect of wood. Pipe the handle. Leave to dry, then dust with black petal dust and clear spirit. Make doorstep from a slab of grey sugarpaste brushed with brown petal dust.*

7

Adding flowers: *Attach flowers around the door with dabs of royal icing. Use a no. 1 tube to pipe centres and paint in the stems with petal dust and clear spirit. Set tulips and leaves at either corner of cottage. Attach ivy to the chimney and petal dust it with brown.*

10

Planting the garden: *Sponge grass with pale green icing. Make path from grey sugarpaste dusted with brown petal dust. Attach ribbon to board. Add groups of flowers to lawn, secure with icing and pipe centres. Position flowerpots and secure with royal icing. Add the cat.*

11

Desert island dream

HAVE TO HAND

Ingredients: *two 23cm (9in) round sponge cakes • jam • buttercream • 1kg marzipan • 1kg sugarpaste • clear spirit • semolina • piping gel • royal icing • selection of paste food colours and petal dusts • flower paste.*

Equipment: *30cm (12in) square cake board • sharp knife • paintbrushes • cut greaseproof bags • greaseproof paper • cocktail stick • spaghetti • parsley cutter • no. 0 piping tube • foam • calyx cutter.*

Main skills: *moulding sponge cake • working with sugarpaste.*

DIFFICULTY	TIME	SUITABILITY

Get away from it all with this wonderful, desert island fantasy cake.

This is the perfect cake for anyone who has ever dreamed of getting away from it all: a beautiful tropical island with warm sunshine and waves lapping the shore. A towel is spread invitingly in the shade of a parasol, while an exotic cocktail and a novel are conveniently to hand. There's even a tube of suntan lotion, a camera waiting to capture the exotic views, and a supply of delicious coconuts. All the island needs now is a castaway in residence!

Give it to someone going on holiday, or taking retirement. Or bake it for a friend or relative who needs a well-earned rest. Don't make it for a honeymoon, though, because there's only room on the island for one!

SHAPING THE CAKE

The cake is made by sandwiching two light, round sponges together with buttercream and jam, then shaping them to create the sloping sides of the island. It is set back a little from the centre of the cake board so that you can make a feature of the seashore and the sea in the foreground. The texture of the sand is achieved by sprinkling fine semolina on to runny royal icing, which has been sponged on to the cake surface.

SEA SCENARIO

The waves which lap at the edge of the island are home to sea creatures such as crabs, starfish and sea urchins. The curling strands of the seaweed, the shells, sea urchins and the five-pointed starfishes are all made from white flower paste brushed with petal dust.

After you have made the leaves for the palm tree and the seashore items, support them on pieces of crumpled greaseproof paper to dry.

This will produce a lifelike sense of movement in the flower paste pieces, as they will dry following the undulations of the paper.

Prop up the items for the seashore around the base of the cake, but secure all the pieces on the top with dabs of royal icing. The sturdy palm tree on top of the cake can be secured with a cocktail stick pushed through its base into the cake, but make sure that this is removed before the cake is served.

The camera, cocktail, suntan lotion and book are all made from sugarpaste. The camera details are piped on, while the cocktail is rolled from several colours with a cocktail stick serving as a straw. You could, of course, make accessories which are particularly suitable for the recipient.

PROFESSIONAL SECRETS
Seashore decorations

• The shells, seaweed and starfish on the seashore are made from flower paste and decorated with petal dust.

• Seaweed strands: Cut out strips of green flower paste using a pastry cutter or edging wheel. Mark them with a cocktail stick and dry them on crumpled greaseproof paper to give them shape. Dust with green, brown and black petal dust.

• Starfishes: Cut these from white flower paste with a calyx cutter. Dry them on crumpled greaseproof paper. Use white royal icing and a no. 1 tube to pipe on the dots, then brush with orange petal dust.

• Scallop shells: Use the template to cut them out and mark the lines with a cocktail stick. Curve into shape and dry on crumpled greaseproof paper. Dust with cream petal dust.

• Razor shells: Shape flower paste into rolls and dust black.

• Sea urchin: Form a pea-sized ball of flower paste and mark it with a pin in rows down from the top. Dust it with red and brown petal dust.

Shaping the cake: Sandwich the two sponge cakes together with jam and buttercream. Shape the sides with a sharp knife, giving the cake a rounded, sloping side from top to bottom all the way round.

1

Covering the cake and board: Brush the cake with jam and coat with marzipan. Dry overnight. Place cake at back of board and brush with clear spirit. Coat cake and board with ivory sugarpaste in one go.

2

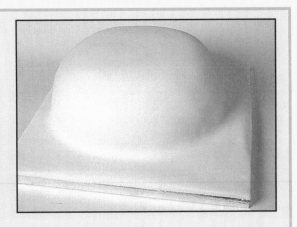

Creating sand effect: Sponge the top of the cake with cream royal icing to represent sand. Make the sandy beach by spreading royal icing on the cake board and sprinkling semolina over the top. Leave to dry.

3

STEP-BY-STEP GUIDE

Creating the sea: *Using paste food colours mixed with water, paint the crabs, starfish and shells on to the cake board. Use a greaseproof paper bag with one end snipped off and piping gel coloured with bright blue paste food colour to pipe the sea around the edge of the board.*

4

Making palm tree: *Roll a 7.5cm (3in) long sausage of flower paste. Snip into it to form scales. Using the template, cut eight leaves from green flower paste. Snip edges and dry over creased greaseproof. Brush trunk and leaves with green, brown and black petal dust.*

5

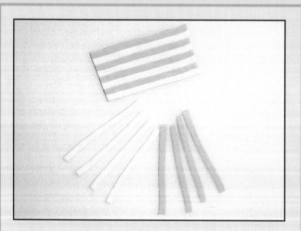

Making the towel: *Colour some flower paste turquoise and roll it out. Roll out some white flower paste. Use a parsley cutter to cut narrow strips of each colour paste. Moisten strips and stick alternate colours together. Roll very lightly to achieve the striped-towel effect.*

8

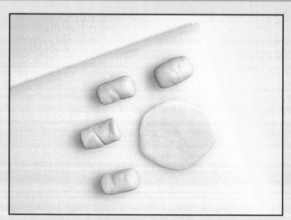

Making the table: *Mould a rounded table top from flower paste, forming the edges into a regular shape. Make four squat table legs out of flower paste and mark them with a cocktail stick to give them a rough-hewn effect. Leave to dry and then assemble them with royal icing.*

9

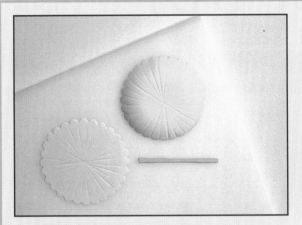

Making the parasol: *Use the template provided to cut the parasol top from lemon-coloured flower paste. Mark in the ribs with a cocktail stick and leave the parasol in the base of a bowl to dry. Make the pole out of a piece of spaghetti covered in brown flower paste.*

6

Assembling the parasol: *Using white royal icing and a no. 0 tube, pipe a design of dots around the edge of the parasol. Attach the pole to the centre of the parasol with royal icing. Invert the parasol and support the pole with a piece of sponge until it is dry.*

7

Assembling the palm tree: *Secure the leaves one by one with dabs of royal icing. Make coconuts from balls of flower paste, texturing them with dabs of royal icing. Pipe the tufts on top with royal icing and a no. 0 tube, then dust them with green, brown and black petal dusts.*

10

Finishing off: *Assemble the table top, securing legs with royal icing. Dust with brown petal dust to give a wood effect. Attach the towel to the cake, then pipe a fringe with white royal icing. Add the seashore items, palm tree, coconuts, parasol and table, plus all the accessories.*

11

Traditional bonnet

This traditional bonnet is lavishly frilled and decorated with ribbon.

HAVE TO HAND

Ingredients: *deep, round 15cm (6in) sponge cake • 18cm (7in) thin, round sponge cake • jam • buttercream • clear spirit • 1kg sugarpaste (500g lemon-yellow/500g lilac)• paste food colours • egg white • royal icing • selection of flower-paste daffodils.*

Equipment: *27cm (11in) square cake board • sharp knife • ribbon-insertion tool • cocktail stick • scalpel • no. 1 piping tube • 2m (2yd) lilac ribbon • lemon satin bow.*

Main skills: *moulding sponge cakes • ribbon insertion • applying frills.*

DIFFICULTY	TIME	SUITABILITY
✓ ✓	⧗ ⧗	🍾

This charming, traditional bonnet, reminiscent of an Easter parade, is coloured in delicate spring shades of lemon and lilac. Viewed in profile, it is set on a sugarpasted board that is coloured the palest lilac, and trimmed with ribbons in toning shades of lilac.

The rim of the bonnet is decorated with a layered, lilac frill, while the bonnet itself is covered in cornelli work. A spray of daffodils adds the final touch.

SHAPING THE CAKE

The shape of the cake is simple to create. Prepare a three-egg sponge, a recipe for which is given on page 115 Bake a third of the mixture in the 18cm (7in) shallow sandwich tin, and the other two thirds in the 15cm (6in) deeper cake tin. This second sponge should be twice the height of the first one. Cut the 15cm (6in) cake in half (horizontally). You will then have three sponge cakes of the same height. Then cut all three cakes in half (vertically). Arrange the halves in a row, cut side down, and sandwich them together with jam and buttercream to give shape to the bonnet. The cake is then coated with marzipan and sugarpaste.

The ribbon-insertion markings around the rim of the bonnet are made with a ribbon-insertion tool while the paste is still soft. The lilac frills are built up to form eight layers and are set off by the deeper lilac of the ribbon-insertion work.

Piping also features strongly on the bonnet. Tiny details are piped around the ribbon insertion, both to help keep the ribbon in place and to add a decorative touch. Cornelli work in lemon royal icing enhances the lemon sugarpaste on the main part of the bonnet. A line is piped just above the ribbon insertions to set the limit for the cornelli work. We have piped all over the rest of the bonnet, working towards the back. A snail's trail around the base of the cake completes the piping detail.

FLORAL ALTERNATIVES

A spray of daffodils, bound with a satin bow, completes this lovely bonnet cake, which would be perfect for a family Easter celebration. You could also attach other spring flowers – such as primroses, forget-me-nots and snowdrops. It would also grace the table at a birthday tea for a female relative of any age.

PROFESSIONAL SECRETS

Spring flowers

• Use a daffodil cutter to make the daffodils from yellow flower paste, brushing them with petal dust and painting the details with paste colour mixed with spirit. Bind three daffodils together, interspersing them with leaves, and finish with satin ribbon tied in a bow.

Three-egg sponge

Ingredients
180g (6oz) margarine
180g (6oz) sugar
3 eggs
220g (7½oz) self-raising flour

Method
Cream together the margarine and the sugar.
Then beat in the eggs, one at a time, adding a tablespoon of sieved flour after each one.
Add the rest of the flour.
Pour the mixture into the two prepared tins. Bake the deeper cake at 180°C (350°F/gas mark 4) for 40 minutes.
Bake the shallower cake at the same temperature for 20 minutes.

Shaping the cake: *Cut the 15cm (6in) cake horizontally, then cut all three cakes vertically and sandwich them together with jam and buttercream in a bonnet shape. Smooth the bonnet rim and edges.*

1

Covering the cake: *Spread jam over cake and coat with marzipan. When dry, brush with spirit and coat with lemon sugarpaste. Cover board with pale lilac sugarpaste. Attach the cake to the board.*

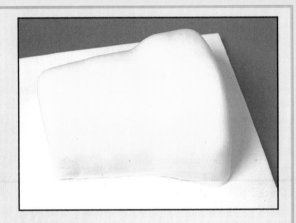

2

Marking ribbon insertion: *Using a ribbon-insertion tool, make the markings for ribbon at 1cm (¼in) intervals at the point where the bonnet rim starts. Do this while the sugarpaste is still soft.*

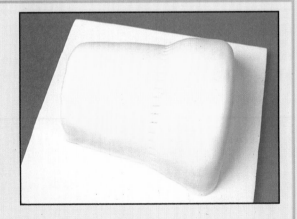

3

STEP-BY-STEP GUIDE

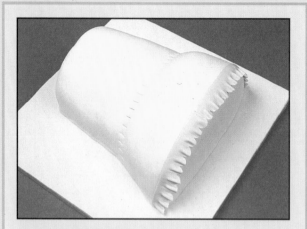

Making the frills: *Colour a mixture of sugarpaste and flower paste with pale lilac paste food colouring. Then, using the template provided, cut strips for the frill. Frill the edges of the strips with a cocktail stick and carefully attach them to the cake with egg white.*

4

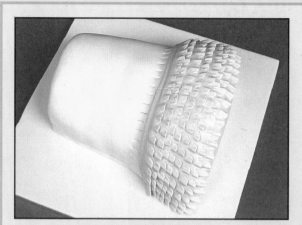

Layering the frills: *Make a second frill in the same way and attach it to the top of the first. Continue in this way until you have built up eight layers of frill, taking you to the base of the ribbon insertion. Make sure that you do not stretch the frills in any way as you attach them.*

5

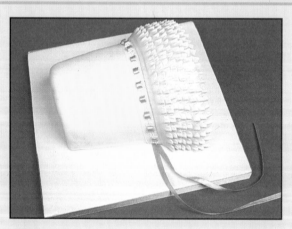

Adding ribbon trim: *Using a no. 1 piping tube and lemon-coloured royal icing, pipe a line above the ribbon-insertion. Attach two ribbon ties for the side of the bonnet with royal icing, draping the ends over the side. Trim the cake board with ribbon in a complementary colour.*

8

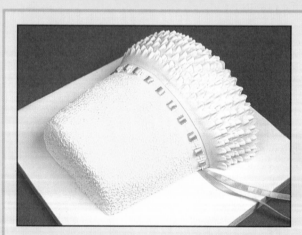

Piping the cornelli work: *Using a no. 1 tube and lemon-coloured royal icing, pipe cornelli work all over the lemon-coloured sugarpaste on the bonnet, starting at the piped line above the ribbon insertion and keeping within the appropriate area.*

9

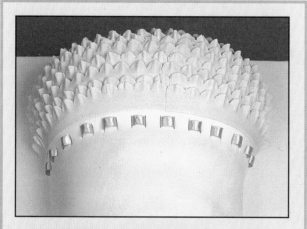

Inserting ribbons: *Cut short lengths of lilac ribbon and insert them into the slots which have already been created with the ribbon-insertion tool. Guide each ribbon into place with the point of a scalpel, making sure that each one is tidily finished.*

6

Piping the details: *Using a no. 1 piping tube and lemon-coloured royal icing, pipe a row of tiny dots on each side of the ribbon inserts to hold them in place. Pipe a tiny decorative motif in between each insertion. Here we piped four little dots around a central dot.*

7

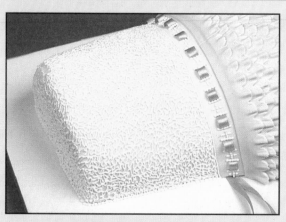

Adding a snail's trail: *Using a no. 1 piping tube and lemon-coloured royal icing, pipe a snail's trail around the base of the cake where it meets the cake board. Begin the snail's trail at the point where the previously piped line meets the cake board.*

10

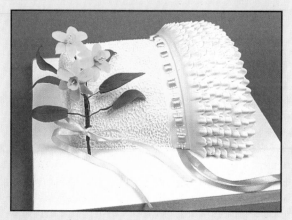

Adding the floral decoration: *Make a spray of daffodils and leaves (as outlined in Professional Secrets on page 115) and decorate it with a lemon-coloured satin bow. Attach the spray to the side of the bonnet and secure it with a dab of royal icing.*

11

Drum roll

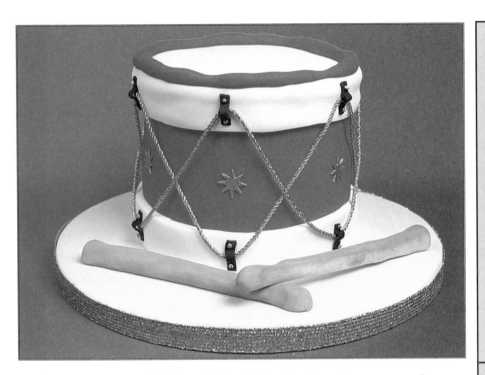

Delight a child with this jolly drum cake, which is surprisingly easy to make.

HAVE TO HAND

Ingredients: *four 18cm (7in) round chocolate sponge cakes • double quantity chocolate fudge icing • 100g white sugarpaste • 600g red sugarpaste • 500g pale chestnut sugarpaste • 200g pastillage • brown, cream and black petal dusts • royal icing.*

Equipment: *28cm (11in) cake board • large sharp knife • string • pins • 3m (3yd) gold braid • scissors • parsley cutter • 1m (1yd) gold ribbon.*

Main skills: *shaping cakes • working with sugarpaste.*

DIFFICULTY   TIME   SUITABILITY

This cake in the shape of a military drum would be ideal for a child's birthday party. The red, white and gold colours are striking and the decoration is simple, both of which appeal to children much more than complicated designs and subtle colours. The cake will also find favour with children as it is a delicious chocolate sponge coated with chocolate fudge icing. As you may have discovered already, many children much prefer sponge cake (especially chocolate!) to a rich, heavy fruit cake.

The drum cake would also be very suitable for celebrating a man's birthday or retirement, especially a man who has military connections.

CREATING THE DRUM

The cake not only looks extremely attractive, it is also very quick and easy to make. It is built up from a stack of round chocolate sponges, then iced and coated with red sugarpaste. It is then banded with white sugarpaste at the top and bottom, and a length of gold braid is zig-zagged around it. This gives the effect of a traditional military drum, a favourite child's toy in Victorian times.

Black sugarpaste 'brackets' are added as supports for the braid, and a pair of simple drumsticks are formed from pastillage. These are dusted with petal dusts to give the effect of wood.

ADDING EXTRA DECORATIONS

We have added an additional (optional) decoration of gold stars in the centre of the diamond shapes formed by the zig-zags of braid. You could, of course, make other shapes, such as teddies or ducks. The stars are easily made by cutting them out out of pastillage, then painting them with gold liquid food colouring. You may prefer to omit these – and the brass studs on the black 'brackets' – as gold food colouring is not edible, and you will have to remove all these items before the cake is cut.

Another advantage of the drum cake is that the plain top is ideal for adding candles, or for piping on an inscription. You might prefer to omit the drumsticks and pipe the inscription round the cake board.

CHOCOLATE FUDGE ICING
If this icing is too oily after it has been mixed, add two teaspoons of rum or clear spirit – but not if the cake is for children!

PROFESSIONAL SECRETS

Chocolate fudge icing

Chocolate fudge icing is delicious, whether it is used to layer a cake, or as a surface coating. Try it on a tea-time cake, a gateau or a dessert cake. Adding rum gives a lovely glossy finish to the icing, as well as a distinctive flavour, but it is not, of course, suitable for a child's birthday cake. However, the finish does not matter for the drum cake as the chocolate fudge icing is covered with a layer of sugarpaste.

• The quantity of chocolate fudge icing given in the recipe below is enough to ice and sandwich an ordinary tea-time sponge cake. For the drum cake, make double the quantity.

Ingredients
60g butter
120g plain chocolate
180g sifted icing sugar
1 egg, beaten
1 tbsp rum (optional)

Method
• Melt the butter and chocolate in a bowl set over a pan of gently simmering water.

• When melted, stir in the beaten egg, then remove the bowl from the heat.

• Beat in the icing sugar until the mixture is thick and glossy.

• Add the rum and beat again. The mixture will thicken as it cools down, so use it quickly before it gets hard to spread.

Shaping the sponges:
Allow the sponge cakes to cool, then shave the tops with a sharp knife to make sure they are flat. Sandwich the cakes one on top of the other with chocolate fudge icing.

1

Icing the cake:
Cover the entire cake with chocolate fudge icing. Work quite quickly, as this type of icing hardens extremely fast and then becomes almost impossible to work with.

2

Covering the top:
Roll out some white sugarpaste. Using the template provided, cut a circle of sugarpaste to cover the top of the cake. Press it lightly into the chocolate fudge icing to hold it in place.

3

STEP-BY-STEP GUIDE

Covering the side: *Colour some sugarpaste bright red and roll out. Measure circumference and height of cake with string and cut paste to cover the side. Press it lightly into the icing to hold in position. Cover the cake board with pale chestnut sugarpaste and set the cake on it.*

4

Adding the white bands: *Use the string again to measure the circumference of the drum. Cut strips of white sugarpaste 3cm (1¹/₂in) deep to make the bands round the top and bottom. Moisten the backs with water and attach them on top of the red sugarpaste.*

5

Forming diamonds: *Return to the starting point and cut off the braid. Secure it at every attachment point with royal icing. Start again at the lower edge and zig-zag the braid round the empty pins to form a diamond pattern. Cut off and secure the braid with royal icing as before.*

8

Making brackets: *To hide the anchor points of the braid, make brackets from strips of black sugarpaste. Cut them with a parsley cutter and attach to the cake with royal icing. Pipe a dot at top and bottom of each bracket to resemble a brass stud and paint with gold liquid colouring.*

9

Hiding the join: *Roll out a long thin sausage of red sugarpaste to to hide the join between the red and white sugarpaste at the top of the drum. Pipe a line of royal icing around the top edge of the drum and gently press the sausage of paste into the icing.*

6

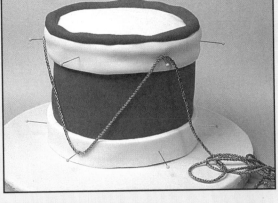

Adding braid trim: *Divide the circumference into six equal sections. Mark these points in parallel along the centre of the white bands with pins. (Stick pins into the paste only, not into the cake.) Secure end of braid with a pin and zig-zag it around drum, hooking round alternate pins.*

7

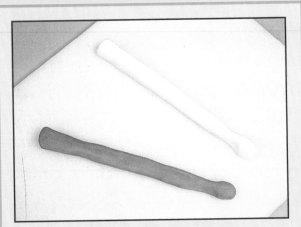

Making the drumsticks: *Mould a pair of drumsticks out of pastillage, flattening one side so that they will rest on the cake board and not roll off. Brush them with a mixture of brown, black and cream petal dusts to produce the wood-grain effect.*

10

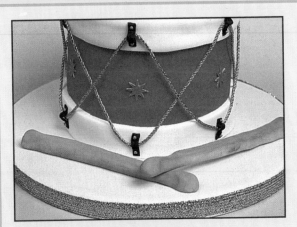

Adding finishing touches: *Trim the cake board with a broad gold ribbon. Position the drumsticks on the front of the cake board, balancing them one on top of the other at the tip. Apply gold pastillage stars to centre of each diamond on side of drum with royal icing.*

11

Swimming pool

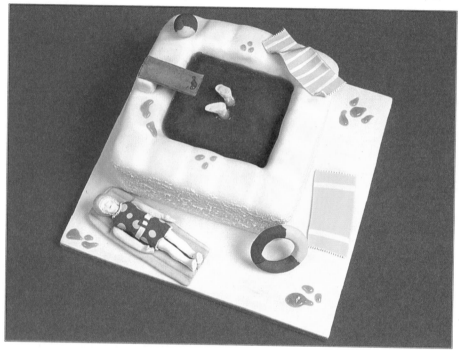

HAVE TO HAND

Ingredients: *2 x 18cm (7in) square sponge cakes • jam • buttercream • 1kg marzipan • 740g sugarpaste • clear spirit • dark blue, red, yellow, lilac, peach and turquoise paste food colours • brown and blue petal dusts • cornflour • royal icing • piping gel.*

Equipment: *30cm (12in) square cake board • sharp knife • large, medium and fine paintbrushes • cocktail stick • piece of foam • no. 1 piping tube • figure mould • knitting needle.*

Main skills: *working with sugarpaste and pastillage.*

DIFFICULTY	TIME	SUITABILITY
✓✓		

Make a splash with this wonderful swimming pool cake, complete with sunbather and swimmer.

Just looking at this cake will remind your friends and relations of their sun-drenched holidays. The cake is shaped as a swimming pool with sparkling blue depths that are created with coloured piping gel.

One bather is diving into the water while the other prefers to sunbathe, stretched out on her lilo beside the brilliant, white, sunbaked walls of the pool, wearing a spotted swimsuit with a definite 1940s' flavour. This theme is echoed by the old-fashioned swimming hat and the pattern on the rubber ring and beach ball.

SHAPING THE CAKE

The cake is made from two square sponge cakes, sandwiched together with jam and buttercream. A square recess is then cut in to the top to form the actual pool. Greater depth is added to the pool by marzipan blocks which are placed around the top edge to build up the sides. They create a realistic, tiled effect. The cake is then covered with sugarpaste, carefully moulded around the cake to preserve the right shape.

The cake is positioned off-centre towards the back of the board so that you have plenty of room to place the figure and accessories around the edges of the pool.

The deep blue of the water in the pool is made by brushing the base of the pool with blue petal dust and adding blue piping gel.

A gust of wind lifts the towel from the side of the pool, water splashes everywhere as the bather dives in and the whole scene is caught in a state of suspended animation – almost like a photograph.

MAKING THE ACCESSORIES

We have placed a lilo, beach ball and rubber ring around the pool, all moulded from sugarpaste. You will probably want to personalise the cake by adding little objects that are suitable for the recipient, such as a book or a cocktail.

You can also dress the figures to suit yourself. You may want to bring the scene up to date by dressing the sunbathing figure in a bikini. The figures are moulded from pastillage, and once you have the knack you can make and dress them to represent particular people that you know.

Give the cake to someone about to go on holiday – or change the accessories and give it to a sports' fan. You could even poise a figure on the side of the pool ready to dive in, or place a child sitting on the side, splashing its feet in the water.

PROFESSIONAL SECRETS

Making the figures

There are plenty of figure moulds available, so choose one which suits the size of your cake.

• Use pink pastillage to mould the figure, which should come in two halves. Join the halves together with royal icing.

• Roll some red sugarpaste and press small spots of yellow on top. Roll it again lightly. Wrap it around the body as a swimsuit, trimming it as necessary. Make the belt from white sugarpaste and the buckle from red.

• Use yellow sugarpaste to make the swimming cap. Pipe an edging around the bottom and neck of the swimming costume, and around the edge of the cap. Attach the arms with royal icing.

• Add facial details with petal dust and a fine paintbrush.

• Use a figure mould to make the swimmer's legs, filled to knee level and trimmed down to the right size.

• Cocktail sticks are used to support the legs in the pool – these must be removed before the cake is cut.

Shaping the cake: *Sandwich the two sponge cakes together with jam and buttercream. Carve out the top of the cake to create the recess for the pool, leaving a rim all around the edge.*

1

Marzipanning the cake: *Coat the cake with marzipan, moulding to shape. Use marzipan to make the blocks. Brush the bases of the blocks with clear spirit and set them around the edge of the pool.*

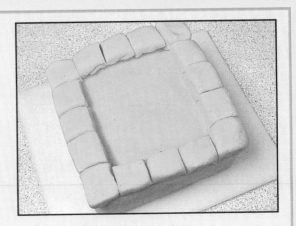

2

Coating the cake and board: *Brush the cake with clear spirit and coat it with white sugarpaste. Coat the board with white sugarpaste and position the cake on it, slightly off-centre and towards the back.*

3

STEP-BY-STEP GUIDE

Dusting and texturing: *Using a large brush, dust the base of the swimming pool with deep blue petal dust and the rim of the pool and the covered cake board with brown petal dust. Using cream royal icing, sponge the sides of the pool to give a textured effect. Leave to dry.*

4

Adding the pool water: *Colour some piping gel with blue, green or turquoise paste food colouring. Spoon it carefully into the pool, swirling it around gently with a teaspoon in order to give the appearance of ripples on the surface of the water.*

5

Moulding beach ball and rubber ring: *Colour some sugarpaste red, yellow and turquoise. Make a small sausage of each colour, push together and roll gently. Join into a circle. Mould the ball from small balls of the three colours, being careful to keep the colours separate.*

8

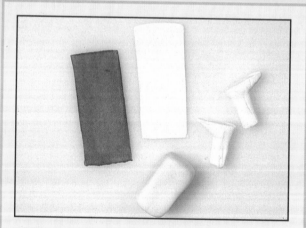

Making the swimmer and the diving board: *Mould the feet and legs from pastillage using a figure mould (filled from the knee downwards). Cut a rectangle of pastillage for the diving board and dust it with brown petal dust. Mould a block of sugarpaste as a diving-board support.*

9

Making the beach towels: *Using the template provided, cut the towels from lilac and peach sugarpaste. Cut strips of white sugarpaste and roll it lightly on top to create stripes. Pull the lilac towel up into folds and leave it to dry. Pipe fringes with white royal icing and a no. 1 tube.*

6

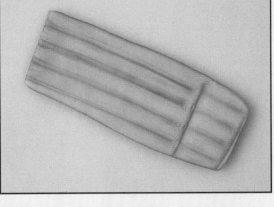

Making the lilo: *Use thickly-rolled sugarpaste and the template provided to cut out the lilo shape. Make the air pockets and pillow divisions with a knitting needle and mould it into shape. Brush it with mid-blue petal dust in order to create a stripy effect.*

7

Attaching the diving board: *Place the block on the side of pool and secure it with royal icing. Position the diving board on top and attach it with royal icing. Push half a cocktail stick into each foot and push it down through the piping gel water into the surface of the cake.*

10

Making a splash: *Position ball and towel on edge of pool. Lay figure on lilo by the edge of pool. Prop up rubber ring at the side and lay out second towel on surface. Pipe splashes of water with piping gel around edges of pool, on the board and around the feet in the water.*

11

Decorating Know-how

Designing a cake

The most successful cakes are those which have been carefully planned in advance. Here we guide you through all the aspects of cake design.

A large part of successful cake decorating comes down to one thing – planning. If you have planned your cake in advance, paying full attention to all the factors that need to be taken into consideration, then you already have a head start.

All cake decorators, whatever their level of skill, should have a notebook for ideas. Jot down your plans and ideas about your cakes, remind yourself of birthdays and other special occasions, and note any themes or special topics that come to mind. You may find that your best ideas come when you are gazing out of a window on a 10-minute bus ride.

At this stage you can move on to planning a cake in more detail. First, consider your own skills. Do not plan an important cake which is based on an advanced skill that you have never used before. All cake decorators have their strong points and preferences. There is no harm in doing something new, but make sure that you are not out of your depth. If you have a wide range of skills and materials at your fingertips, so much the better – but you can still be very successful with limited resources. Get organised and give yourself plenty of time, since some decorations will need to be made in advance and you may need time to track down certain items in specialist shops.

CAKE CHECKLIST

The person for whom the cake is intended will influence your choice of theme. Is it a novelty cake reflecting the recipient's job or hobby? Will it be a feminine cake, topped with flowers, or a country scene painted on a plaque? Once you have decided upon a theme, you can then make the rest of your design decisions.

DECORATING DECISIONS

The cake's size is governed by the number of people it has to serve, (though you can make an extra, plain layer for a wedding cake just for cutting and passing around to the guests). The shape of both cake and board will also influence your design.

What kind of inscription are you going to use? Do you wish to include a side decoration? There are many options, from broderie anglaise and extension work to corner designs and collars. Decide on a colour scheme and check that the cake will not clash with decorations at the venue. Once you have considered every angle, check that the cake looks balanced. It is a good idea to draw and colour the cake first, as you would a dress design, or make templates and experiment with layouts. Then you can begin your cake with confidence.

PLANNING YOUR CAKE

Link two cakes with a central floral arrangement and an inscription.

Floral arrangements can be off-set and the theme continued on the side of the cake.

The inscription should be balanced with the rest of the cake-top design.

Emphasise a shaped cake with a matching collar, board and tiny runouts.

Frills are a very pretty way of adding volume to a cake, and they do not compete with the cake top.

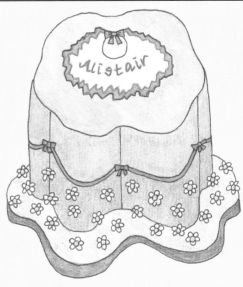

Inscriptions that sit on a curve can save space on a petal-shaped cake.

Add height to a cake with a floral arrangement that tapers at the base.

Smaller flowers around the base should complement the top floral decoration.

PLANNING A CAKE

1 Choosing a theme: Ideas can come from many sources, such as magazines, cards, photographs and postcards. Build up a collection of these items. This cottage was chosen for grandma's birthday.

2 Colour schemes: Find the colours that work best with your chosen design. Experiment with them on a white tile, mixing them for more unusual colours. Make sure that you keep a note of their names.

3 Side design: The side design should always complement the cake top and never detract from it. Here an embroidered design has been chosen and traced from a template.

4 Inscription: Look for examples of lettering and reject those that do not suit the cake. They may be too modern or too elaborate. Consider your choice of lettering next to every other element of the design.

5 **Oval shape:** Make a cake-top template and experiment with the positioning of the design. Here the cottage has been placed at the bottom left and balanced by the inscription on the top right.

6 **Round cakes:** Here the cottage has been placed centrally, with the inscription above and below it. Once you have developed a good 'eye' for design, you will begin to place designs instinctively.

7 **Shaped rectangle:** The cottage is placed on the right and the lettering to the left of the cake. The effect is well balanced, and neither aspect of the design is squashed.

8 **Petal-shaped:** Petal shapes are a little more difficult to design. The cottage is placed to the bottom left of the cake and the inscription is ranged around it.

Cutting and fitting a simple drape

*This elegant sugarpaste drape is not only easy to make,
but is also very pretty to look at.*

HAVE TO HAND

Ingredients: *20cm (8in) round
sponge or fruit cake • 1.25kg
sugarpaste • 75g marzipan • royal
icing • peach, pink and green paste
food colours • pink petal dust •
cornflour • small blossoms.*
Equipment: *nos. 1 and 2 piping
tubes • 25cm (10in) round cake
board • greaseproof paper • small
pair of scissors • string • soft
paintbrush for petal dusting •
scalloped wheel cutter.*
Main skills: *positioning and
decorating drapes.*

DIFFICULTY   TIME   SUITABILITY

This sugarpaste drape sits
gracefully on top of the cake
and hangs like a tablecloth. The
effect is extremely pretty, especially
if the sides have been covered in
sugarpaste in a complementary
colour and the drape is decorated.
Drapes are particularly suited to
curved cakes – round, oval or petal
shaped – rather than square ones.

CREATING A STRAIGHT EDGE
The method used here involves creating a straight edge at the top of the
cake so that the drape hangs attrac-
tively. We have used a sponge cake
and the top is covered with marzipan.
The side is sugarpasted and the sugarpaste trimmed where it meets the

marzipan. This creates a straight
edge rather than a curved one – a
very important consideration when fitting a drape on a cake.

When covering a fruit cake, the
procedure is slightly different,
although the principle is the same.
The cake is first covered entirely with
marzipan, then the sides are sugarpasted. The effect will be the same,
as long as you remember that the
top and the sides of the cake must
be covered separately in order to create the straight edge.

ROLLING THE DRAPE
The sugarpaste should be rolled to
the approximate shape of the cake,

and in this case we used a scalloped
wheel cutter to create the pretty
effect around the edges. Try not to
stretch the drape as it is placed over
the cake.

DECORATING THE SIDES
A drape focuses attention towards
the sides of the cake, so care should
be taken to produce a delicate
design which enhances the movement of the drape.

Dust the drape with a mixture of
cornflour and pink petal dust. The
piped foliage is then added and pink
blossoms are placed near the edge
of the drape. The design is extremely
pretty and very pleasing to the eye.

FINISHING THE DRAPE

Here, an embossing stamp has been used to imprint a rose design on the drape. The roses are coloured with peach and green petal dust.

A lace and border cutter with a heart-shaped blade has been used to cut a short frill which is joined to the drape. Small shells cover the join.

A broderie anglaise frill cutter and a five-hole eyelet cutter are used to produce a large frill. The daisy shapes and frill are outlined in white.

Here, the edge of the drape has been overpiped with very dark pink royal icing. The inner point of each scallop is decorated with a piped dot.

helpline   **Attaching a frill**

If you decide to attach a frill to your drape, you must leave the drape to dry for at least two or three days, until it is quite firm before adding the frill. Cut the frill from a mixture which contains equal quantities of sugarpaste and flower paste using a Garrett frill cutter.

When you are joining one section of frill to another which has already been placed on the cake, fold back the cut end of the second section before attaching it to the cake, and then carefully place it over the end of the first section.

Attach the frill to the cake by painting the edge of the drape with egg white and gently press the frill on to the albumen-covered part of the drape, taking care not to stretch the paste. Then set aside for a couple of hours to allow the frill to dry thoroughly. Use a decorative piped finish, such as a row of small shells or bulbs to cover the join between the drape and frill.

Use string to get the correct measurement for your drape, measuring from the point from where you want the drape to fall on the side of the cake, then

across the top of the cake and down the other side. If you decide not to attach a frill, allow the drape to fall fairly near the base of the cake, leaving the sugarpasted sides of the cake in view.

If you are adding a frill to the drape, though, you must take into account the extra length that this will create, and make the drape smaller in order to compensate. If you are adding a design to the top of the cake, keep it very simple – anything elaborate will deflect attention from the drape itself.

CUTTING AND FITTING

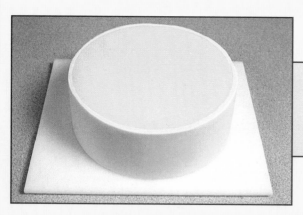

1 Covering the cake: Cut a marzipan circle for the top of the cake. Cut pink sugarpaste to fit the depth and circumference of the cake. By using this method you will achieve the necessary sharp edge.

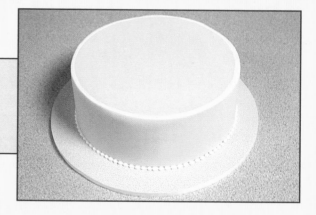

2 Piping a row of shells: Cover the cake board with pink sugarpaste or paper and attach the cake. Pipe a row of shells around the base of the cake with white royal icing and a no. 2 tube.

3 Positioning the drape: Use string to measure across and down the cake to where the drape will sit. Cut a circle of paste as wide as this measurement, using a scalloped wheel cutter. Place it over the cake.

4 Adjusting the drape: Once the drape is in place, adjust the frilled effect by pulling it away from the side of the cake at intervals to create the effect of fabric. Don't stretch the drape as you do this.

A SIMPLE DRAPE

5 Drying the drape: Before adding any decoration, let the drape dry thoroughly for two to three days. It is best to place some greaseproof paper over the cake to prevent dust falling on to the drape's surface.

6 Adding colour: Once the drape has dried, use a soft brush and some petal dust to lightly dust the edge of the drape. If you find the colour of the petal dust too vivid, mix it with cornflour.

7 Piping the design: Using green icing and a no. 1 piping tube, pipe foliage 1cm (½in) from the edge of the drape. Make sure the space in between the edge of the drape and the foliage is not too large.

8 Adding the blossoms: Once the foliage is dry, attach small blossoms in position, as shown, with royal icing. Make sure you use pastel colours which blend well with the delicacy of the design.

Using crimpers

A set of crimpers enables you to create a wide range of different patterns both quickly and easily.

Crimping is not a difficult technique, but it takes a little practice because you have to work very quickly – especially if the crimped design covers much or all of the cake's surface – before the surface of the sugarpaste begins to dry. If this happens, the sugarpaste will begin to crack as you work and spoil the design.

Once you have mastered the art, however, the different crimping tools available will allow you to create a wide variety of designs.

CRIMPING TOOLS
The most commonly available crimping tools come in two widths – half and full size. It is better to use the larger size to start with, so that you can work quickly and so that there is less risk of the paste drying out. The basic patterns are single and double open scallops, single and double closed scallops, chevron, and straight edge, plus diamond, heart and holly-leaf shapes.

The scallop and chevron tools are ideal for building up an all-over pattern based on a simple guideline – the diamond pattern on the cake shown here was built up from rows of 'V' shapes crimped with a double closed scallop tool. This produces a pattern with subtle curves within it; a chevron crimper used in the same way would produce straight lines, giving a much more formal effect.

A straight-edged crimper can be used to write inscriptions, but the lines can create a rather mechanical effect. A heart crimper is quite versatile, as it can also be used to build up flower and butterfly shapes. When using crimpers, dust the ends frequently with cornflour in order to prevent sticking.

PLANNING THE WORK
Because crimping can only be carried out successfully while the sugarpaste is still soft, it is important to plan exactly how you are going to carry out the design before starting work. If it is to be repeated on all four sides, cover the three not being worked on with polythene, taped in place to exclude air. Alternatively, work the crimped design on panels of sugarpaste, leave to dry, then attach to the sides of the cake. Cover the joins between the panels with piping.

CRIMPER DESIGNS

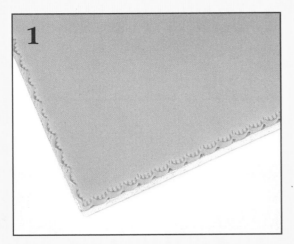

Crimping is one of the most popular methods of decorating the edge of a sugarpasted board. Here, a small crimper has been used to imprint the pattern.

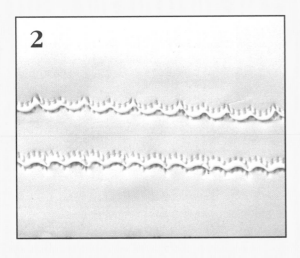

This crimped side design can be left as shown, or a decorative ribbon can be placed between the two rows of crimping to add an extra touch of colour.

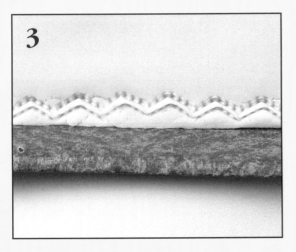

As an alternative to a row of small piped shells, the join between a sugarpasted cake and board can be decorated using a crimped design.

DESIGN TOUCH

The diamond-shaped crimped design illustrated in this article gives a similar effect to smocking, but it is much quicker and easier to carry out. The only element missing is the additional colour added when smocking stitch is piped on to ribbed and pleated sugarpaste. If you wish to add colour to the design shown here, it can be done is a variety of ways. One is to overpipe the diamond pattern using a no. 0 piping tube and coloured royal icing. Another is to lightly dust the diamond-shaped panels using a soft brush and petal dust.

For an extra special touch, you could always pipe tiny coloured flowers in the middle of each diamond, accompanied by a couple of tiny piped leaves. These could be piped in the centre of every diamond-shape panel, or alternatively, you could just add flowers to a few selected patterns. If you choose to adopt the last option, it would be better to use crimpers to decorate only one, or at the most two, sides of the cake. The other sides should be left plain.

CRIMPING A

1 **Marking the 'V' shape:** Cut a piece of greaseproof paper to the same width as the cake. Put crimper at a 45° angle to the top and mark its width with a pencil. Move crimper to opposite 45° angle, and mark again.

2 **Folding the template:** Fold the paper on the marked 'V' shape, then continue folding until the whole strip of paper is used up. While still folded, cut off top of paper to produce a row of even 'V' shapes.

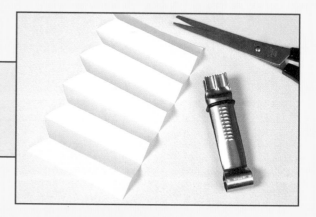

3 **Pinpricking the template:** If working on a panel of sugarpaste, hold the template in place and mark the top and bottom points of the 'V' shapes with a pin. On a cake, tape the template in position first.

4 **Starting the crimping:** Remove the template. Following the marked points, crimp the top row of the zig-zag pattern with the crimping tool, working as quickly as possible.

SIDE PANEL

5 **Beginning the diamond pattern:** Crimp a second row of 'V' shapes under the first so as to create a diamond pattern. Provided the crimping tool is held straight, a regular pattern will form naturally.

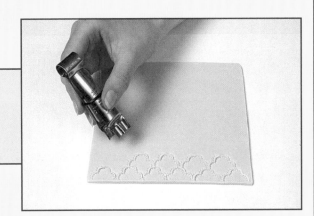

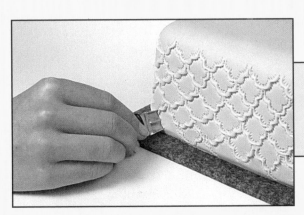

6 **Completing the diamond pattern:** Continue crimping across the sugarpaste until the whole surface is covered with the diamond pattern. Make sure that the diagonals line up neatly all the way down.

7 **Neatening the base:** To conceal the join where the bottom row of crimper work meets the cake board, pipe on a line of shells using a no. 2 tube and white royal icing.

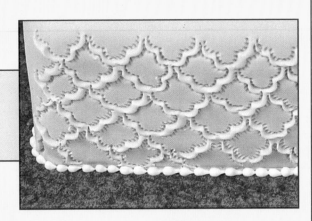

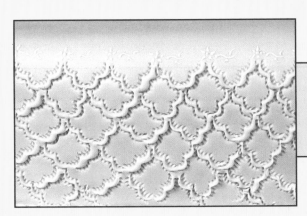

8 **Neatening the top:** Using a no. 1 piping tube, pipe small flowers and leaves in order to provide a finishing touch where the points of the first row of 'V' shapes meet the top of the cake.

Pressure-piping techniques

Pressure-piped runouts can look wonderful placed on cakes, plaques or even pastillage cards.

HAVE TO HAND

Ingredients: • quantity of royal icing at stiff peak consistency • egg white or albumen • selection of paste food colours.

Equipment: nos. 1, 2, 3 and 4 piping tubes • greaseproof or tracing paper • pencil • acetate • small sheet of glass • fine paintbrush • cranked palette knife.

Main skills: pressure piping.

DIFFICULTY   TIME   SUITABILITY

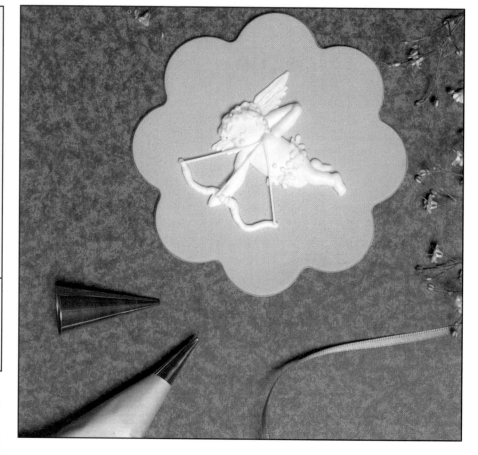

The technique of pressure piping is used to produce two-dimensional figures, and decorations such as flowers, bows and lines of piping suitable for cake tops and sides. With pressure piping, you can build up figures so that they have the quality of bas-relief work. You do not need to pipe in the outlines first with pressure piping – the consistency of the icing is stiff enough to hold its shape, unlike the icing used for runouts in bas-relief.

MAKING THE ICING

The consistency of the icing is very important. While it is being pressure-piped, it should be soft peak, but it is best to make the icing up to full peak consistency first, then soften it with a little egg white. Larger areas require a softer icing than others – for example, the face and the tummy of the cherub featured above.

Practice is vital too, as the smooth finish of the work depends on the amount of pressure you exert, and the movement of your hand as you pipe. Practice will demonstrate the icing consistency that is best to work with. Most pressure piping work uses piping tubes nos. 1, 2, 3 and 4.

PIPING THE FIGURES

When working on a figure, decide in advance which tubes you will need, and have piping bags ready, filled with the right consistency icing.

You can work pressure piping directly on to the cake if you are con-fident. Otherwise, trace the template on to greaseproof or tracing paper, cut around the shape, and place it on a sheet of glass. Secure this with a sheet of acetate over the top.

Use a cranked palette knife to remove the finished work when it is dry. Tiny, fragile details – such as birds legs – are either piped directly on to the cake, or painted on with food colouring when the figure is placed in position.

Pressure-piped figures can be worked in any colour. Children, for example, love brightly coloured animals. However, to work purely in white produces an elegant and artistic effect which is highly distinctive.

PRESSURE PIPING A BLACK CAT

Using a no. 3 tube and black royal icing, pipe an oval shape, tapering it towards the the neck for the cat's head.

Next, using the same tube, pipe an elongated oval shape to form the body of the cat. Make sure that it connects to the head.

With the no. 3 tube, pipe two tiny ovals for the front paws, a curve for the back leg and a curly tail on top. Smooth the icing with a paintbrush.

Pipe the ears in black, the nose in brown and the cheeks and eyes in white. Add the eye details, and pipe a pink tongue with a no. 2 tube.

Alternatives

PRESSURE PIPING A SWAN

To pipe the swan, use a no. 2 or 3 tube and begin by piping the sweep of the neck. Add the head and beak and then the body, building up the shape smoothly. Shape the wing in the background first, with rows of piping and a fine paintbrush. Outline the icing in the foreground and fill in the feathers with rows of piping. Paint in the eye in black with clear alcohol and food colouring. Pipe the beak in yellow icing.

Cherub template

PIPING THE CHERUB

1 **Piping the right arm:** Pipe in the right arm of the cherub with a no. 3 piping tube, varying the pressure in order to form the contours of the wrist and elbow.

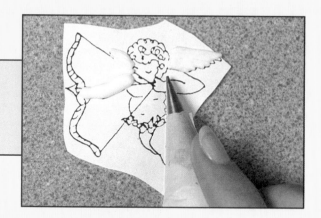

2 **Piping the wings:** Pipe in the wings with a no. 1 tube, using a back-and-forth motion and working from top to bottom. Then, take the no. 3 piping tube again and pipe in the upper part of the left arm.

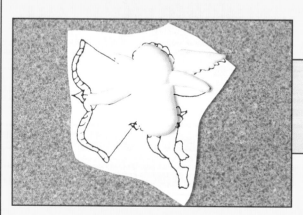

3 **Adding the face and tummy:** Pipe in the face with a no. 3 tube and a softer consistency icing in order to gain a smooth effect. Then, use the same tube and icing to pipe in the tummy.

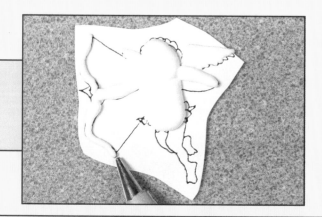

4 **Piping in the bow:** Return to a stiffer icing and a no. 2 piping tube. Starting at the top of the bow, pipe the section down to the cherub's arm. Pipe the bottom section separately.

5 **Piping the forearm:** Using a no. 3 tube and stiff royal icing, pipe the forearm of the cherub and the clenched fist. Use a paintbrush to mark an indentation where the fist begins.

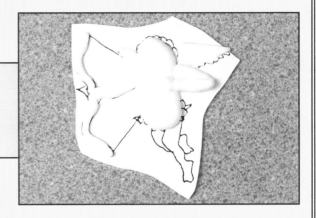

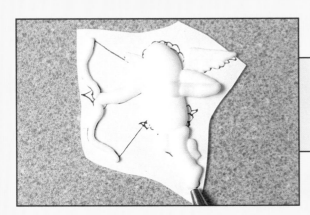

6 **Piping the legs:** Using a no. 3 piping tube, pipe in the bent leg in two sections. Leave this to dry. Then, pipe in the other leg, using pressure to form the contours of the thigh, knee, ankle and toes.

7 **Adding details:** Using a no. 1 tube, add tiny lines for the fingers holding the bow, and wavy lines for the hair. Fill in the tip of the arrow, and add wavy lines for the garland around the tummy.

8 **Finishing off:** Use the no. 1 tube to complete the finer details, including the eyes, nose, navel and bow string. Set the finished figure aside and allow it to dry before attaching it to a cake or plaque.

Colouring with petal dust

Skilful colouring using petal dust can transform simple designs and ideas into something very special.

HAVE TO HAND

Ingredients: *modelling paste (flower paste and sugarpaste) • pastillage paste • selection of petal dusts • cornflour • clear alcohol.*

Equipment: *baby moulds • selection of paintbrushes • ice-cube tray • tile (for mixing colours) • parsley cutter • basket.*

Main skill: *colouring with petal dusts.*

DIFFICULTY	TIME	SUITABILITY
✓✓		

Petal dust is a very versatile colouring medium. It can be brushed lightly on as a powder tint, mixed with cornflour for a more delicate touch, or used with clear spirit and painted on. You can buy a wide range of colours and mix them together for many subtle variations.

COLOURING TECHNIQUES

Here we have used two pastillage babies – one dark skinned, and one fair – as an example of how effective petal dusting can be. They could be used as a centrepiece at a christening, or perhaps at a new-baby party. If taken out of the basket, they can be placed on the blanket and then put on to the top of a cake.

However, petal dust is most commonly used to colour flowers and frills. Flowers, in particular, demand a high level of realism when it comes to colouring and markings, and it is worth developing your skills with petal dust. Be warned that petal dust has a tendency to spill and it is very hard to remove marks if any of the dust ends up in the wrong place.

You will need a selection of brushes to use with petal dust, from very fine ones to large ones with fluffier heads. Make-up brushes – such as those used for loose powder or blusher – are ideal for dusting colour on to large areas, but make sure that you only use them for cake-decorating purposes. A large white tile can be used as a palette upon which you can mix your colours.

MAKING THE BABIES

The decorative babies were made in special moulds. Fill the moulds, and leave to harden overnight. Then gently ease the babies out of the moulds. Here, only the front half of each baby has been used. If you wanted to join the two halves together, use white royal icing to glue the two halves and to smooth over the join before applying the petal dust.

HANDLING PETAL DUST
When painting with petal dust, use an ice-cube tray and put some of each powder in a separate compartment.

COLOURING THE BLANKET

Pad the basket with sugarpaste. Roll modelling paste thinly. Use a parsley cutter to mark vertical and horizontal lines on the paste, but don't cut it.

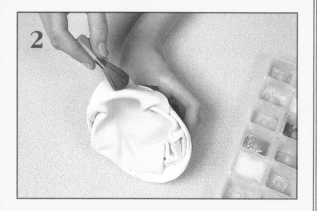

Line the basket with the paste blanket, folding cut edges under. Leave to dry. Brush on a mix of yellow petal dust and cornflour. Dust off excess.

Mix deep and pale yellow petal dusts with a tiny drop of spirit, and paint tiny flowers in some of the squares on the blanket with a fine brush.

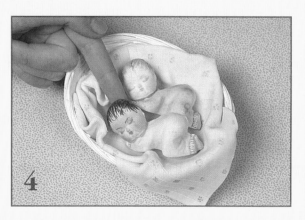

Arrange the finished babies in the basket. Take care that the blanket is not damaged at all during this process.

helpline

THINGS TO WATCH

Petal dust is one of the most versatile of colouring agents, because it comes in so many different colours and can be mixed to provide many different shades. Also, because it contains no glycerine, it does not affect the drying time for royal icing work – such as runouts. However, unlike paste and liquid food colouring, it is difficult to control. The dust particles are so fine that, unless you are very careful, they can get everywhere. So it is very important that you never dip a brush into a pot of petal dust and then attempt to brush your decoration without first removing any excess dust from the brush.

Also, if you wish to dust a specific area of a flat surface, it is best to cover the adjoining areas with a greaseproof mask so that the colour does not stray.

When colouring a decoration that requires a dark shade of a particular colour, it is best to brush the item several times rather than try to apply one thick layer of petal dust.

If you want to produce a pale shade of a colour, you can lighten the petal dust with cornflour. *Simply mix the cornflour and petal dust together on a palette, just as you would a paste colouring, then dust the excess off the brush before you start to colour.*

When painting with petal dust, it is best to mix the powder with a clear spirit, such as vodka or gin. The alcohol evaporates faster than water, and this will speed up the drying process. You will only need a very tiny amount of spirit, so you can buy a miniature bottle and keep it just for this purpose.

DUSTING AND PA

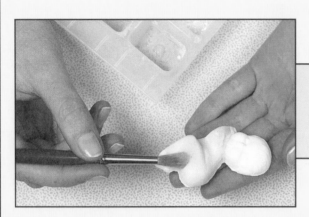

1 Beginning the work: Colour one of the romper suits with peach petal dust, using a medium-sized paintbrush. Do not colour the feet and head. Brush off any excess dust using a brush with a large head.

2 Colouring the second romper suit: Use lilac petal dust and a medium-sized paintbrush. Mix more petal dust with a tiny drop of spirit. Use a fine brush to add ribbing details at the neck and wrists.

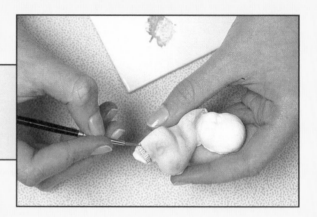

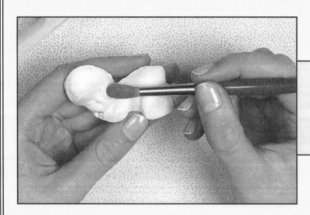

3 Adding the details: Add the ribbing details to the peach baby. Mix dark brown, terracotta, and cream petal dust together, and brush them on to the baby's face with a medium-sized paintbrush.

4 Petal dusting the face: Use peach and cream petal dusts mixed with cornflour to produce the paler skin tones of the lilac-suited baby. Dust the face, hands and feet.

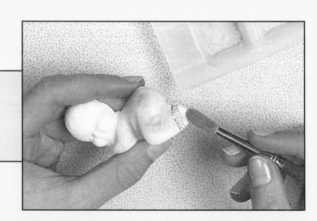

NTING THE BABIES

5 Adding the hair: Dust the hands and feet of the peach-suited baby with the skin tone that you have mixed for him. Mix dark brown and black petal dust with a drop of clear alcohol and paint in the hair.

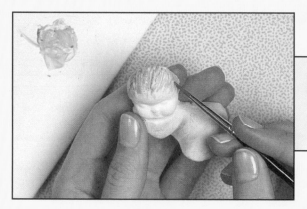

6 Adding the fair hair: Mix some yellow petal dust with a touch of dark brown and a drop of clear spirit, and carefully paint in the hair of the lilac-suited baby with a fine brush.

7 Painting the features: Use a very fine paintbrush and a paler version of the relevant hair colour to paint in the eyelashes and eyebrows on each baby. Use an even paler version for the lips.

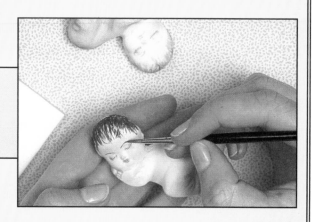

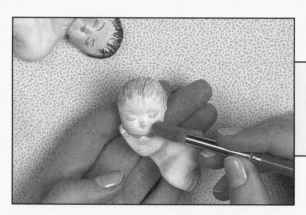

8 Finishing off: Use a fine paintbrush to paint the collar details on to the suits of each baby. Add a small amount of pink to each of the skin-tone colours, and brush carefully on to the cheeks.

Colouring chocolate

Use pretty petal dusts to create a wide range of colourful chocolate.

There is a wide range of chocolate bars available, but they tend to come in the conventional forms of milk, plain or white chocolate. Here, we show you how to add a wide range of colours to homemade chocolates, which you can give as a special treat to a friend or serve at a children's party.

Coloured chocolate is best used to add details to milk, plain or white chocolate for a heightened decorative effect. You can add colour only to white chocolate, but milk and plain chocolate can be used elsewhere in the figure or mould.

USING PETAL DUST

Petal dust is a very effective method of colouring small quantities of chocolate. Liquid food colourings should be avoided, since they are water-based and so could affect the consistency of the chocolate. The advantage of petal dust is that there is an enormous range of colours to choose from – and you can create even more through clever mixing. Make some for a friend (using their favourite colours) and place them in a basket tied with a matching ribbon. A few little coloured chocolates or lollipops make wonderful and relatively inexpensive party bags for young children. You can buy special lollipop moulds (and the sticks) at good cake-decorating outlets.

CHOOSING COLOURS

You can colour chocolate any colour you like, but bear in mind that some colours – such as blue – do not have much edible appeal, especially as far as adults are concerned. Solid areas of very brightly coloured chocolate can be off-putting, so use colour with caution and add only a little at a time until you have the right shade. It is more effective to use small touches of colour, rather than producing big blocks of coloured chocolate.

HANDLING CHOCOLATE

The other important consideration is the handling of chocolate. Warm hands can spoil the shape of chocolates and leave fingerprints, so keep your hands cool by running them under the cold tap. Handle your chocolates as infrequently as possible. Once they have been turned out of the mould, use a cranked palette knife to move them.

ADDING COLOUR
Adding petal dust can cause chocolate to set quickly. Keep the bowls of chocolate over hot water while you work.

COLOURING IDEAS

These small flowers have been layered – either with two different types of coloured chocolate, or one layer of coloured and one layer of white chocolate. The effect in both cases is extremely attractive.

These lollipops make ideal treats for children. You can layer the design (as in the case of the diamond), marble it, or paint details on to it. Stick them in a block of florist's foam and let the children help themselves!

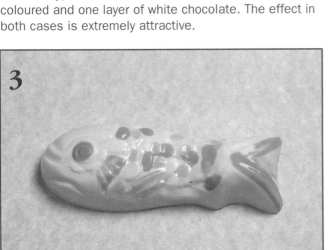

With small figure moulds, fill in the details with coloured chocolate and a fine paintbrush. This white-chocolate fish has been brightened up with orange, pink and green-coloured chocolate.

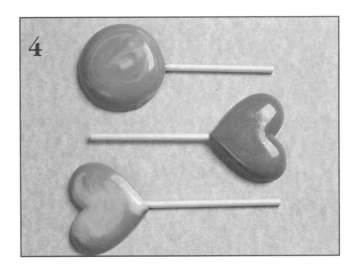

The marbling effect here is achieved by placing white chocolate in a mould and swirling some coloured chocolate around it with a paintbrush. Do not mix too thoroughly, or you will lose the marbled effect.

helpline   MIXING COLOUR

When colouring chocolate, do not worry if you make a mistake and suddenly realise that you do not like the colour that you have mixed. If the colour is too bright, it can be rectified by adding other shades of petal dust.

If you want to weaken the colour, simply add more melted white chocolate. Get to *know which colours certain combinations of petal dust produce. For example, adding blue petal dust to an unwanted, bright yellow will tone it to green. You can also create a marbled effect by trailing one colour through another. Adults will probably appreciate pastel shades, while children love bright colours.*

ADDING COLOUR

1 Melting the chocolate: Break the chocolate into small pieces. Melt the dark and white chocolate separately in small bowls over a pan of hot water, stirring well.

2 Polishing the moulds: Wash the moulds in warm, soapy water and dry them well. Polish them with some cotton wool to ensure they are clean and also to give the finished chocolates a shine.

3 Measuring out the chocolate: Divide the white chocolate mixture between three separate pots. Don't worry if it begins to set – each little pot can be stood in hot water to melt the chocolate again.

4 Adding colour: Add your chosen colours of petal dust to the melted chocolate. Don't be over-generous. Start with only a little and mix it in very well before adding any more.

5 **Transferring the image:** Using the coloured chocolate and a fine paintbrush, paint in the details in your chosen moulds. Then leave them until the coloured chocolate has set thoroughly.

6 **Making small cut-outs:** When the coloured chocolate has set, fill the painted moulds with dark or white chocolate. Make sure that the chocolate is level with the top of the moulds.

7 **Removing any air bubbles:** Tap each mould sharply on the table as you fill it in order to get rid of any air bubbles and also to level the surface of the chocolate. Place the moulds in the fridge at once.

8 **Emptying the moulds:** Leave the chocolates to set in the fridge for five or 10 minutes. Then leave to stand at room temperature for a while. Ease them out of the moulds by giving the moulds a sharp tap.

Designing simple collars

Once you have mastered the skills for designing a run-out collar, you will always be able to transform your cakes into something special.

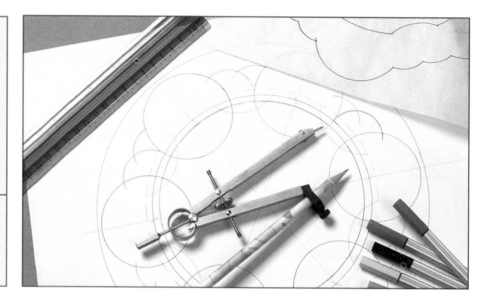

Collars are a very attractive addition to any cake, and they can transform a simple design into something extremely special. There are many possibilities for collar shapes – especially when you can design your own, thus making the cake absolutely unique.

It may seem daunting – especially if you haven't picked up a compass since you were at school – but if you persevere, you will get results. On page **154** we give a step-by-step guide to designing a collar for a 18cm (7in) cake. By following it, you will gradually understand how a full collar is designed. Once you have this information, you can carry on and create your own wonderful ideas.

PRINCIPLES OF COLLAR DESIGN

There are several basic principles of collar design which must be remembered before you start. The first is that of balance. The collar must not

be wider than the cake board, otherwise it will look top heavy. Also, the collar should not sit too far inwards on the cake, or else it will squash the cake-top design. By their very nature, run-out collars are delicate and fragile, so they are best suited to royal-iced cakes.

The design process involves drawing the boundaries of your cake and board on paper so that you have set limits within which to design. The design is divided into sections, and we recommend that you use a selection of coloured pencils to make things clearer.

MAKING YOUR OWN DESIGNS

When you have a free moment, experiment with some designs by setting the compass at different widths so that you can either produce slight curves or a very rounded effect. Or mark certain points around the cake and join them with a ruler.

You can also trace a smaller, more intricate pattern, and repeat it around the cake section by section.

If you are not confident enough to run out a full collar, you can run out several sections and attach them bit by bit. But remember that when attaching sections, you must incorporate another design, such as an overlay, which will cover the join. A quarter collar is often more suited to square cakes or to those cakes which only require a collar at the cake corner.

USING COLOUR

Don't forget to plan the colour scheme for your collar. They often look very attractive when picot-edged or outlined in a different shade or colour. You may find yourself becoming an enthusiast about collar design and, if you do, you will find that there are a range of books available which go into the subject in some depth.

DESIGN IDEAS

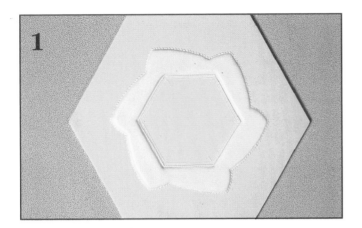

The inner line of this collar echoes the hexagonal shape of the board. Section the cake design into six segments and draw straight lines between adjacent points.

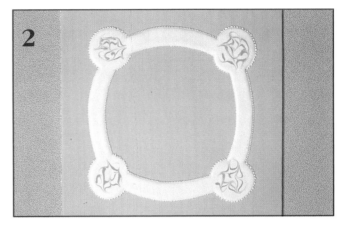

The collar design here is based on four small circles at each corner of the cake joined by very gentle, curved lines. A marbled effect is created within each circle.

This simple design features a scalloped outer edge and a more intricate inner edge. It would look attractive when teamed with a circular or scalloped board.

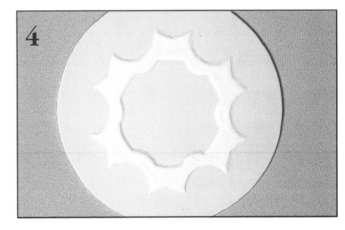

The outer line features six curved lines interspersed with a simple crown shape. The inner line is also a combination of curves and straight lines.

helpline   BISECTING A CAKE

The fewer number of segments you divide your circle into, the simpler the design will be. With more intricate designs you will have to divide your cake into more sections.

Dividing your cake into thirds or multiples of the number three is relatively easy. If you set your compass to the radius of the cake, you can mark six sections on the cake by placing the point on the outer edge, then marking off one section along the circumference, and then moving the needle

to that spot and continuing in the same fashion. If you set your compass to half the radius of the cake, you will end up with 12 sections, and so on. You can bisect the angles on a cake in this fashion as long as the number of sections on your cake is a multiple of either three or four.

Once you have marked the circle into thirds or quarters, you can then also use a protractor as an easy way of dividing the cake into further sections.

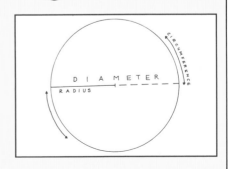

DESIGNING A

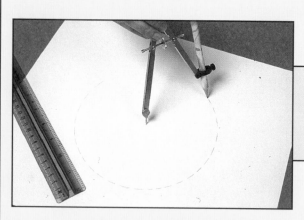

1 **Measuring the cake circumference:** Measure your cake tin or finished cake and use a compass to draw a circle to this size with a broken line. This broken line is known as the 'cake line'.

2 **Measuring the board:** Measure the board – the diameter gives you the outer limit for your collar. Use a green crayon to draw this line. Then draw an inner green circle 5mm (¼in) smaller than the cake.

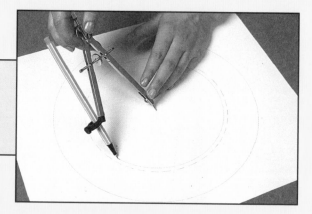

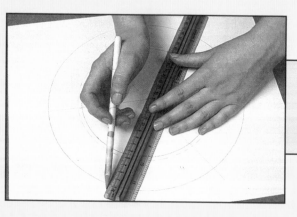

3 **Marking sections:** Set compass to the radius of your cake. Place the point on the inner circle and mark a line. Repeat this all around the circle. Then join each mark to its opposite mark with a ruled line.

4 **Marking small circles:** Place the compass point where a dotted and a ruled line meet. Set the compass width to 3.5cm (1½in) and use a pink crayon to draw a circle. Do this at each intersection.

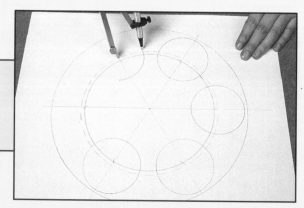

COLLAR

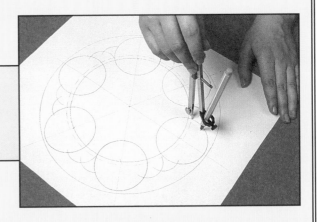

5 **Adding arcs:** Set compass at 2cm (³/₄in). Place point where a pink circle meets the cake line and draw an orange arc outside the circle. Repeat all the way around, bisecting the adjacent orange arc.

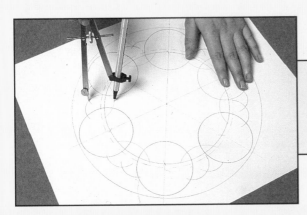

6 **Adding detail:** Keeping the same radius, position the compass needle where two orange arcs intersect and use a yellow pen to draw another arc, this time joining two points on the inner green circle.

7 **Marking the innermost circle:** Use a red pen to draw another inner circle 5mm (¹/₅in) smaller than the green inner line and 10mm (²/₅in) smaller than the cake line. Set compass point at the cake's centre.

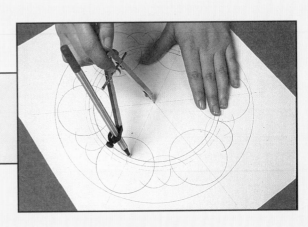

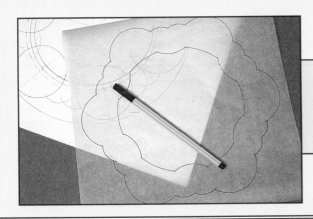

8 **Tracing the design:** Trace over your design so that you have very clear lines to follow for the runout. Some of the lines will be redundant, so it is important to have a finished design you can follow.

Tempering chocolate

Couverture chocolate is a luxury product which has to be put through a heating and cooling process called tempering before it can be used. The results, however, are well worth the time and trouble.

Couverture chocolate may be the most expensive type of confectioner's chocolate, but it does produce the best results. It requires tempering – a process which involves heating the chocolate to a specific temperature, cooling it on a marble slab, then reheating it before use. The finished chocolate has a high-gloss finish and what is known as 'snap' – it will break crisply and cleanly when set.

Couverture chocolate is available in plain, milk and white varieties. The plain variety is made from cocoa mass, sugar and cocoa butter. Full cream milk and other fats are added for milk couverture chocolate. Each variety is tempered using different temperatures, being allowed to cool in between so that the two different types of fats contained within the chocolate, which have different setting points, melt and then solidify.

The higher temperature is reached first so that at the second heating only one set of fat crystals will melt, while the other will remain solid.

USING TEMPERED CHOCOLATE

When using tempered plain chocolate, be sure to keep it at 31-32°C (89-90°F) by stirring it every now and then and putting it back on top of the saucepan of hot water occasionally.

Use tempered chocolate for coating home-made chocolates, piping, or making figures in moulds. The beauti-ful Easter egg illustrated here is made from plain chocolate, decorated with an inscription and a snail's trail piped in white chocolate.

SECRETS OF SUCCESS

When tempering chocolate, always work in a cool room. If the chocolate does not set when tested, you will have to temper it again. Be careful not to mark the mould with your fingers after polishing it, since any greasy marks will prevent the chocolate being released from the mould.

When coating a mould with chocolate, always use a dry brush. Also, make sure that steam from the hot water doesn't get into the chocolate. Moisture can cause it to thicken at the wrong time and develop a bloom.

Finally, try to avoid handling the finished chocolate, otherwise you risk leaving fingerprints on it.

TEMPERING CHOCOLATE TECHNIQUE

1 **Melting the chocolate:** Put the plain chocolate into a heatproof glass bowl and set the bowl over a saucepan of hot (not boiling) water. Stir constantly with a wooden spoon until the chocolate has melted.

2 **Heating the chocolate:** Continue stirring while checking the temperature with a thermometer. When the chocolate reaches 48-49°C (105-107°F), remove it from the heat immediately.

3 **Pouring the chocolate:** Quickly pour the melted chocolate out on to the marble slab. Do not scrape all the chocolate out of the bowl – leave a coating behind.

4 **Working the chocolate:** Turn chocolate on the marble slab and work it with a scraper. Be ready to do this quite quickly, since the chocolate can start setting immediately, depending on room temperature.

helpline   TEMPERATURES AND TIPS

Plain chocolate
Melt to 48-49°C (105-107°F)
Cool to 28°C (86°F)
Rewarm to 31-32°C (89-90°F)

Milk chocolate
Melt to 45°C (103°F)
Cool to 27°C (85°F)
Rewarm to 29-30°C (87-88°F)

White chocolate
Melt to 40-42°C (98-100°F)
Cool to 26°C (84°F)
Rewarm to 29°C (87°F)

The temperatures used for tempering couverture chocolate vary according to which type is being used. They should be followed precisely, so a thermometer is essential.

You will also need a marble slab to work the chocolate on so that it cools down rapidly after the initial melting. The chocolate you buy may come with manufacturer's

instructions as to what temperatures to follow. If these are different from the ones we recommend, follow them, as different brands vary in their composition.

5 **Checking the temperature:** Keep checking the temperature of the melted chocolate with the thermometer. When it drops to 28°C (86°F), it is ready to be returned to the bowl for reheating.

6 **Reheating the chocolate:** Put the chocolate back in the bowl and reheat it to 31-32°C (89-90°F), stirring it constantly with a wooden spoon. Check the temperature with the thermometer.

7 **Spreading the chocolate:** Using a palette knife, spread some chocolate on to the marble slab. It should set quickly. If it takes longer than three minutes, go back to step 2 and repeat the process.

8 **Lining the mould:** Polish the mould with cotton wool and use a dry pastry brush to coat it with a thin layer of chocolate. Take great care not to mark the inside of the mould with your fingers.

9 **Applying a second layer:** Keep the chocolate at 31°C (89°F); return it to the heat from time to time and stir. Refrigerate the mould for a few minutes to cool it before applying a second layer of chocolate.

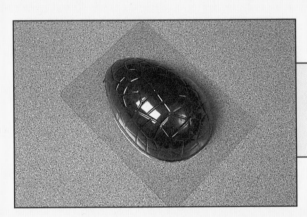

10 **Completing the layers:** Check the mould for any thin spots and, if necessary, apply another layer of chocolate. The chocolate has set in the mould when it has an opaque appearance.

11 **Turning out the chocolate:** When the chocolate has set hard, tap the mould firmly on the work surface. It is fragile, so turn the chocolate on to a cloth to protect it from damage.

12 **Joining the halves:** Use the remaining melted chocolate and a fine paintbrush to paint the edge of one of the halves. Press the two halves together and leave to set before decorating.

Making fondant icing

Making fondant icing is a highly skilled process that can bring great satisfaction to the enthusiastic cake decorator.

HAVE TO HAND

Ingredients: *1kg cube sugar •*
300ml water • 175ml liquid glucose
• cooking oil.

Equipment: *2 palette knives (or*
scrapers) • sugar thermometer •
wooden spoon • large marble slab •
pastry brush • large, copper-
bottomed saucepan.

Main skills: *making fondant icing.*

DIFFICULTY   TIME   SUITABILITY

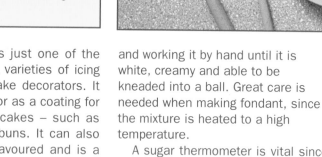

Fondant icing is just one of the many different varieties of icing available to cake decorators. It is used as a filling or as a coating for sweets and small cakes – such as eclairs and choux buns. It can also be coloured and flavoured and is a popular choice for chocolate fondants and peppermint creams.

FOOLPROOF FONDANT

Fondant icing differs from sugarpaste in that it is made to a different consistency and involves a heating process which is absolutely crucial to its success. It is made by preparing a white paste in advance, which then has stock syrup added to it to bring it to a pouring consistency. It requires skill to make, so if you are short on time or experience, it might be better to buy it from the shops.

Fondant icing is made by boiling sugar and glucose, then cooling it and working it by hand until it is white, creamy and able to be kneaded into a ball. Great care is needed when making fondant, since the mixture is heated to a high temperature.

A sugar thermometer is vital since the temperature of the mixture is checked at three different stages in the process. The mixture becomes extremely hot at one stage, so be on your guard against splashing yourself. Do not make it when children are in the vicinity.

When the temperature of the mixture has reached 116°C/240°F, it is carefully poured on to an oiled marble slab and left to cool. (The marble slab helps the mixture to cool rapidly.) If you are worried that the mixture will run over the edge of the slab, look for special, oiled metal bars which can be used to form a retaining square or triangle on the work surface. The end result should have a rather fine texture. When you have finished, wrap it closely in cling film and store in a sealed container in a cool, dry place for up to a month.

FINISHED FONDANT

Once made, fondant can either be used in its paste form and rolled (it is rather like sugarpaste but not as elastic), or (more usually) reheated to pouring consistency. In the latter case, gently reheat the fondant in a double boiler to 38°C/100°F (no higher or it will lose its gloss). Stock syrup and other flavourings are then added.

A key word in the making of fondant icing, as with many cake decorating skills, is patience. Do not be tempted to rush the process during the early stages by turning the heat up too high.

MAKING FONDANT ICING

1 Oiling the marble slab: Use a pastry brush to lightly brush a marble slab with cooking oil — you will need quite a large slab to ensure that the mixture does not run over the edges.

2 Dissolving the sugar: Place the sugar cubes and water in a saucepan and heat gently until the sugar dissolves, stirring occasionally with a wooden spoon. Do not allow the mixture to boil.

3 Adding glucose: While the sugar dissolves, warm the glucose. Check sugar-solution temperature with thermometer. When it reaches 107°C/225°F, add glucose. Turn up heat and bring to boil, but do not stir.

4 Brushing with cold water: While the sugar is boiling, brush cold water constantly around the inside edges of the saucepan to prevent the sugar from crystallising.

---

helpline

ADDING STOCK SYRUP

Stock syrup is a mixture of refined caster sugar and water, brought to the boil and then cooled. It is very versatile and can be used for a number of cake-decorating purposes. The sugar must be completely dissolved before you bring it to the boil and while it boils it must not be stirred at all. To make it you will need 240g of caster sugar for every 300ml of water.

Leave the fondant paste for 24 hours before reheating and adding the stock syrup. Place the fondant in a clean bowl over a saucepan of hot water and stir until it has melted. Add 1 tbsp of stock syrup. Continue to heat the mixture, adding more syrup if necessary, until it coats the back of the spoon. It can then be coloured and flavoured as you desire.

5 Fast boiling: Keep an eye on the temperature all the time and continue fast boiling until the mixture reaches 116°C/240°F. Do not stir it, and watch out for splashing.

6 Standing in cold water: When the mixture reaches 116°C/240°F, remove the saucepan from the heat and put it immediately into a bowl of cold water to cool. Leave it to stand for two minutes.

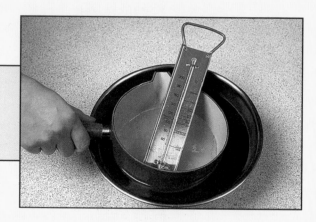

7 Pouring the mixture: Start to pour the mixture on to the centre of the oiled marble slab. It is important that either the slab is large or that the mixture is contained by metal bars.

8 Pouring the rest of the mixture: Pour the remaining mixture out on to the slab but do not scrape the mixture from the pan, since fine crystals can form on the sides of the saucepan.

9 **Turning the mixture:** When the temperature drops to 38°C/100°F, start to turn the mixture with an oiled palette knife. The cooling process is rapid, so be prepared to work quickly.

10 **Using palette knives:** Using two oiled palette knives or scrapers, continue turning the mixture. As you work the mixture, it will become more opaque and start to thicken.

11 **Working the mixture:** Work the mixture for some time. When it becomes white and crumbly, it has reached the required texture. This process takes at least 30 minutes.

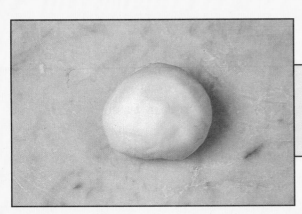

12 **Kneading the fondant:** With moist hands, work the fondant into a ball and knead it until it is smooth. This takes between five and 10 minutes. Cover with a damp cloth and leave for 30 minutes.

Colouring flowers

Dipping paste flowers opens a wide range of possibilities for adding special colours and effects.

HAVE TO HAND

Ingredients: paste food colours • isopropyl alcohol • white vegetable fat • petal dusts • flower paste.

Equipment: flower stand • jam jar • fine paintbrush.

Main skills: colouring and dipping flowers.

DIFFICULTY	TIME	SUITABILITY

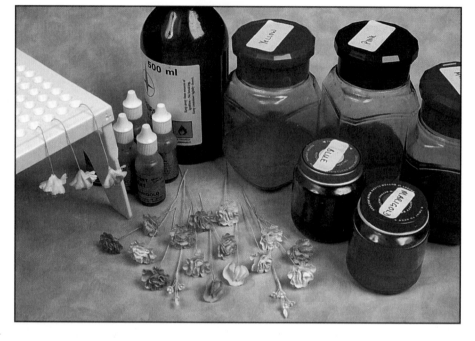

Dipping flowers is a very effective way of adding colour to them and it also makes a change from other methods of colouring cake decorations.

Here, the flowers are dipped in an alcohol-based mixture that has an extremely high percentage proof, such as isopropyl alcohol. This is only available at the discretion of your local pharmacist and it is vital that it is kept tightly sealed and well away from little hands. The higher the percentage of alcohol, the faster it will evaporate. This ensures that the dipped flower will dry very quickly and also helps to avoid any damage that can be caused by flower paste coming into contact with water.

DIPPING THE FLOWERS

Once you have obtained the alcohol you need to find a good solid jar with a top wide enough for the flower to pass through. Pour enough alcohol into the jar to cover the flower and then mix some paste food colour into it. It does not matter if the colour looks exceptionally dark. The flower will still look pale on the first dipping, and to achieve very vibrant colours you will need to dip more than once.

Once you have dipped the flower, raise it to the top of the jar and hold it suspended while you twirl it gently around in the enclosed space so that the surplus alcohol falls back into the pot and does not splash on to your hand. If any does, wash it off straight away with cold water.

The flower paste from which the flowers are made should contain white vegetable fat. If it does not, add some to the paste before you roll it out to make the flowers. Use dry flowers on a wired stem and gently lower each one into the dipping solution so that it can absorb the colour. Once you have removed the flower from the pot, dry it on a flower stand. If you wish, you can suspend it upside-down in the stand so that the excess colour runs to the rim of the flower and gives it a darker edge. This creates a very pretty effect which enhances the overall look of the flower.

TWO-TONE FLOWERS

If you want a differently coloured centre for your flower, you can use the 'resist' method. This involves painting part of the flower with vegetable fat – effectively, sealing it off. This means that you can create pretty, two-tone flowers quite easily.

Above all, do remember that the liquid is dangerous and highly inflammable. Keep it away from children at all times and handle it very carefully, disposing of it by washing it down the sink. The mixture will keep for a little while if you intend to dip more flowers, but sediment will accumulate on the bottom of the jar – so give it a gentle stir before re-using it.

FINISHED FLOWERS

These purple carnations show the colour that can be achieved by dipping flowers once (left), twice (centre) and three times (right).

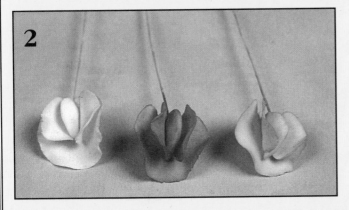

Produce colour changes by dipping first in one colour and then another. For example, the sweet pea has been dipped into pink first and then into purple.

Use lustre dust to enhance the finished, dipped flowers. In this case, mother-of-pearl dust adds a sparkle, but you could use a toning shade to deepen areas of colour on the flower.

These colours were produced by using five liquid colours. Some were dipped once, some several times. Others were dipped in two different colours, or in a mixture of two colours.

DESIGN TOUCH

If you have any left-over paste flowers from another cake in various pastel shades, you can dye them using the dipping method until they are all the same colour. You can also wire tiny flowers into groups before dipping them so that you can colour the whole group together. Make sure that the wire stems are long enough to enable complete dipping, since you should avoid putting your hand into the jar itself.

You could also colour other flower-paste decorations in the same way. Tiny, plunger-cutter blossoms can be placed in a little muslin bag or sieve. The dipping method is particularly useful for a big occasion (such as a wedding) when you may want to colour a considerable quantity of pastillage decorations in a shade to match, for example, the bridesmaids' dresses. For those of you who like to work ahead, you can make plain white flowers in advance and dip them when the time comes in your preferred colour. When mixing colours, add a little at a time until you have reached the correct shade.

METHOD 1

1 **Setting up the jar:** Pour some alcohol into a jar, enough to ensure that you can dip the whole flower in without damaging it on the base of the jar. Add the liquid colour to the jar.

2 **Dipping the flower:** Place the lid firmly on the jar and shake it well to mix the colour thoroughly. Remove the lid and dip the flower into the jar, gently twirling it around to achieve an even colour.

3 **Removing the excess liquid:** Gripping it firmly by the stem, raise the flower towards the neck of the jar and then twirl it around gently in order to remove the excess liquid.

4 **Re-dipping the flower:** Remove the flower from the jar and replace the lid. Leave the flower to dry on the flower stand. If you want the flower to be a deeper colour, repeat the process.

METHOD 2

1 Brushing on the fat: Melt a small amount of white vegetable fat over a low heat. Using a fine paintbrush, brush the fat on to the edges of the petals. Leave to set.

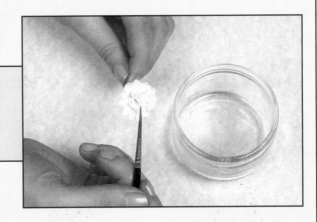

2 Dipping the flower: Add the liquid colour to the jar of alcohol and shake it well with the lid firmly in place. Then remove the lid and dip the flower into the liquid.

3 Removing excess liquid: Grasping the stem firmly, lift the flower and then twirl it around in the neck of the jar to remove any excess liquid. Be careful not to hit the petals on the side of the jar.

4 Finishing off: Dip the flower as many times as is necessary in order to obtain the shade of colour that you require. You can achieve other effects by painting on the melted fat in stripes.

Crystallising flowers

A very simple method of using fresh flowers as cake decorations is to crystallise them.

HAVE TO HAND

Ingredients: edible flowers • caster sugar • rose water or orange water • flower paste • gum-arabic powder (or egg-white solution).

Equipment: fine paintbrush • tweezers (metal or plastic) • absorbent kitchen towel • scissors.

Main skill: crystallising flowers.

DIFFICULTY	TIME	SUITABILITY
✓	⌛	

Using crystallised flowers is a very quick and simple method of decorating cakes. They can look wonderful on tea-time cakes and gateaux. However, there are a number of important considerations to bear in mind when choosing the flowers that you wish to crystallise.

CHOOSING FLOWERS

Make sure that you have chosen an edible flower. Any of the following are suitable: honeysuckle, primroses, pansies, heart's ease, violets, sweet peas, mint, pinks and nasturtiums. Rose petals are particularly effective, but you must check very carefully with a reference book before using any other variety of flower.

Only certain flowers are suitable for crystallisation in their entirety. Others, such as the rose, must be dismantled and scattered as petals on a cake or board. Choose flowers which have a bright, clear colour and a flat shape. You should look for even-sized, undamaged petals that are quite strong.

If a flower does not meet these requirements, it will be very difficult to crystallise. This is because the flowers have to be coated with a solution to preserve them, and with some flowers it is almost impossible to cover every part of the petal with the solution. Flowers with a bell or trumpet are very hard to crystallise since they lose their shape easily. Also, some tiny flowers can be overpowered by the sugar coating, so your choice needs to be just right.

Flowers should be picked on a dry day, and washed and dried immediately to avoid any possibility of mould developing. If they are stored correctly, they will keep for two or three months when placed in a box between absorbent kitchen paper.

COATING THE FLOWERS

Once you have chosen your flower, you must give it a protective coating to preserve it. The petal or flower must be entirely covered with either an albumen or a gum-arabic solution. The method and the finished result are just the same, but flowers coated in the gum-arabic solution can be stored for longer. Both methods are better than using raw egg white.

The flowers are liberally dusted with caster sugar and left to dry overnight in a warm, dry spot – either on kitchen paper in the airing cupboard, or supported by a wire rack. For fast results, you can dry them on a baking sheet in a very slow oven for about eight minutes. The end result is very pretty and provides a quick and effective way of decorating a simple tea-time cake.

DIPPING ROSE PETALS

1

Choose roses that are starting to open as the petals need to lie fairly flat. Carefully detach the petals, wash them, and gently pat them dry. Hold them very carefully with a pair of tweezers.

2

Dip each petal into the gum-arabic or albumen solution, covering it completely. Then shake it gently so that any excess mixture runs off it.

3

Still using the tweezers, dip the petal into the sugar. The petal should be covered by a fine, even coating. Do not damage the petal by holding the tweezers too tightly.

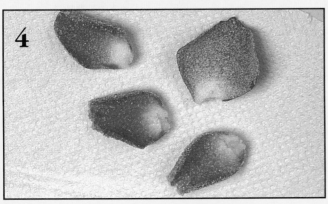

4

Remove any excess sugar by gently shaking the petals, then lay them on a kitchen towel in a warm, dry place to dry overnight.

DESIGN TOUCH

When you crystallise edible flowers, you might also like to crystallise some fruit at the same time. Both fruit and flowers are an attractive and simple way to decorate a cake. Try crystallising grapes or gooseberries. You can use them to decorate small cakes, making them look extremely tempting. The procedure is exactly the same as for the flowers, but they do not last quite as long and should be eaten within 12 hours. When you are ready to place the fruit and flowers on the cake, position them gently around the top or board. If you are unhappy with the result, you can reposition them, but do not handle them too much. (You could attach them with dabs of royal icing.) If you have any tiny, crystallised petals, you can use them to spell out the recipient's name on top of the cake.

CRYSTALLISING HEART'S EASE

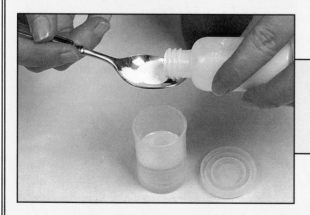

1 **Making the gum-arabic solution:** Put two tablespoons (30ml) of rosewater into a small screwtop container. Add two teaspoons (10ml) of gum-arabic powder.

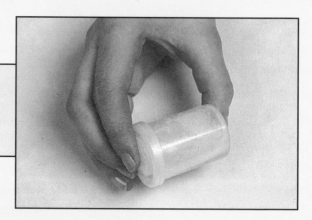

2 **Shaking the solution:** Don't worry if the solution is lumpy when it is first mixed. Simply put the lid on the container and shake it vigorously. Then leave it to stand until the mixture is completely clear.

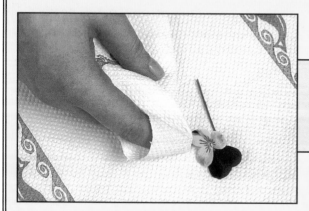

3 **Cleaning and drying the petals:** Wash the flowers very gently and pat them dry with absorbent kitchen paper. Take great care to ensure that they remain undamaged.

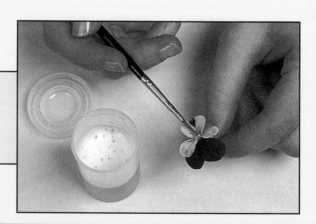

4 **Brushing with gum arabic:** Using the gum-arabic solution and a fine paintbrush, paint the back and front of the petals. Cover every bit of them in order to avoid any later growth of mould.

5 **Sprinkling with caster sugar:** While the gum arabic solution is still wet, sprinkle a thick layer of caster sugar over the back and front of the petals. Do this over a piece of kitchen paper.

6 **Shaking off the excess sugar:** To achieve a smooth finish, hold the flower upside-down and twirl it gently between your thumb and forefinger in order to shake off any excess sugar.

7 **Trimming the stalks:** Trim away most of the stalk so that the flower lies relatively flat. You need only very little stalks when using flowers to decorate the cake.

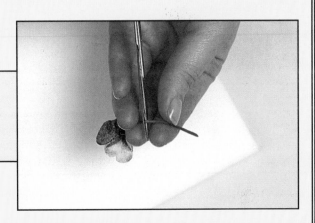

8 **Finishing off:** Lay the flowers on absorbent kitchen paper and leave them in a warm, dry spot – such as the airing cupboard – for 24 hours, turning them over once or twice.

Piping on tulle

Tulle shapes decorated with piping make extremely beautiful, delicate decorations for all types of celebration cakes.

Once you have mastered the technique of cutting and shaping tulle, you can make all manner of decorations for your cakes. Items such as churches and cradles – decorations traditionally used on Christmas and christening cakes – appear much more delicate than pastillage models when made using this method. They are, however, also surprisingly sturdy.

SELECTING TULLE

You can buy tulle in most large department stores or specialist fabric shops. Silk, cotton and nylon varieties are all available, but the first two are expensive and only available in a limited range of colours. Nylon tulle comes in a wide range of colours and is also much stiffer than either silk or cotton. If you can find the colour you want in a nylon tulle, you can cut and fashion it without using a stiffening solution. Soft tulle can be stiffened using a sugar solution (see Professional Secrets, page **173**) and shaped as it dries.

MAKING A TULLE FRILL

Perhaps one of the simplest ways of using tulle is to fit a frill around a cake. This is particularly suitable for novice cake decorators who find cutting and attaching a sugarpaste frill, section by section, a time-consuming and complicated procedure.

For a full frill, cut a length of tulle three times the diameter of the cake, then gather it at the top and hold it in position with glass-headed pins before you secure it with a length of ribbon. The bottom edge of the frill is then edged with piping. A random pattern of small dots could be piped on the surface of the frill to give it a little added colour.

If you use a fairly stiff tulle for the frill, then it will be easier to handle than sugarpaste and also less likely to be accidentally damaged.

You can then add some tulle decorations, such as the flowers, bootees and butterflies shown here, cut from the same shade of tulle piped with complementary colours of royal icing.

IDEAS FOR USING TULLE

This pretty flower has petals and leaves cut from tulle. The petals are outlined in pink royal icing and the leaves in green. The leaves, which also have piped veins, are shaped by drying them over a former.

This blue bootee has a pastillage sole and a tulle upper that is attached with royal icing and supported with pins until dry. The fabric texture is created with cornelli work, and the trim is a tiny, piped shell border.

This lacy butterfly begins with a pair of tulle wings. These are outlined in royal icing and covered with a pattern of veins. When dry, they are set onto a still-wet piped body, supported at an angle on sponge.

The tulle frill is half the depth of the cake and three times its circumference. The top is gathered up to fit, and attached with ribbon. The scalloped edge and random dot pattern are piped on with royal icing.

PROFESSIONAL SECRETS

Working with tulle and net

• The tulle we have used is made from nylon. It is inexpensive, especially as you will not need large amounts, and comes in white, cream and pastel colours.

• If you cannot get the colour you require, the tulle can be dyed by soaking it for two to three hours in paste or liquid food colouring diluted with boiling water. This will produce pastel colours.

• For stronger colours use a fabric dye, following the maker's instructions carefully.

• Nylon tulle is a stiff fabric and so only suitable for making decorations that are either flat, or that curve in one direction.

• To mould more complicated shapes – such as wedding bells or wedding slippers – in tulle, you need to use fine-grade cotton net and stiffen it with sugar solution.

• Make the solution by adding three parts caster sugar to one part water. Boil it for just long enough to dissolve the sugar.

• Dip the net in the solution until coated. While still wet, mould it into the required shape, using a former or your hands. As it dries, the sugar will stiffen the fabric.

• Cotton net is usually cream, but it takes colour better than nylon net. You can easily colour it by adding liquid or paste food colouring to the sugar solution.

MAKING A TULLE BOW

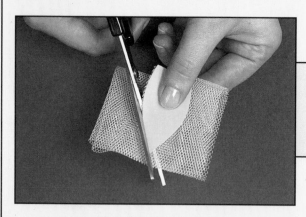

1 Cutting the bow loops: Make a pattern for the loops. Fold a square of tulle in half vertically and then horizontally. Place the pattern against the fold and cut two bow loops.

2 Cutting the tails: Fold a longer piece of tulle in half and use the template provided to cut the tails for the bow. Hold the template firmly to prevent it slipping as you cut.

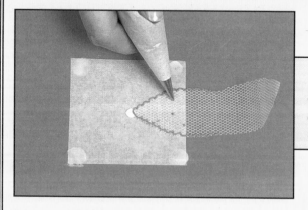

3 Beginning to decorate: Fix wax paper to a work surface with dabs of white royal icing. Attach one end of bow loop. Using a no. 0 tube, pipe deep pink scallops round half the outer edge. Add random dots.

4 Folding into half-bow shape: Carefully fold the free end of the bow loop into the centre, lining it up with the decorated half. Attach it with a dab of white royal icing.

5 **Completing the decoration:** Using a no. 0 tube and deep pink royal icing, repeat the piped design on the second half of the loop, scalloping the edges and piping randomly placed dots over it.

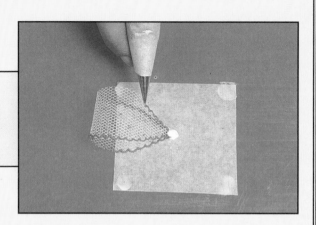

6 **Adding the second bow loop:** Attach a second loop to the centre with a dab of white royal icing. Pipe scallops and dots as before, then fold over and attach. Complete the design on the top of the loop.

7 **Creating the tails:** Attach the tulle tails with dabs of white royal icing. Use the deep pink royal icing again to pipe scallops around the tails, then decorate the scallops with dots as for the loops.

8 **Finishing off:** Finally, roll the centre piece of the bow into a tube and attach it with royal icing. Use a glass-headed pin to hold it in place while you pipe on the scallops and dots.

Secrets of Success

Corner designs

**Coloured frills, placed at the corners of a square cake,
add attractive details to a simple design.**

HAVE TO HAND

Ingredients: *sugarpasted square cake*
• flower paste • sugarpaste • pink
food colouring • royal icing • egg
white • small blossoms.

Equipment: *Garrett frill cutter •*
greaseproof paper • scissors • glass-
headed pins • nos. 1 and 2 piping
tubes • sugarpaste roller • cocktail
stick • paintbrush.

Main skills: *• making and positioning*
frills • colouring paste.

DIFFICULTY   TIME   SUITABILITY

Corner designs are a very effective way of adding detail and shape to a simple, square cake, and there are many interesting designs with which you can experiment. What's more, if you like to royal ice your square cakes but are still inexperienced at this technique, then adding extra decoration can be an effective way of masking less than perfect corners!

When a cake has a simple top design which you do not wish to clutter, like this one, a side decoration is the ideal way to add to the appeal of the cake. Frills also bring a softer, more feminine touch to an otherwise plain cake.

THE CORNER DECORATIONS
The corners of our featured cake are decorated with frills cut with a Garratt frill cutter. Each frill is coloured a different shade of pink and then layered according to shade. They are attached to the cake with egg white. Finally, a larger white frill is placed at the top of the corner and sweeps down the side of the cake until it reaches the base.

ACHIEVING THE RIGHT ANGLE
The success of the cake depends to a large extent on achieving the correct angles for the placement of the frills, and you will be guided in this respect by a greaseproof-paper template which will keep your lines straight.

When you have decided upon the size of the frill, make a triangular template. It is up to you how far up the cake you would like the frills to sit, and how wide you wish them to be but they should be neither too big nor too small. Each frill is positioned only 5mm-1cm ($^1/_4$-$^1/_2$in) higher than the one underneath, so that the darker colour just peeps out from below the lighter colour on top, giving a subtle grading of colour tones.

MAKING THE FRILLS
Frill paste is made with a mixture of flower paste and sugarpaste in equal proportions in order to give just the right consistency. You need to make four different shades of your chosen colour. Here we have made dark pink, mid pink, light pink and a very pale pink according to the method stated in step 2 on page 178. You may prefer to choose a different colour but it is advisable to stick to pastel shades. When the frill is made, use a cocktail stick to soften and frill the edges a little further.

FINISHING TOUCHES
A tiny row of shells is piped in white royal icing with a no. 1 piping tube along the white frill where it meets the rest of the cake in order to disguise the join. Add a final touch to this very attractive cake by adding tiny pink and lilac blossoms to the sides.

MAKING A

1 Cutting the template: Cut a small triangle out of greaseproof paper and place it against the corner of the cake as shown. Make a line of pin pricks on the cake around the edge of the triangle.

2 Colouring the paste: Colour the paste until you have a very pale pink. Remove a quarter of the paste. Apply more colour to the remaining paste and continue in the same way until you have four different shades.

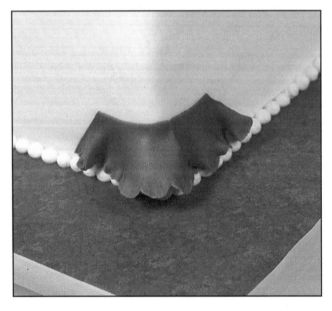

3 Attaching first frill: Cut a small frill from the darkest paste. Soften the edges with a cocktail stick. Attach to the cake with egg white. Cut the ends at an angle, using the pin marks as a guide.

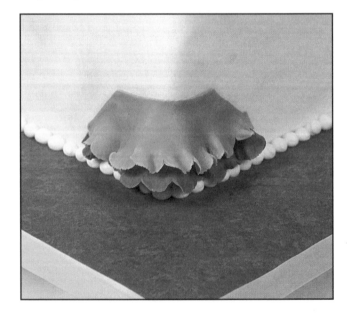

4 Attaching second frill: Cut a frill from the mid-pink paste. Soften the edges and attach to cake in the same way as before. Lift edge up with a paintbrush. The first frill should show by only about 5mm-1cm (¹/₄-¹/₂in).

CORNER DESIGN

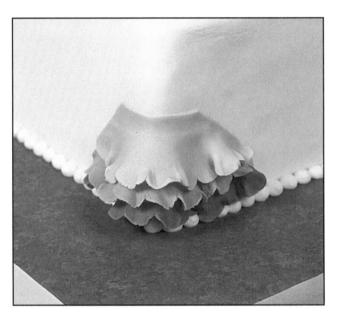

5 Adding third frill: Cut a frill from the light pink paste, soften the edge of the frill, and attach above the second frill as before. Cut to fit the angle, checking that you are following the marked lines.

6 Adding the final pink frill: Cut a frill from the lightest pink. Soften the edge and attach as before. Make sure you trim the ends so that they follow the shape of the original pin-pricked triangle.

7 Attaching the final frill: Attach a long white frill over the pink frills, running all the way down to the base as shown. Position the frill, then trim the outer edge to follow the original triangle shape.

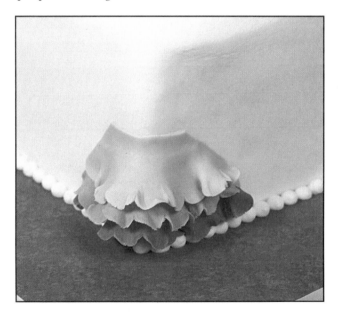

8 Piping a row of shells: Use a no. 1 piping tube and white royal icing to pipe a line of small shells or dots which follow along the line of the white frill where it meets the side of the cake.

IDEAS FOR CORNER DESIGNS

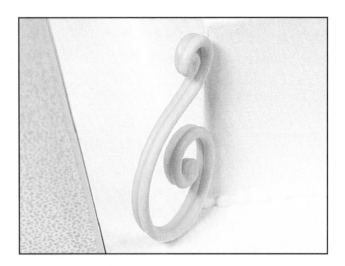

1 Elegant piped scrolls attached to each corner of a royal-iced cake will make it look larger. Pipe the scrolls on to wax paper and leave them to dry before attaching.

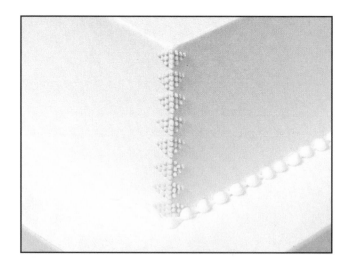

2 This simple corner design comprises two rows of triangles built up from small dots of royal icing that run from the top to the bottom of the cake.

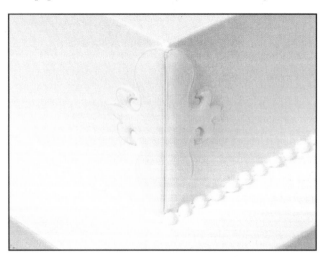

3 Delicate white runouts are placed on neighbouring corners of this cake. The runouts have been flooded using white icing and edged in yellow royal icing.

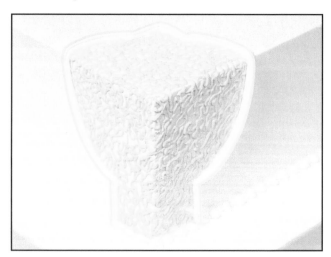

4 Yellow cornelli work, encased inside a piped design, makes an attractive finish for a royal-iced cake. This type of piping is useful for hiding flaws in the coating.

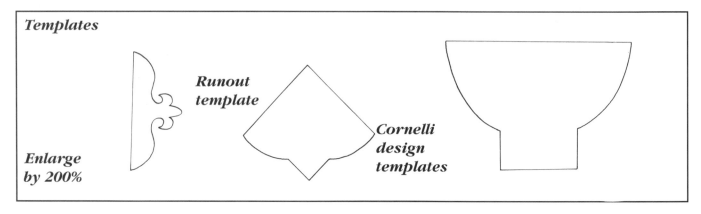

Templates

Runout template

Cornelli design templates

Enlarge by 200%

Extension-work panels

These various techniques for lace and extension work will help you to create delicate and intricate designs.

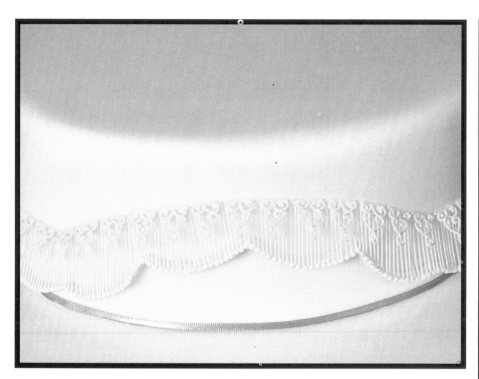

Cakes in which lace and extension work feature strongly can look very beautiful indeed. They may seem complicated, and you certainly need time and patience, but the end result will be well worth your efforts.

The main feature of the cake shown here is the lace and extension work piped around it in pale yellow royal icing. If you have not done much of this type of work before, remember that white icing piped against white icing does not show up very well, and it will be easier to see if you use a pastel colour.

PIPING THE DESIGN
Firstly, the design is scribed on to the side of the cake, and then the bridgework is piped along the lower curved line. If you have not had much experience of piping along a curved scribed line, you can pipe in a series of dots first as a guide.

Then, by piping from dot to dot, you can create a regular curve. The bridgework is built up by overpiping the same scribed line and leaving it to dry for 24 hours.

PIPING STRAIGHT LINES
When you begin to pipe the extension work you must maintain very straight lines. Hold a piece of straight card gently against the cake and follow its line as you pipe. Then pipe another straight line 2.5cm (1in) above it. These lines will act as guides and keep your lines straight when you begin to pipe them only millimetres apart.

Keep a sable paintbrush to hand in order to neaten your work and to remove any hanging edges by tucking them under the bridge. Each line should be finished in this way. Use the paintbrush to keep the top line neat. Ideally, you should work with a tilting

turntable – the extension work will be easier to pipe if the cake is angled towards you. When you pipe, pull the line of icing slightly away from the cake.

ADDING LACEWORK
The delicacy of lacework makes it an ideal partner for extension panels. It can either be used to outline the top of the panels, or added to extension work flounces as an additional element in the decoration. To pipe lace pieces, place the design you have chosen under a piece of wax paper or acetate. Pipe a row, then gently slide the paper or acetate down and pipe further rows. It's always a good idea to make about twice as many pieces as you will need as being so delicate, they are extremely fragile.

MAKING EXTENSION

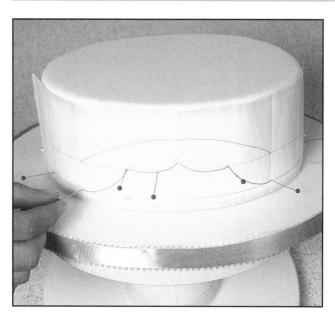

1 Scribing the template: Trace the template provided on to greaseproof paper and cut it out. Secure it to the cake with glass-headed pins. Place the cake on a tilting turntable and scribe around the template.

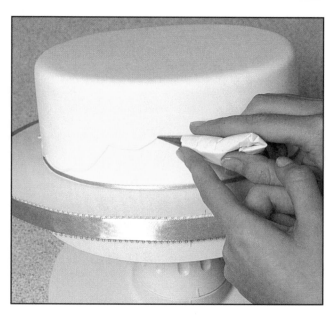

2 Starting the bridgework: Using a no. 2 tube and lemon-coloured royal icing, pipe along the scribed line and leave to dry. Overpipe this with another line (again with the no. 2 tube), and then pipe a third line.

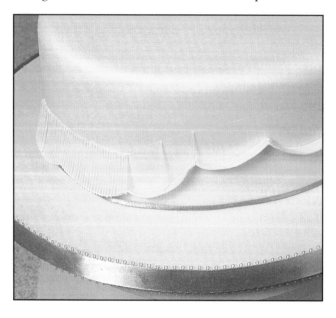

5 Piping the extension work: Hold a straight edge up against the cake, to guide you with your first piped lines. Using a no. 1 tube, pipe a straight line from the top scribed line down to the bridge.

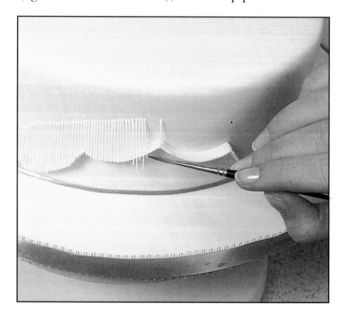

6 Tidying the extension work: As you pipe the straight lines, pull the tube slightly away from the cake. Use a paintbrush to tuck the ends of the icing under the bridge. Keep the top line neat.

WORK PANELS

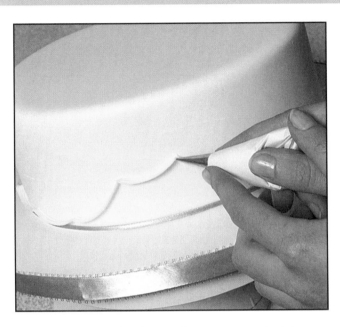

3 Completing the bridge work: Using a no. 1 piping tube, continue to build up the bridgework. Overpipe the scribed line and leave to dry. Do this a second and then a third time.

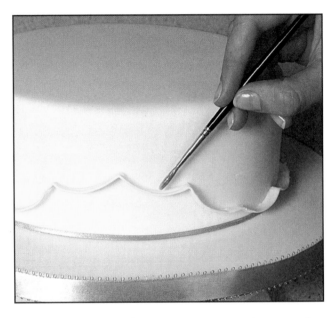

4 Neatening the bridge: Using runny royal icing and a fine sable paintbrush, paint over your six lines of bridgework. This will create a unified look to the separate lines of piping – as if they were one piece.

7 Piping a line of dots: When the extension work is dry, use a no. 0 piping tube and lemon-coloured royal icing to pipe a tiny row of dots along the bridge itself as an extra decorative touch.

8 Adding the lace pieces: Lift the lace piece with a cranked palette knife and attach it to the cake with tiny dots of icing. With a paintbrush, position the lace so that the narrow end faces up and falls into place.

PANEL DESIGNS

1 The centre section of this extension-work panel consists of vertical lines decorated with flowers. Side sections are piped on the slant, then partly overpiped with lilac lines running the opposite way. Small bulbs frame the panel.

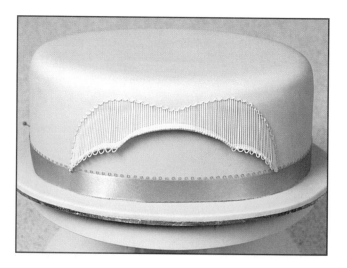

2 This curved panel shaped like a bird's wing is built up with simple vertical extension work piped in cream. The outline is embellished with a row of loops in pale lilac, changing to small bulbs on the central arch at the base.

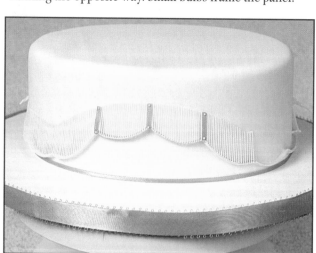

3 The bridgework on this scallop-shaped panel has been overpiped in lilac so that it shows through the lines of extension work. A final touch is a strip of ribbon at each scallop intersection, decorated with two bulbs of icing.

4 This triangular-shaped extension-work panel is built up from three scallops surmounted by a raised top one. The plain vertical extension work is hail-spotted in white, and the top decorated with lace pieces in pastel shades.

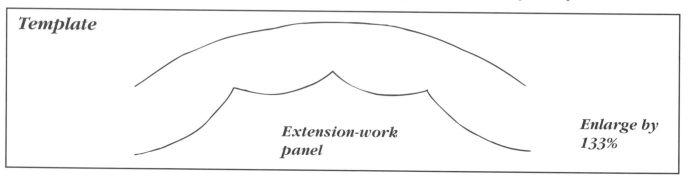

Template

Extension-work panel

Enlarge by 133%

Making pastillage cards

Pastillage paste dries to a hard, porcelain-like finish and is ideal for making beautiful greetings cards to mark special occasions.

Pastillage paste, also known as gum paste, is similar to flower paste, but it is made without any fat. This means that it is less pliable, but can still be rolled out very thinly. It dries very hard, with some of the qualities of porcelain, making it suitable for modelling into boxes, plaques and cards. However, like porcelain, it can shatter easily, and should be handled with care.

ROLLING AND DRYING

There are many recipes for making pastillage paste. The one we give in Professional Secrets on page 188 is quick and easy, and is a good way of using up leftover royal icing. If you don't have any, make up a fresh batch of royal icing and proceed in the same way.

Roll out pastillage paste very thinly, using cornflour to prevent it sticking to the board. After cutting, pastillage paste should not be moved until it has dried, to avoid the danger of stretching it out of shape. Do the cutting on your drying surface, and cut carefully: work from each corner inwards only as far as the centre point of the line – if you cut beyond the centre, you will distort the shape – and do not drag while cutting. While the cards are drying, gently turn them over once to stop them bowing.

To assemble cut pieces of pastillage paste, use piped lines of royal icing. Support sections with pieces of foam sponge while they dry. It is useful to assemble cards on to a surface which will support them and help to protect them from damage. A small, round cake board, covered in either coloured sugarpaste or paper, is ideal.

DECORATING IDEAS

A card modelled in pastillage makes an ideal gift for any sort of occasion (we give some examples on page 188), and it will last for a long time if handled carefully. The components of the flower-filled card illustrated here can all be made in advance and assembled at the last minute. The flowers are made from coloured flower paste, cut to shape with carnation cutters, and wired on to covered floristry wire, ready for use. Loops of ribbon, secured by a hook at the top of the wire, are ideal for these types of arrangements, filling the gaps between the flowers and hiding the sugarpaste supporting them.

CUTTING RECTANGLES
Instead of creating a template for your pastillage card, you could always use a small greetings card.

MOULDING AND DE

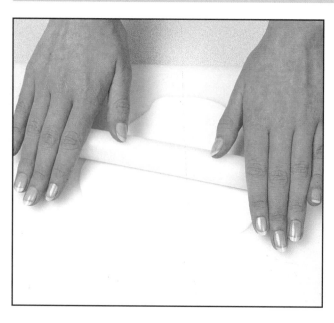

1 Rolling out the paste: Dust the work surface with cornflour and roll out the pastillage paste until it is about 3mm (¹⁄₈in) thick. Transfer the rolled paste to your drying surface before starting to cut it out.

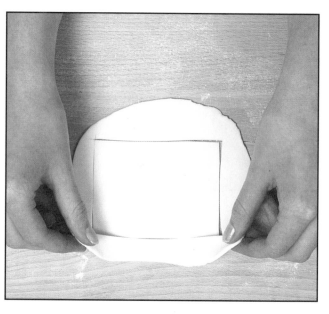

2 Cutting out the back of the card: Make a rectangular template and place it on the paste. Using a scalpel, cut out the shape. Work from each corner only as far as the centre of the line to avoid any distortion.

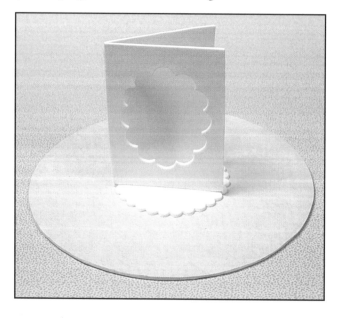

5 Assembling the card: Centre the plaque on the cake board and fix it in place with a dab of royal icing. Join the two halves of the card together along the piped line. Position the card on the plaque.

6 Fixing the card: Using a no. 2 tube and royal icing, pipe a fine line along the lower edge of the card to hold it in place. Support with pieces of foam until it is dry. Pipe a snail's trail down the back to hide the join.

CORATING A CARD

3 Cutting out the front of the card: Cut another rectangle for the front of the card. Then, carefully cut out a central opening, using a scalpel and a template, or a suitably shaped cutter. Leave it to dry.

4 Preparing the stand: Cut a plaque of pastillage on which to stand the card, and leave it to dry. Cover a small round cake board. Pipe a line of royal icing down one long edge of the plain rectangle.

7 Adding flowers: Roll some sugarpaste into a small ball and put it inside the card, just behind the base of the cut-out. Trim the flower wires to length required and stick them into the sugarpaste with tweezers.

8 Adding ribbons: As you continue to add flowers, fill the gaps between them with wired ribbon loops, until the sugarpaste is completely hidden. Add any extra ribbon decorations, securing with a dab of royal icing.

DESIGN IDEAS FOR CARDS

1 To make this monogrammed card, cut two pastillage rectangles, join them together, and hide the join with a snail's trail. Run out the required monogram in white royal icing, and paint it with silver food colouring. Attach it to the card. Pipe blue lace pieces with a no. 1 or 0 tube, and use them to frame the monogram.

2 For this good luck card, cut a rectangle for the back and a horseshoe shape for the front. Colour them pale yellow with petal dust. Pipe a brush-embroidered, four-leaf clover in the centre. Write 'Good Luck' on the horseshoe in white, overpiped with green. Pipe small clover leaves at inside corners. Attach the horseshoe to the back.

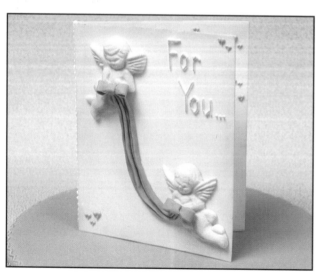

3 To create this Valentine card, cut two rectangles and colour their edges with pink petal dust. Make two cherubs using a mould. Dust them pink and stick on to card. Attach a pink flower-paste drape and bows. Decorate with piped hearts and write 'For You' on the front and 'My Valentine' inside in white royal icing overpiped in pink.

PROFESSIONAL SECRETS

Working with pastillage paste

Ingredients:
1tsp gum tragacanth
240g royal icing
sifted icing sugar
paste food colouring (optional)

Method:
- Place the icing sugar in a mixing bowl, and sprinkle the gum tragacanth over the top.

- Cover the bowl with a damp cloth and leave the mixture to stand for 10 minutes.

- Turn the mixture out on to a work surface dusted with sifted icing sugar.

- Knead the mixture until smooth, adding extra icing sugar as required to obtain a stiff paste.

- If you wish to colour your pastillage paste, add some edible paste food colouring while kneading the mixture, and continue kneading it until an even shade has been achieved.

- Once the paste has been made, it should be used immediately. Otherwise, it will begin to harden and be difficult to cut into the required shapes.

- Pastillage paste can be made in advance and stored until needed – provided it is enclosed in a polythene bag and placed in a sealed, plastic container.

Texturing sugarpaste

***There are numerous ways of texturing sugarpaste –
so use your imagination and liven up your cakes.***

Texturing sugarpaste is fun, as well as being an easy way to add interest to a variety of cakes. Use your imagination and you will develop a whole range of ideas and skills which can quickly be pressed into service when a cake is required.

CHOOSING EQUIPMENT
You can buy special rollers from cake-decorating shops to provide instant textured decoration, or you can make your own at home from a variety of implements. You will find that sharp pointed scissors, scalpels, pastry wheels and cocktail sticks are useful and versatile, so make sure that you have a supply of them in your tool box.

Look out for other household objects which can be used to imprint textures and patterns – imprinted lids or bottle tops, for example. It's even worth having a look at the modelling tools which are now available for children to use. The important thing is to be aware of your environment – it should provide a constant source of ideas for you.

USING ROLLERS
If you are using a roller, be careful to roll the sugarpaste evenly, otherwise you may get an uneven texture on the finished piece. Marzipan spacers, placed at either end of a rolling pin, can be used as a guide. Always work with soft, pliable sugarpaste, dusting it liberally with icing sugar to prevent it from sticking.

Sugarpaste can be textured to produce precise symmetrical patterns – either by using rollers, or by working free-hand with a variety of equipment. Generally speaking, you should roll and texture the paste before cutting it, although there are occasions – such as when you are working on smaller details – when you can cut the paste first and then texture it.

TEXTURING TIPS
Texture can add interest, either to large surface areas of cake, or just to details. It can, however, be difficult to texture large areas of paste and cover the cake without distorting the pattern, so if you need to develop confidence, start with smaller areas on the cake and board.

Try adding textured details first – such as hearts, buttons, balloons, stars and hats. You can also try making animal fur, clothes for a clown, or texturing the tyres on cars and engines .

Texturing is particularly useful when making cakes for children, since they respond to colour and love to touch things, and they will find textured cakes very stimulating. Overleaf wc feature a charming teddy for you to make, or you could try the igloo illustrated above, which is simply made from white sugarpaste, and then scored with a scriber to give the effect of ice.

MAKING THE TEDDY

1 Creating the fur: Cut a simple teddy shape from mid-brown sugarpaste. Snip into the surface on the arms and legs with small, sharp-pointed scissors to give the impression of fur.

2 Making the head: Cut the head from mid-brown sugarpaste. Add a pink sugarpaste nose and black sugarpaste eyes. Use a cocktail stick to score the ears and mouth and to texture under the nose.

3 Adding the suit: Roll out some deep blue sugarpaste, and roll it out using a ribbed roller. Cut out a suit for the teddy bear, then carefully lift and place it in position, using a cranked palette knife.

4 Finishing touches: Use yellow sugarpaste for honey jar with a roll for the rim. Pipe icing for the spilled honey. Texture brown sugarpaste with a basket-weave roller and cut basket shape. Add handle and bananas.

TEXTURING TECHNIQUES

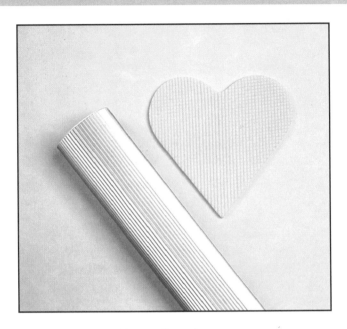

1 To achieve this effect, roll out the sugarpaste using spacers to ensure that the paste is the same depth throughout. Roll in one direction with the ribbed roller, then in the other direction before cutting out.

2 Here we have quilted the rolled sugarpaste with a quilting wheel and cut it out carefully. Don't press too hard with the wheel, or you will cut through the paste. Do not disturb the pattern when you move the heart.

3 Use a pastry cutter or cake-decorating wheel to create this particular texture. Make even lines diagonally, and then repeat in the opposite direction, making sure that the spacing is kept even.

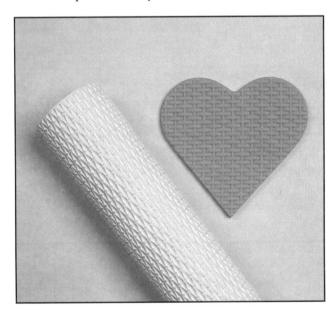

4 You can create this effect very simply with a basket-weave roller. Again, be very careful when moving the cut-out design, and do not stretch it in any way, or you will distort the finished effect.

IDEAS FOR TEXTURING

1 Create the owl's feathers by snipping the sugarpaste – but not too deeply. Mark round the eyes with a cocktail stick, and then make shaggy eyebrows from thin strips of sugarpaste textured with a cocktail stick. Snip the ends.

2 Cover the cake in blue and cut the swan from white sugarpaste. Texture the wings with a cocktail stick, and frill the edges for a feathered effect. Add neck and head from white sugarpaste, and make a yellow beak and black eyes.

3 Use a boxwood roller to provide the netting on the racquets and the net. Texture grey and white sugarpaste first before cutting the ovals for the racquets and strips for the net. Add sugarpaste handles and surrounds, and a ball.

4 Cut the cracker from red sugarpaste, and texture it with a ribbed roller. Attach the cracker to white sugarpaste cake. Add gold foil trim and petal-dusted, flower-paste holly sprigs. Add shop-bought lettering, or pipe your own.

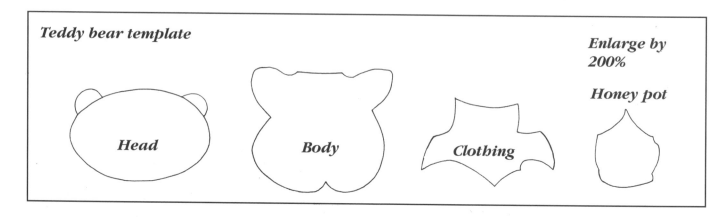

Teddy bear template

Enlarge by 200%

Honey pot

Head

Body

Clothing

Cake board finishes

HAVE TO HAND

Ingredients: *sugarpaste • selection of paste food colourings • royal icing • petal dusts • granulated sugar • clear alcohol.*

Equipment: *crimpers • embossing tool • ribbon insertion tool • no. 1 piping tube • pastry cutters • basket-weave roller • paintbrush • piece of foam • ribbon.*

Main skill: *decorating cake boards.*

DIFFICULTY   TIME   SUITABILITY

There are many ways to decorate cake boards. Here we show you some quick and effective methods.

The cake board is often overlooked as a design factor in cake decorating, but it should always be thoroughly considered when you are planning your cake. It is an essential part of the overall look and balance of the cake and must not be disregarded.

The cake board should certainly be a discreet part of the design – you do not want it to detract from the cake itself – but there are many ways in which you can add extra special details which enhance your chosen style of decoration.

COLOUR SCHEMES
Many people prefer to cover the cake and the board in the same colour. This is a sensible decision, especially if you are inexperienced. If you wish to use different colours, start by experimenting with gentle pastel shades so that you avoid a clash of colours.

You can have more fun with colour when working on a cake for children, since they often love bright, sensational effects. You may want to treat the board as an integral part of the whole scene by using it to capture the effect of grass, water or snow.

METHODS OF COVERING
First, decide on the shape you want your board to be. If you do not have much experience, it is better to choose a board which is the same shape as the cake and will enhance it. Simple shapes, such as squares and circles, are easier to cover, although you can buy boards in many different shapes and already covered in silver or gold.

Cover the cake and the board separately. They can be covered in one move, but if they are you will find that it is harder to get a good angle around the base of the cake. You might choose to cover your board either with sugarpaste or royal icing, fabric or paper.
As you gain experience you may even use more exciting materials – such as wood or clear acrylic, for example.

WORKING WITH SUGARPASTE
In the following pages we concentrate on covering boards with sugarpaste, and we have used a range of design techniques, including marbling, embossing, crimping and painting. We also look at how to give texture to boards – either through the use of tools, or by using sugarpaste sponged with runny royal icing.

If you want to add ribbon to the side of the cake board, it is important to choose the ribbon first and then mix your sugarpaste to match. It is very frustrating to have to search for a ribbon to match a board and be unable to find the right colour. If you take the trouble to plan things carefully in advance, you won't go far wrong.

DESIGNS ON

1 Crimping: Crimp around the edges of the cake board with a crimping tool before the sugarpaste has dried. The same crimped design can also be repeated around the sides of the cake.

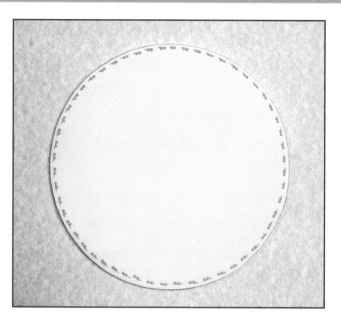

2 Piping: Pipe a row of scrolls around the edge of the board with a no. 1 piping tube. Here we have piped tiny 'S' and 'C' scrolls, but you can always use a design which suits the rest of the cake.

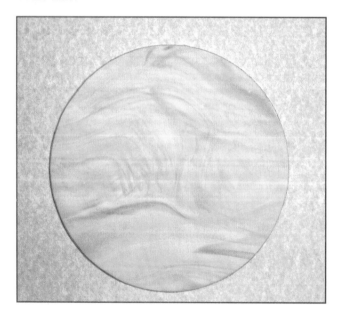

5 Marbling: Create varied and interesting colour effects by using marbled sugarpaste. Here we have used yellow and blue paste food colours and white sugarpaste. If you prefer, you could use pre-coloured sugarpaste.

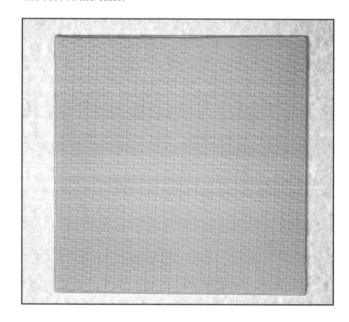

6 Texturing: Textured boards can look very effective. Here, blue sugarpaste has been textured with a basket-weave roller. A basket-weave finish is particularly suited to square cake boards.

SUGARPASTE

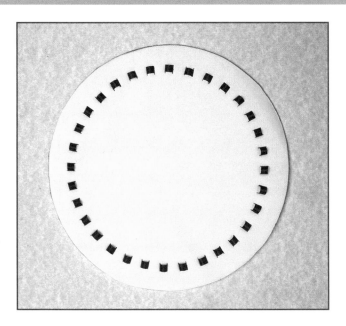

3 Ribbon insertion: Use a ribbon insertion tool to make slots around the board while the sugarpaste is still soft. Leave to dry, then insert the ribbon. The width of the ribbon should suit the size of the board.

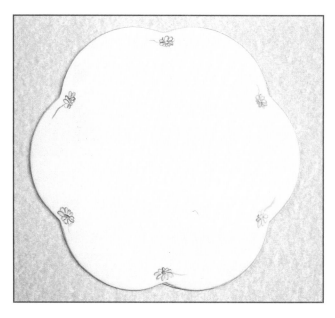

4 Painting: Paint your own design on to the sugarpaste with food paste colours and alcohol. Here a pink floral design has been painted on to emphasise the scallop shape of the board.

7 Inlaid: Use a cutter to cut shapes out of the sugarpasted board. Then cut the same shapes in a different colour sugarpaste and insert them into the original spaces, as we have done here with these holly leaves and berries.

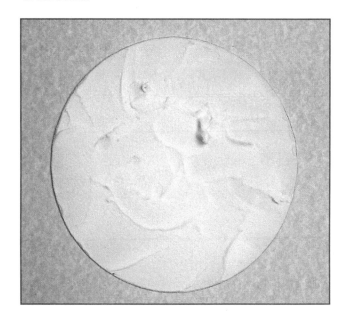

8 Snow-covered: Cover the board with white sugarpaste, and then roughly apply soft royal icing. Leave it to dry for a while and then sprinkle it with a covering of caster or granulated sugar.

DESIGN IDEAS

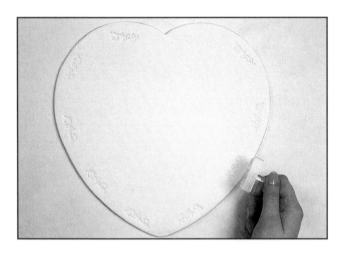

1 To emboss sugarpaste, roll it to a thickness of 5mm (¼in) and then cover the board. Use an embossing tool to mark tiny floral motifs around the edges of the cake board.

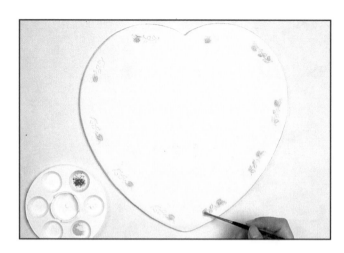

2 Use green petal dust to paint in the foliage and a colour – such as peach – for the petals. Use a fine brush to apply the dust and make sure you remove any excess beforehand.

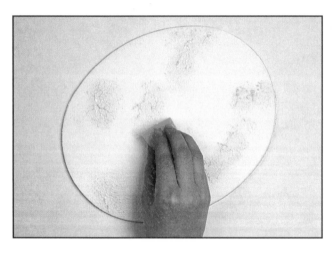

1 When sponging a cake board you can either use food paste colouring and alcohol, or runny royal icing for more texture. Press lightly on the board with a piece of foam.

2 When the first colour application has dried, go over the board with a second colour in exactly the same way with a small piece of foam. Here we have used lilac and peach.

Alternatives

COVERING CAKE BOARDS

Apart from the usual methods of covering cake boards with sugarpaste or royal icing, there are some rather more unusual ways of presenting your cake.

The most important factor to remember is that, regardless of how a board is covered, it must be thoroughly hygienic. Paper should be food-grade and should not

contain anything which can contaminate food. You can buy this at specialist sugar-craft shops, although wallpaper is often just as good, as long as you use greaseproof paper between the cake and the board.

Fabrics, especially watered and raw silks, are often a good choice for cake boards. Choose plain fabrics since fussy, detailed or

loud designs are less likely to suit your cake – although tartan is an exception to this rule. If you want to be really adventurous you can use acrylic plastic, or even varnished wood which make a very unusual-looking base.

Lastly, be on the look-out for surfaces which will serve as cake boards and unusual shapes which you will be able to cover.

Inlaying side designs

Inlaid designs around the side of a cake are versatile and attractive and can be adapted to suit a number of special occasions.

Inlaid side designs are a very attractive and unusual way of enhancing the sides of a cake. Once you have mastered the basic principle of this technique, you will find that there is no end to the many versatile ways in which it can be put to use.

Here we have inlaid woven flower paste on to the sides of a sugarpasted cake, and we also offer a variety of suggestions for those of you who are interested in this method of cake design.

COVERING THE CAKE
The cake is covered with marzipan and then left to dry. This is usually the stage at which the marzipan is covered with clear alcohol or cooled boiled water in order for the sugarpaste to be properly attached. In this case you must avoid brushing the areas where you are going to place the inlay. If you forget, and brush the whole cake, you will find that the sugarpaste will attach itself too firmly

to the marzipan and you will be unable to remove it. If you wish, you could make a template for the side of the cake which indicates where the inlay will sit, and use it to mark the inlay pattern on the surface of the marzipan.

CUTTING THE INLAY
Once the cake has been covered with sugarpaste you must then get to work immediately, since inlays should be cut while the sugarpaste is still soft. You could either use a shaped cutter, or else make a template and then use a scalpel – it really depends on what you are most comfortable with.

Remember that the shape of the inlay must suit the design of the cake and should be neither too small nor too large. When you cut the inlay, you will feel the point at which you reach the marzipan

because, having already dried, it will feel firmer than the sugarpaste.

PLANNING THE SHAPE
You can cut any shape you please – circles, diamonds, hearts or stars – but remember that the more intricate the shape, the harder it is to do. Plan the inlay design to fit with the rest of your cake. The inlays can be the same shape as the cake board, or match it in colour. You could use a basket-weave roller for the board and the inlay, or use the similar technique of marzipan marquetry. There are many options; just consider the rest of the cake when making your decision.

Fortunately, you can make as many inlay pieces as you wish and experiment with a few first. You need only attach your best efforts to the cake, thus ensuring a successful end result.

1 Cutting the side inlay: Cut a section of sugarpaste from the side of your cake while the sugarpaste is still soft. Use a card template to help you to position the cutter.

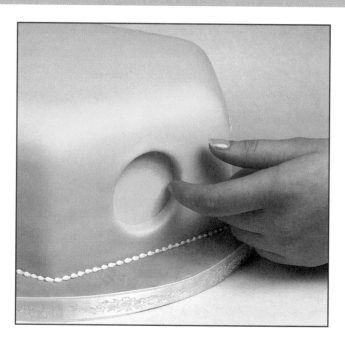

2 Smoothing the edges: Gently smooth the edges of the cut-out section with your finger. Make sure that you do not distort the shape in any way.

5 Starting to weave: Lay the white strips out flat. Bend back every other strip. Place a pink strip across the white ones. Paint with sugar glue where the strips meet.

6 Finishing the section: Continue to weave until you have an area at least as wide as the cutter. You need to work quickly before the paste dries.

A SIDE INLAY

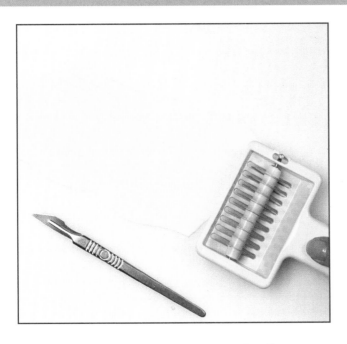

3 Cutting the white strips: Roll out some white flower paste and cut it into strips with a parsley cutter. Each strip should be about 5mm (¼in) wide.

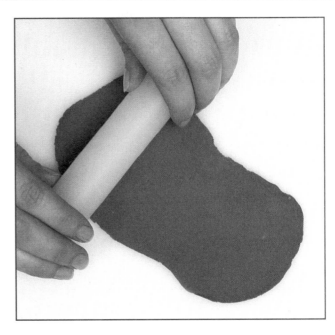

4 Cutting the pink strips: Colour some flower paste pink and roll it out. Cut it into strips with a parsley cutter in exactly the same way as before.

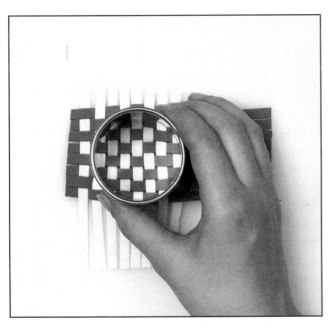

7 Cutting out the inlay: Cut a section out of the woven flower paste with the same cutter that was used to cut a section from the cake.

8 Fitting the inlay: Place the woven flower-paste inlay in the cut section of the cake and secure it with royal icing. Cover the join with a picot edge or row of shells.

DESIGN IDEAS

1 Make a runout to fit the inlay. Pipe filigree work with a no. 0 tube. Attach the runout to the inlay piece and place on the cake. Pipe a picot edge to cover the join.

2 Pressure-pipe a stork on to the inlay piece and pipe in the background details. Once the inlay has been attached, pipe a picot edge to cover the join.

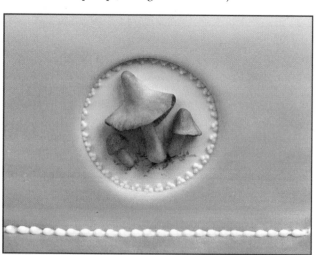

3 Make some little bas-relief mushrooms. Leave them to dry, then brush with petal dust. Petal dust the inlay piece, add mushrooms and attach to the cake. Pipe a picot edge.

4 Paint directly on to the sugarpaste cutout with paste food colour and clear alcohol. Use a picture to guide you if you wish. Pipe a tiny line of shells over the join.

---

helpline   WEAVING WITH FLOWER PASTE

When weaving with flower paste, it dries quite quickly, so once you have rolled and cut the strips you need to work fast.

First roll both the flower-paste balls to a thickness of 5mm (¹/₄in) each. The method we have used is called the 'warp and weft' method and involves the following process.

Each sheet of paste must be cut into strips with a parsley cutter. The white strips form the 'warp' part of the weave – that is, the lengthways strip through which the 'weft' weave is fed.

With a paintbrush, lift up and bend back every other white strip. Then place a pink strip across the flat strips, keeping it straight and tight. Then position the bent back strips over the pink strips. Then bend back the alternate white strips (which were

not touched last time) and proceed in exactly the same way. Wherever two strips cross, attach them with a dab of sugar glue.

You can make a quick sugar glue by mixing two-thirds of a cup of water with about 30g (1 oz) of sugarpaste. Heat the mixture in a microwave until softened, sieve into another bowl, then mix in about two-thirds of a cup of clear spirit.

Inlaid top designs

Add dimension and interest to the top of your cake with these stunning, yet simple, inlaid top designs.

An inlaid top design can add interest and depth to your cakes, both by framing special features and by allowing you to experiment with shape and colour. There are various methods of creating inlays, which can be placed either on the side or the top of the cake. One way is to coat the cake with a layer of marzipan and one of sugarpaste. The inlay is then cut out and another decorated section attached in its place.

Here, though, we show you a different method in which the cake top is ready to have other features attached to it as soon as the inlay section has been cut out.

COVERING THE CAKE

The secret is to coat the top of the cake with two layers of sugarpaste. The cake is first covered with marzipan in the usual way and left to dry. Then, a layer of sugarpaste is added to the top of the cake only. This will form the inlay base itself, so you need to make sure that it is in the correct colour and is absolutely smooth. When this is dry, another layer of sugarpaste is added to the entire cake.

The inlay piece is cut while the outer layer of sugarpaste is still soft. As the section is cut away, it reveals the first layer of sugarpaste – normally in a contrasting colour. The double layer means that you will end up with a lot of sugarpaste – a bonus for a child's party!

CHOOSING A SHAPE

Choose an appropriate cutter to cut out the inlay piece. There are many shapes from which to choose. Cutters come in a variety of shapes – animals, letters, hearts and numbers – as well as in more formal shapes, such as petals, ovals and geometric designs. If you want a larger inlay section, which will create a frame-like effect around the edge of the cake top, use a cake tin which you can cut around with a scalpel or sharp knife.

If you have not done much of this kind of work before, it is easier to work with cutters and cake tins which give a solid outline, rather than making complicated templates which you have to cut around.

The inlay piece can either be large, thereby taking up most of the cake top, or small, perhaps placed to the side of the cake. There are many options available to you when you plan your design. Here, tube embroidery is piped around the inlay. The central feature of the inlay is a sugarpaste baby, wrapped in a frilled, flower-paste shawl. The design is perfect for a christening cake.

MAKING THE

1 Covering the cake: Cover the cake with marzipan then put a layer of sugarpaste on the top only. Smooth the edges with your finger. Leave to dry for a few days.

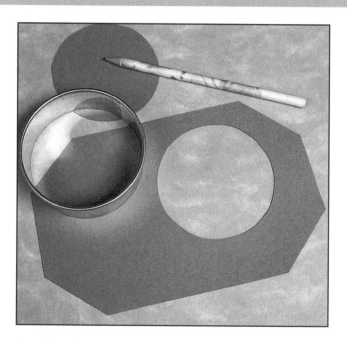

2 Making the templates: Make a card template to the same size as the top of the cake. Draw your inlay piece in position on the template and then cut it out.

5 Cutting the inlay: Use the cutter to cut out the inlay piece from the top of the cake. If you place your template on the cake top, you will know exactly where to cut.

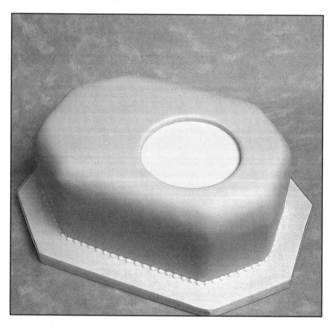

6 Smoothing the inlay: Remove the top layer of sugarpaste. Smooth the edges of the inlay with your fingers, making sure that you do not push it out of shape.

TOP INLAY

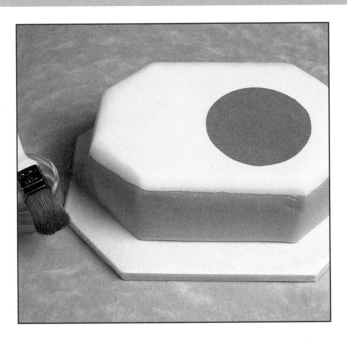

3 Brushing the cake: Brush the cake with clear alcohol. Use the card inlay cut-out to mask the area where your inlay will sit. It must not be brushed with alcohol.

4 Covering with sugarpaste: Cover the entire cake with sugarpaste and pipe a row of shells around the base. Do not leave it to dry, as the inlay must be cut immediately.

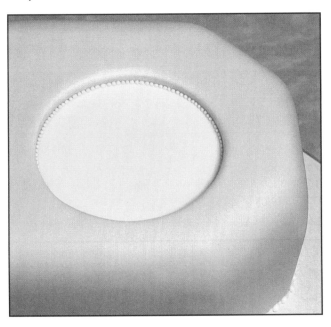

7 Covering the join: Cover the join around the edge of the inlay by piping a row of dots – either in the same colour, or a complementary one.

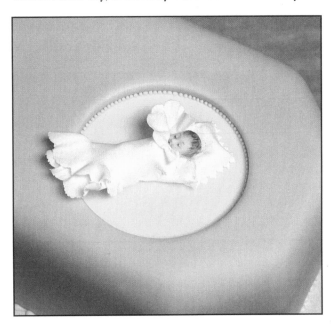

8 Adding the baby: Add the central feature (in this case, a sugarpaste baby) to the inlay and attach it to the cake with royal icing.

DESIGN IDEAS

1 A sugarpaste bas-relief clown with clothes made from flower paste has been attached to a bright-red square with a yellow inlay section. A line of blue and white bulbs has then been piped around the edge of the inlay.

2 This teddy bear-shaped inlay has been made with a cutter. Dust the inlay with brown petal dust and then paint in the features. Make sure that any excess petal dust is shaken off the brush first.

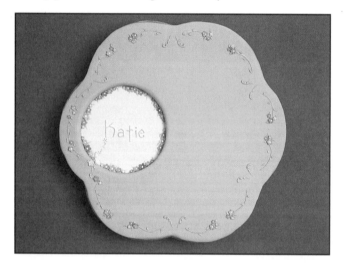

3 A piped inscription has been placed to one side of this lilac, petal-shaped cake. Peach-coloured blossoms and some tube embroidery have been placed around the inlay and around the edges of the cake.

4 Marbling can create the prettiest effects of all. Here, the under layer of sugarpaste has been marbled in pink and the top layer left plain. The central feature is floral and the effect of the plain, white roses is simple but effective.

Alternatives

DECORATING THE INLAY

However you decide to decorate the inlay, it should echo the ideas and techniques that are used elsewhere on the cake.

Piping a snail's trail or a line of shells with a no. 1 tube are obvious choices to disguise a join, but there are plenty of other ideas. Try adding run-out lace pieces around the edge of the inlay, or attach a delicate, narrow ribbon in the same colour as the one placed around the board.

The area around the inlay can also be decorated in many ways. We have used tube embroidery, but you can choose other techniques, such as broderie anglaise, in the same or a contrasting colour. For example, if the inlay is pink, you can pipe matching tube embroidery around the inlay on to a pale cream background.

Curved runout techniques

**Extend your range of skills by making curved
runouts which can be attached to circular and oval cakes.**

HAVE TO HAND

Ingredients: *run icing • paste food
colouring • clear alcohol.*

Equipment: *cake tin • no 1. piping
tube • wax paper or acetate • greaseproof paper • scissors • pencil •
paintbrush • angled desk lamp.*

Main skills: *making and handling
curved runouts.*

DIFFICULTY	TIME	SUITABILITY

Curved runouts are made in almost the same way as the flat variety, but they are curved during the drying process in either a concave or convex former. They can then be placed on a curved surface, such as the sides of an oval or circular cake.

This technique opens up many more possibilities for the enthusiastic cake decorator. If you have decided upon a flat runout for the top of your cake, you will be able to repeat the design on the sides – and of course some motifs, such as leaves, are actually more effective if they are dried on a curve.

If you have never attempted to make curved runouts before, it is advisable to start with small ones. Use a motif that can be flooded in sections rather than in one piece.

PIPING THE RUNOUT
Once you have selected the design, trace it on to greaseproof paper in the normal way and then place it under wax paper or acetate. At this stage there are two ways in which you could proceed. The runout can either be flooded while it is on a flat surface and then quickly moved to dry on a curved surface, or you can tape the motif and the wax paper on to the side of the former and pipe directly on to the curve. If you are working in different colours, or flooding and drying the motif section by section, you will have to use the latter method.

Pipe the outline of the motif first with a no. 1 piping tube. When it is dry, flood the motif section by section with run icing of a thicker consistency than usual in order to prevent it from running down the curve. The runout is then left on a curve or former to dry under an angled desk lamp. You can always improvise when using formers. Many household objects will serve this purpose.

ATTACHING THE RUNOUT
If the runout is to sit flush against the side of the cake, you must use a former that is rounded to exactly the same degree as the cake. Often the best way to do this is by using the same tin that the cake was baked in. If you are making a large runout which will extend right around the cake, you will have to account for the extra width added by marzipan and sugarpaste as they will alter the curve of the cake.

Curved runouts can also be very attractive when they are attached to the cake at certain points only. See our suggestions on page 208, or experiment with designs which will be enhanced by a curve, such as figures of people, animals and flowers. Don't forget to run out a few spares – just in case of damage.

PIPING CURVED

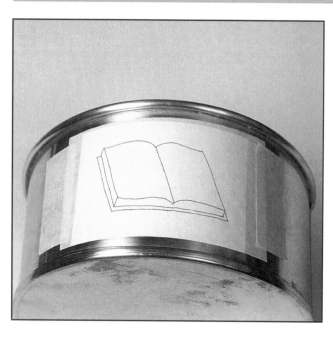

1 Securing the template: Tape the motif on to a curved surface, such as a cake tin. Place a piece of wax paper or acetate over the top and tape it securely in place.

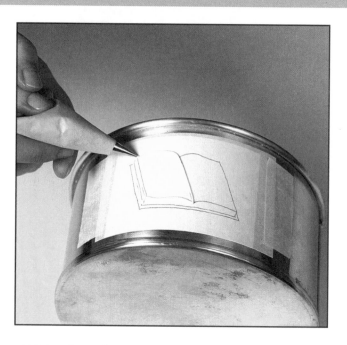

2 Piping the outline: Pipe the outline of the book with a no. 1 piping tube. The way the outline is piped creates a two-dimensional effect.

5 Levelling the pages: Use a fine paintbrush to neaten the runout and to shape it. Then leave it to dry for 24 hours before painting it.

6 Painting the runout: Use clear alcohol and brown paste food colouring to paint the book cover and to add the print to the pages. Then leave to dry.

RUNOUTS

3 Flooding the right-hand page: Flood the right-hand page of the book and some of the page edges on the left-hand side. Dry under an angled desk lamp for ten minutes.

4 Flooding the left-hand page: Flood the left-hand page of the book and the remaining page edges. You may find it easier to turn the tin around while you work.

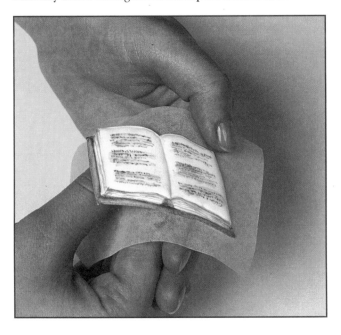

7 Detaching the runout: Remove the runout from the wax paper by holding it in your hand and peeling it away from the paper very gently.

8 Attaching the runout: Decide on the point where the runout is to be placed and attach it carefully to the cake with royal icing.

DESIGN IDEAS

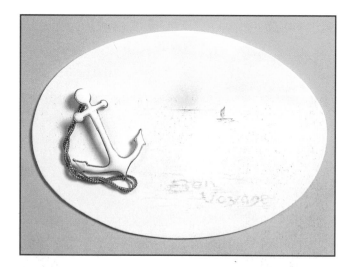

1 This anchor has been painted with gold food colouring around the edges and has gold thread, dried in a twist, added to it. It is twisted and attached to the plaque at certain points only, in order to achieve a raised effect.

2 Monograms can look extremely attractive when dried on a curved surface. This one has been outlined in one colour and then piped in another. You can attach these runouts either to a flat or a curved surface.

3 Leaves look more realistic if they are dried on a curve; they can also be attached liberally all over the cake. Run them out in green-coloured icing. If you wish, add extra markings with paste food colour when the runout is dry.

4 Run-out baskets can be dried on a curve and then attached to the side of the cake. Here, flowers have been added by first piping in green foliage and then attaching tiny blossoms that were cut with a blossom cutter.

Alternatives
CURVED CAKE DECORATIONS

If you are not sure whether a curved runout will suit your cake decoration, you can save time and energy by experimenting with it first in sugarpaste. The process is much quicker since you would simply have to cut out the design and then leave it to dry on the former in exactly the same way. Or if you want it to sit flush against the side of the cake, you merely attach it with royal icing before it dries. Pastillage can also be used to make curved decorations. Take the idea of the shaped basket, but roll it using a basket-weave or other textured roller. Runouts are delicate and ideally suited to a royal-iced cake; but on a sugarpasted cake, either sugarpaste or pastillage decorations would suit very well. Try a range of different figures and motifs.

Decorating with ribbon

With a little imagination, ribbon can be used in many ways to add gaiety and colour to your cake.

HAVE TO HAND

Ingredients: *royal icing.*

Equipment: *no. 1 piping tube •
selection of ribbons in three widths•
scissors • tilting turntable • pins •
scriber • greaseproof paper.*

Main skills: *working with ribbon.*

DIFFICULTY	TIME	SUITABILITY

Ribbon is an effective and relatively simple method of decorating cake tops, sides and boards, since it adds colour and texture to a design in a variety of different ways.

You are probably already more skilled with ribbons than you realise. Think of the ways in which you use ribbons in other circumstances – when wrapping parcels for example, or plaiting hair. You can use exactly the same techniques to decorate cakes. Plaited ribbons can be used to trim cake boards or to overlay wider ribbons – the options are endless.

RIBBON ARRAY

Keep a selection of ribbons in different colours and sizes handy. Sometimes a beautiful ribbon will turn up, and sooner or later you will be able to use it on a cake. Use ribbons in graduated widths, and in toning or complementary colours. It's great fun to play around with ribbon finishes, putting colours together on the sides of the cake until you get the effect that you are happy with.

Decorative trails and tassels made from ribbon make a quick, easy and opulent-looking decoration. Other quick finishes include ribbon rosettes (secured with floristry wire) and ribbon loops (made in the same way), which can be used to fill out gaps in sprays of paste flowers. Ribbon decorations are faster to effect than piping, and have a high impact due to the colours used. You can also mix textures, placing a thin satin ribbon upon a velvet one, and so on.

Double-sided satin ribbon is a particularly good choice since it looks good from all angles – essential when making bows and loops. All ribbons come in a huge range of colours, from the palest pastels to bright jewel colours. Take a look around the haberdashery section of a large department store. You will find many lovely decorative pieces.

SECURING RIBBONS

The tension of a ribbon is important, so position it with a pin first. When you are happy with the placement, take the pins out and secure the ribbon with royal icing. Alternatively, attach one end of the ribbon to the cake with icing and then pin the ribbon a little further along. This will enable you to place the length of ribbon correctly, without detaching the end from the cake.

Make sure that the cake surface is completely dry before you start work, and remember that royal icing takes a little time to set after you have secured each ribbon.

The easiest way to apply ribbon around a cake is to place the cake on a turntable, secure one end to the centre back, and then gradually turn the turntable, positioning the ribbon as you go and returning to the starting point.

You can also use ribbon in conjunction with unusual wrapping paper. Cover the board and then position the cake (with a piece of greaseproof paper underneath it). It's amazing how quickly this can transform a cake.

209

WORKING WITH

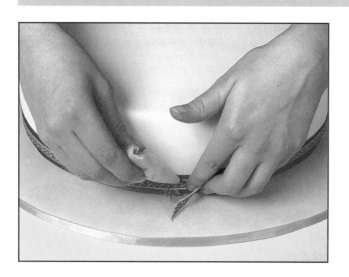

1 Beginning the design: Place the cake on the board and use a broad satin ribbon to hide the join. Secure the ribbon with royal icing at the centre back of the cake. Pin a second layer of ribbon at one end. Position it centrally around the first ribbon and secure it with icing.

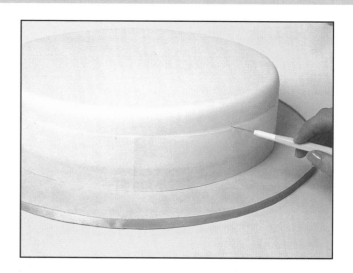

2 Using a template: Measure the circumference of the cake and divide it into equal measurements, according to the number of swags required. Make a template which corresponds to the measurement of the cake and mark the position of the swags on it. Use a scriber to mark the cake.

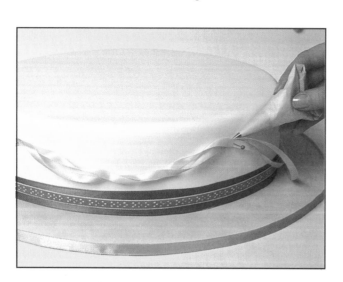

3 Twisting the ribbons: Twist together two lengths of narrow ribbon in contrasting colours and secure them with pins at either end on the cake. Secure with dabs of royal icing and remove the pin. Make sure that you achieve the right degree of tension so that the ribbons do not slip.

4 Securing the swags: Secure the swags all around the cake with royal icing and attach the tiny bows – made from the narrowest ribbon – over the attachment points. Pin them first to hold them in place, then secure them with royal icing and remove the pins.

RIBBON

1 Beginning the design: Apply the first pale ribbon on a light diagonal across the top of the cake about a third of the way in, and secure it at either end with dabs of royal icing. Apply a second, deeper ribbon, making a crossover point slightly off centre. Pin first and then secure with royal icing.

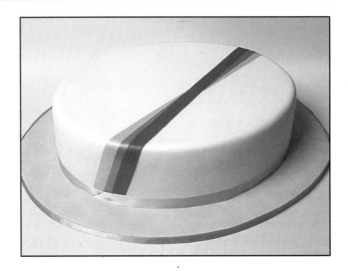

2 Adding the third ribbon: Attach the third ribbon (deepest shade) to the top, crossing over in the same way. Secure it with royal icing. Next, attach a layer of ribbon (the palest) to hide the join between the cake and the board. Place the join so that it coincides with the lower edge of top ribbons.

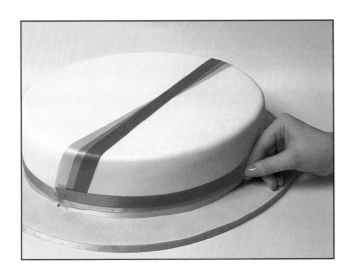

3 Continuing the base design: Position the second base ribbon on top of the first, positioning it carefully half-way up. Keep all the joins in the same place and secure the ribbon with royal icing. Repeat with the third, deepest shade of ribbon.

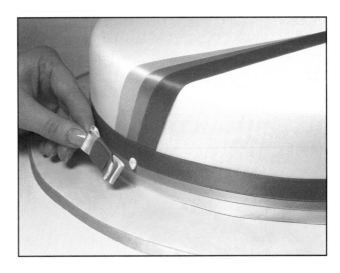

4 Finishing touch: Make a simple ribbon decoration from flat loops of ribbon, stuck down with royal icing and with the join hidden by a loop of ribbon. Use this to cover the ribbon joins. Apply royal icing to the ribbon bands and place the decoration on the cake.

DESIGN IDEAS

1 Side design: Attach a wide ribbon at the base of the cake to hide the join between the cake and the board. Plait together three narrow satin ribbons in toning colours and attach them to the cake side above the first ribbon.

2 Loops: Loosely attach a purple ribbon at the base of cake and secure it with a pin. Wind the lilac ribbon around the purple, threading it between purple ribbon and board, giving a looped effect. Adjust these and secure with icing.

3 Cake boards: The largest board is trimmed with turquoise velvet overlaid with lemon satin. The second features a three-colour effect in different widths. The smallest is trimmed with multicoloured chiffon ribbon.

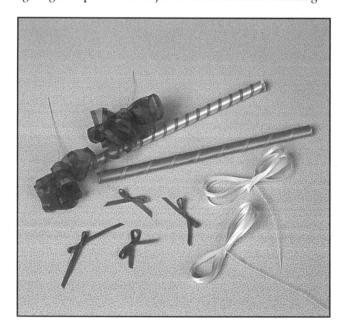

4 Rosettes: For a rosette, concertina a length of wide ribbon, twist some floristry wire around the centre to hold it, and fluff it into position. You can also wrap ribbon around dowelling to support light items on a cake top.

Cake Templates

Cocoa-painted cake

HOW TO USE YOUR TEMPLATES: Lay a sheet of tracing paper over the various templates and trace on to the paper. You may find it easier if you then cut the paper so that each template is separate. Using a scriber, trace the template shapes on to the rolled marzipan or sugarpaste.

Top templates

Side templates

Embroidered book cake

HOW TO USE YOUR TEMPLATES: Lay a sheet of tracing paper over the various templates and trace on to the paper. You may find it easier if you then cut the paper so that each template is separate. Using a scriber, trace the template shapes on to the rolled marzipan or sugarpaste.

Embroidered book template

A special cake for Christmas

HOW TO USE YOUR TEMPLATES: Lay a sheet of tracing paper over the various templates and trace on to the paper. You may find it easier if you then cut the paper so that each template is separate. Using a scriber, trace the template shapes on to the rolled marzipan or sugarpaste.

THE FIRST DAY OF CHRISTMAS

Gold rings

Pear tree

French hen

Calling birds

Turtle dove

Pears

Partridge

Fantasy frills

HOW TO USE YOUR TEMPLATES: Lay a sheet of tracing paper over the various templates and trace on to the paper. You may find it easier if you then cut the paper so that each template is separate. Using a scriber, trace the template shapes on to the rolled marzipan or sugarpaste.

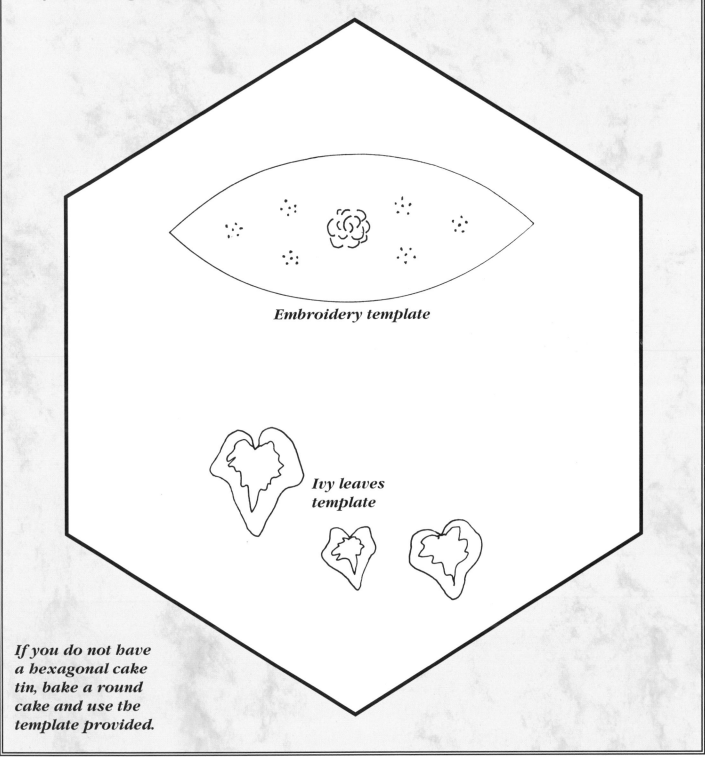

Embroidery template

Ivy leaves template

If you do not have a hexagonal cake tin, bake a round cake and use the template provided.

217

With love from Ted

HOW TO USE YOUR TEMPLATES: Lay a sheet of tracing paper over the various templates and trace on to the paper. You may find it easier if you then cut the paper so that each template is separate. Using a scriber, trace the template shapes on to the rolled marzipan or sugarpaste.

Narrow frill

(Frill cutters are available for both these frills from cake-decorating supply shops.)

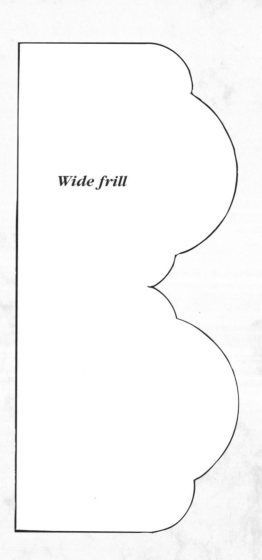

Wide frill

Teddy bear

Golden-wedding cake

HOW TO USE YOUR TEMPLATES: Lay a sheet of tracing paper over the various templates and trace on to the paper. You may find it easier if you then cut the paper so that each template is separate. Using a scriber, trace the template shapes on to the rolled marzipan or sugarpaste.

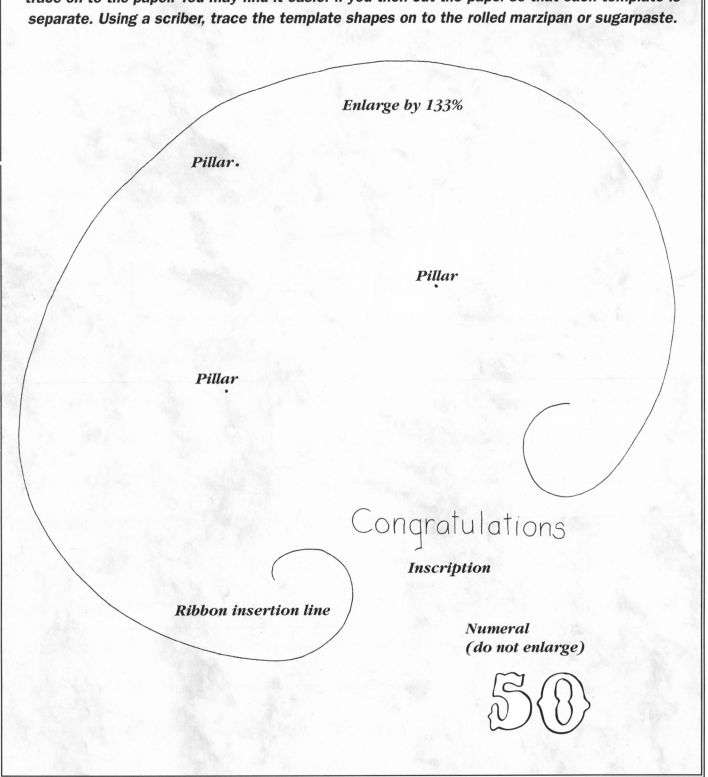

Enlarge by 133%

Pillar.

Pillar

Pillar

Congratulations

Inscription

Ribbon insertion line

**Numeral
(do not enlarge)**

Mildly marbled

HOW TO USE YOUR TEMPLATES: Lay a sheet of tracing paper over the various templates and trace on to the paper. You may find it easier if you then cut the paper so that each template is separate. Using a scriber, trace the template shapes on to the rolled marzipan or sugarpaste.

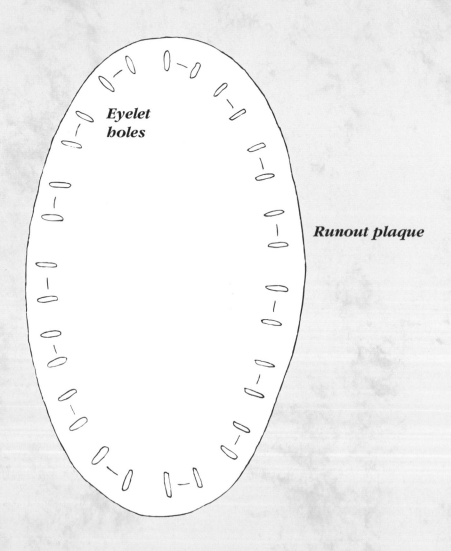

Eyelet holes

Runout plaque

A time for celebration

HOW TO USE YOUR TEMPLATES: Lay a sheet of tracing paper over the various templates and trace on to the paper. You may find it easier if you then cut the paper so that each template is separate. Using a scriber, trace the template shapes on to the rolled marzipan or sugarpaste.

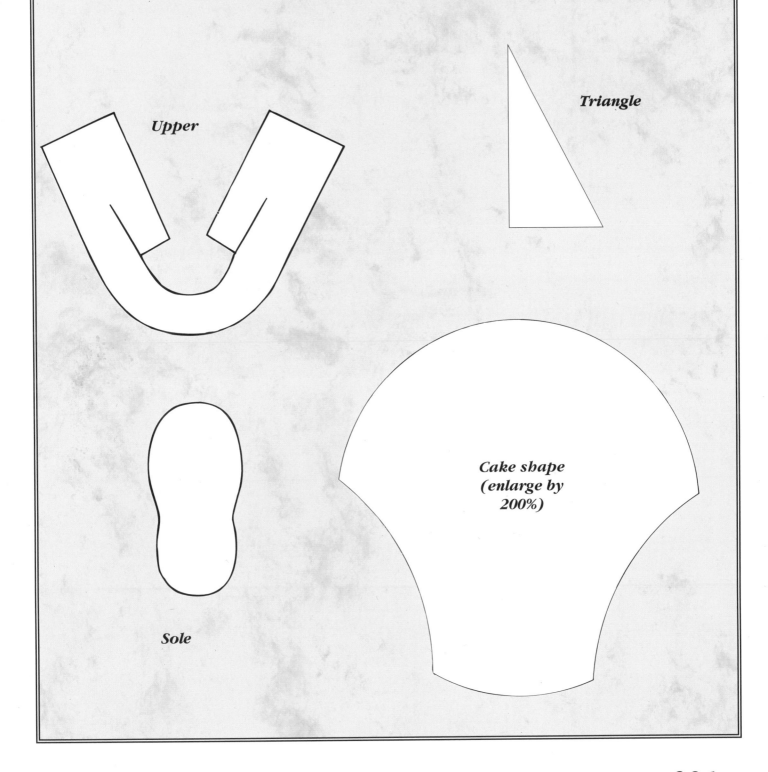

Triangle

Upper

Sole

Cake shape
(enlarge by
200%)

Spring celebration

HOW TO USE YOUR TEMPLATES: Lay a sheet of tracing paper over the various templates and trace on to the paper. You may find it easier if you then cut the paper so that each template is separate. Using a scriber, trace the template shapes on to the rolled marzipan or sugarpaste.

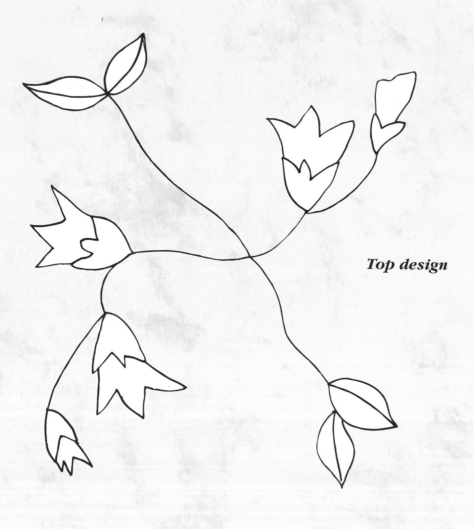

Top design

Small flower

Large flower petal
(cut seven)

Two hearts entwined

HOW TO USE YOUR TEMPLATES: Lay a sheet of tracing paper over the various templates and trace on to the paper. You may find it easier if you then cut the paper so that each template is separate. Using a scriber, trace the template shapes on to the rolled marzipan or sugarpaste.

Large heart template

Enlarge by 130%

Dressing-table cake

HOW TO USE YOUR TEMPLATES: Lay a sheet of tracing paper over the various templates and trace on to the paper. You may find it easier if you then cut the paper so that each template is separate. Using a scriber, trace the template shapes on to the rolled marzipan or sugarpaste.

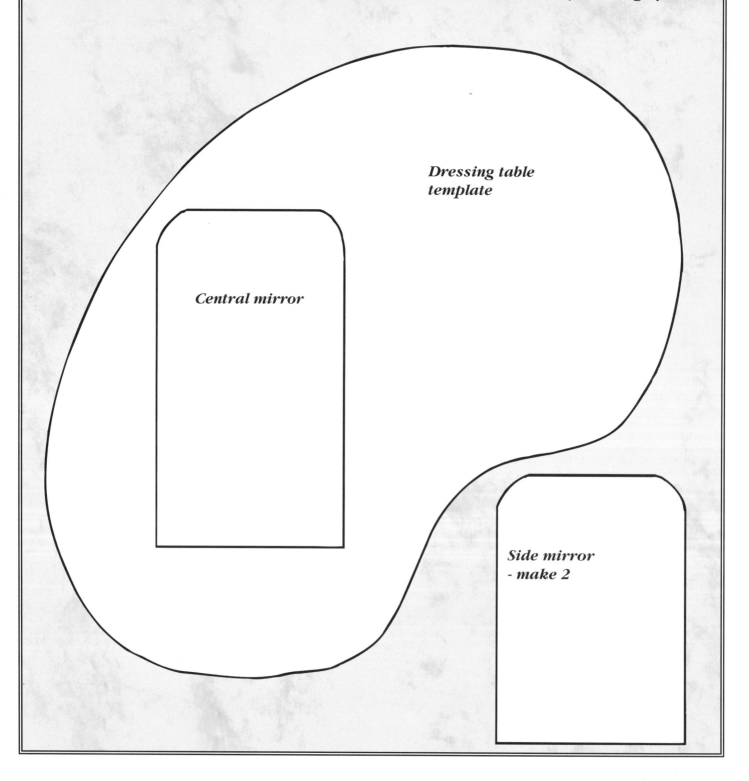

Dressing table
template

Central mirror

Side mirror
- make 2

Artist's palette

HOW TO USE YOUR TEMPLATES: Lay a sheet of tracing paper over the various templates and trace on to the paper. You may find it easier if you then cut the paper so that each template is separate. Using a scriber, trace the template shapes on to the rolled marzipan or sugarpaste.

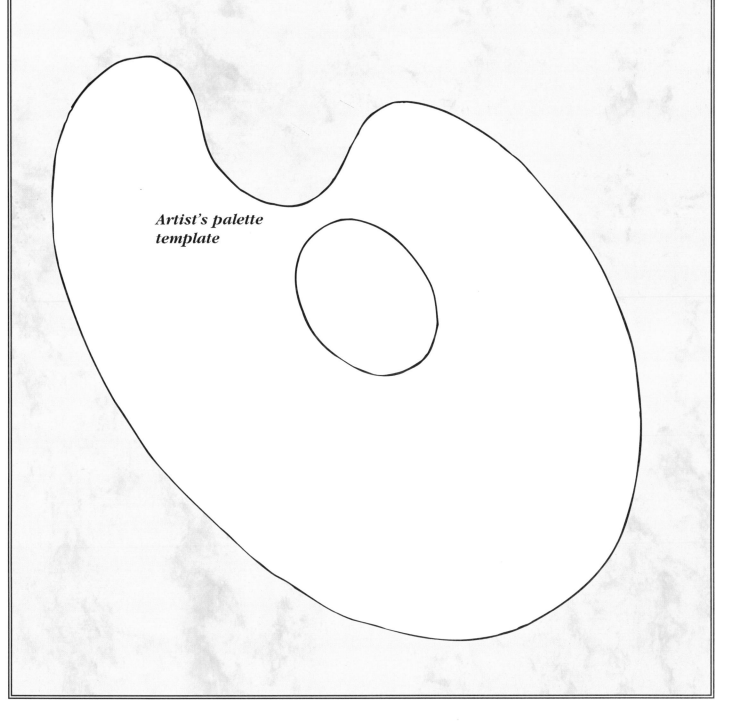

*Artist's palette
template*

DINOSAUR cake

HOW TO USE YOUR TEMPLATES: Lay a sheet of tracing paper over the various templates and trace on to the paper. You may find it easier if you then cut the paper so that each template is separate. Using a scriber, trace the template shapes on to the rolled marzipan or sugarpaste.

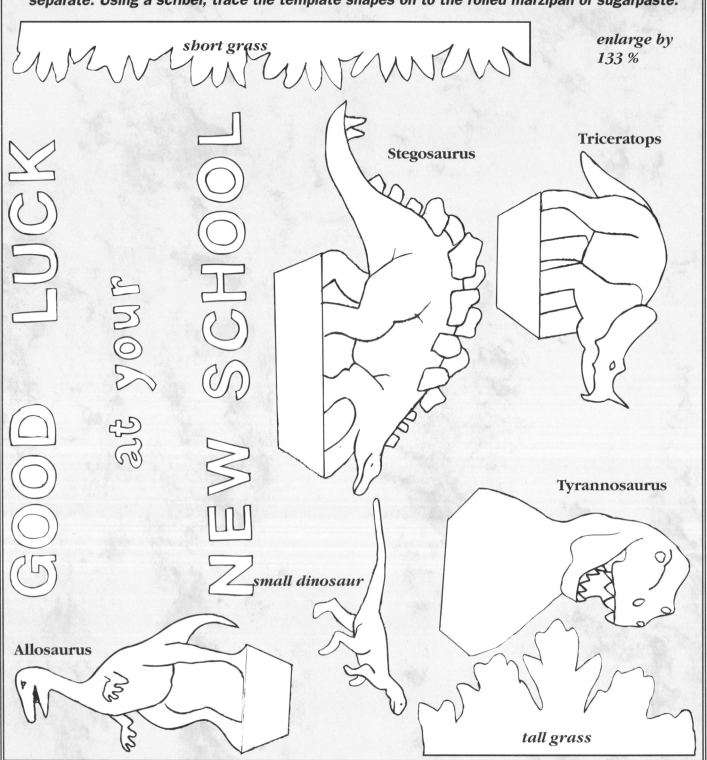

short grass

enlarge by 133 %

GOOD LUCK

at your

NEW SCHOOL

Stegosaurus

Triceratops

small dinosaur

Tyrannosaurus

Allosaurus

tall grass

Autumn flower basket

HOW TO USE YOUR TEMPLATES: Lay a sheet of tracing paper over the various templates and trace on to the paper. You may find it easier if you then cut the paper so that each template is separate. Using a scriber, trace the template shapes on to the rolled marzipan or sugarpaste.

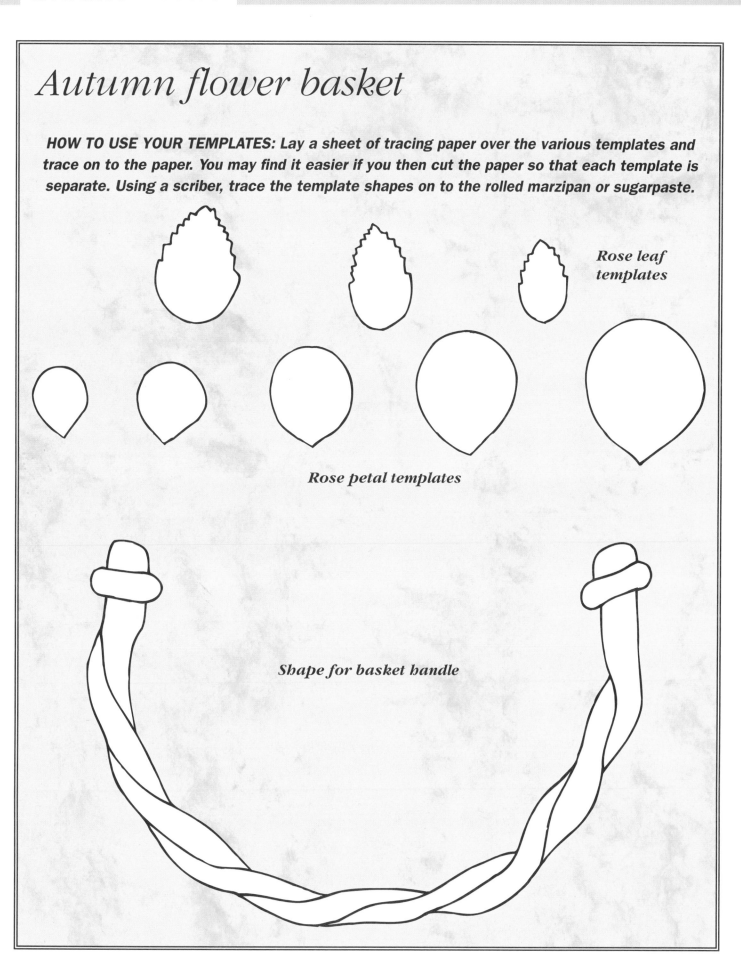

Rose leaf templates

Rose petal templates

Shape for basket handle

Little fat hen

HOW TO USE YOUR TEMPLATES: Lay a sheet of tracing paper over the various templates and trace on to the paper. You may find it easier if you then cut the paper so that each template is separate. Using a scriber, trace the template shapes on to the rolled marzipan or sugarpaste.

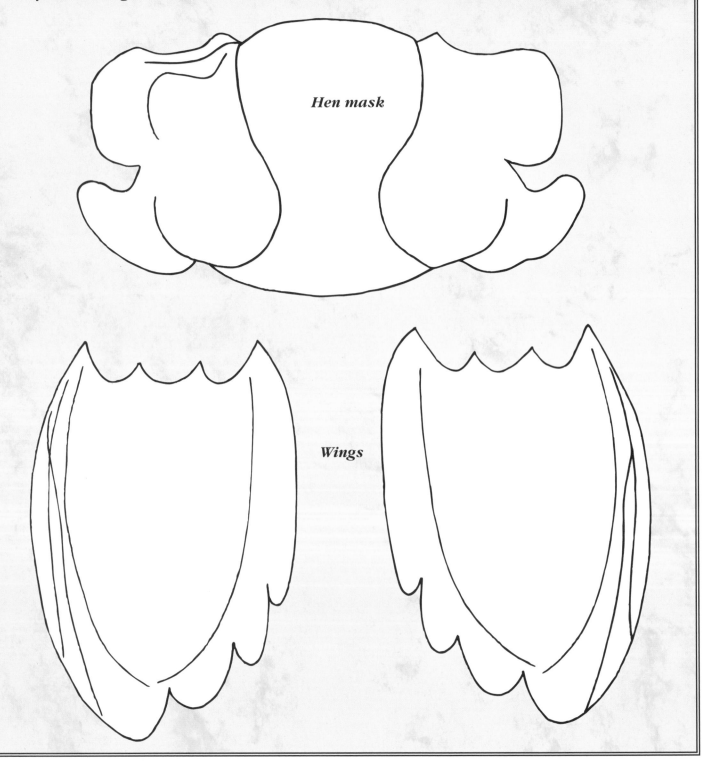

Hen mask

Wings

Robins in the snow

HOW TO USE YOUR TEMPLATES: Lay a sheet of tracing paper over the various templates and trace on to the paper. You may find it easier if you then cut the paper so that each template is separate. Using a scriber, trace the template shapes on to the rolled marzipan or sugarpaste.

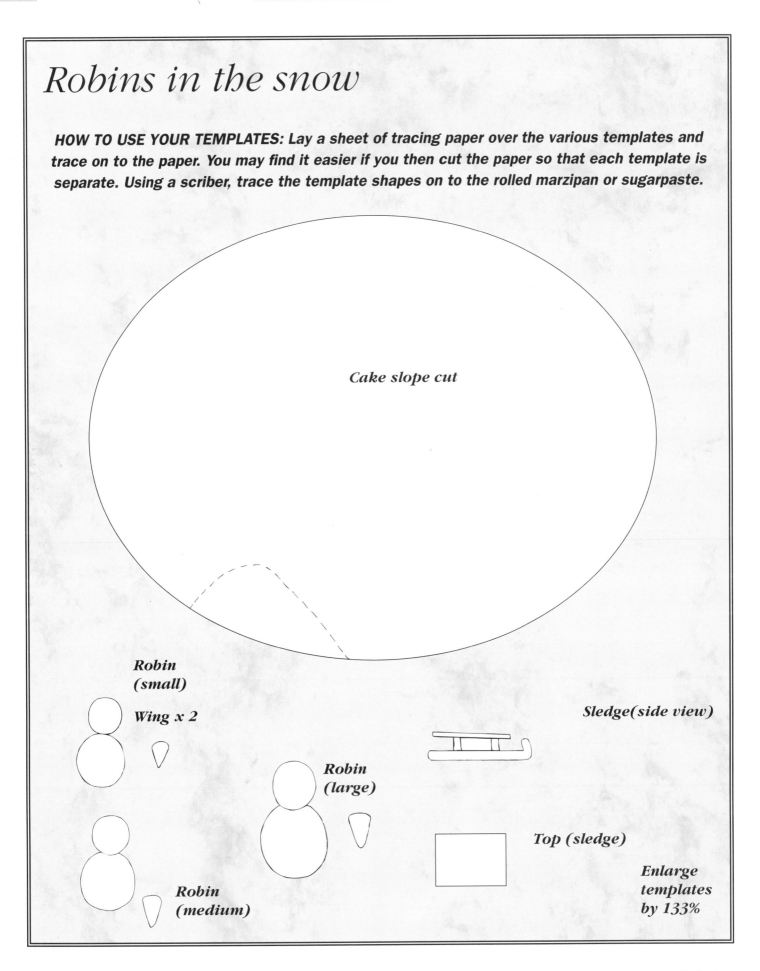

Cake slope cut

Robin (small)

Wing x 2

Robin (large)

Sledge(side view)

Top (sledge)

Robin (medium)

Enlarge templates by 133%

Clamped-car calamity

HOW TO USE YOUR TEMPLATES: Lay a sheet of tracing paper over the various templates and trace on to the paper. You may find it easier if you then cut the paper so that each template is separate. Using a scriber, trace the template shapes on to the rolled marzipan or sugarpaste.

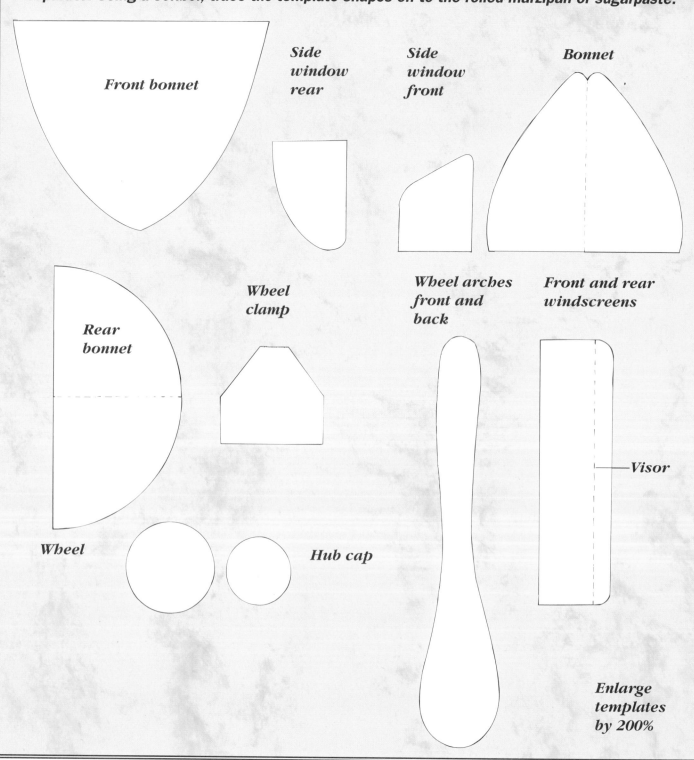

Front bonnet

Side window rear

Side window front

Bonnet

Rear bonnet

Wheel clamp

Wheel arches front and back

Front and rear windscreens

Visor

Wheel

Hub cap

Enlarge templates by 200%

Time for bed

HOW TO USE YOUR TEMPLATES: Lay a sheet of tracing paper over the various templates and trace on to the paper. You may find it easier if you then cut the paper so that each template is separate. Using a scriber, trace the template shapes on to the rolled marzipan or sugarpaste.

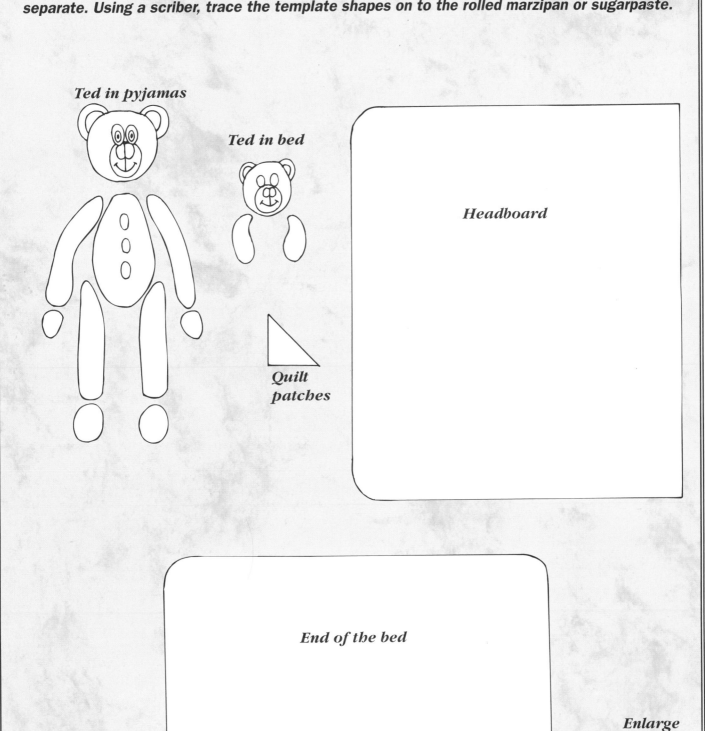

Ted in pyjamas

Ted in bed

Quilt patches

Headboard

End of the bed

Enlarge by 133%

Bees around the honey pot

HOW TO USE YOUR TEMPLATES: Lay a sheet of tracing paper over the various templates and trace on to the paper. You may find it easier if you then cut the paper so that each template is separate. Using a scriber, trace the template shapes on to the rolled marzipan or sugarpaste.

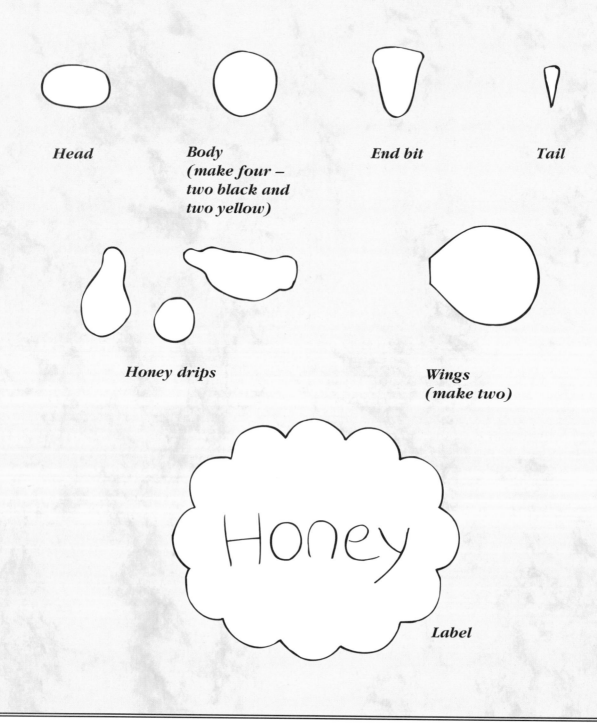

Head

Body
(make four –
two black and
two yellow)

End bit

Tail

Honey drips

Wings
(make two)

Label

Back to the Sixties

HOW TO USE YOUR TEMPLATES: Lay a sheet of tracing paper over the various templates and trace on to the paper. You may find it easier if you then cut the paper so that each template is separate. Using a scriber, trace the template shapes on to the rolled marzipan or sugarpaste.

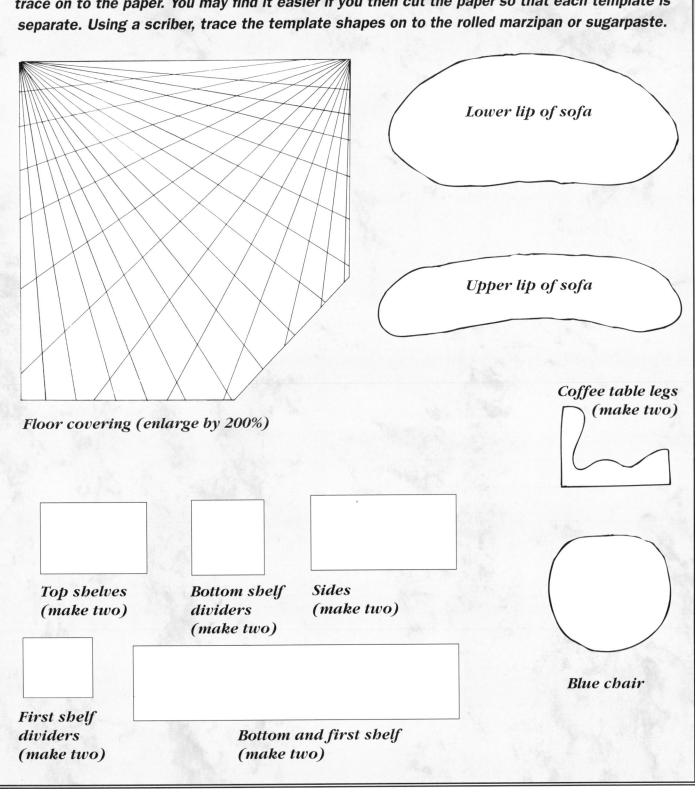

Floor covering (enlarge by 200%)

Lower lip of sofa

Upper lip of sofa

Coffee table legs (make two)

Top shelves (make two)

Bottom shelf dividers (make two)

Sides (make two)

Blue chair

First shelf dividers (make two)

Bottom and first shelf (make two)

Cosy cottage

HOW TO USE YOUR TEMPLATES: Lay a sheet of tracing paper over the various templates and trace on to the paper. You may find it easier if you then cut the paper so that each template is separate. Using a scriber, trace the template shapes on to the rolled marzipan or sugarpaste.

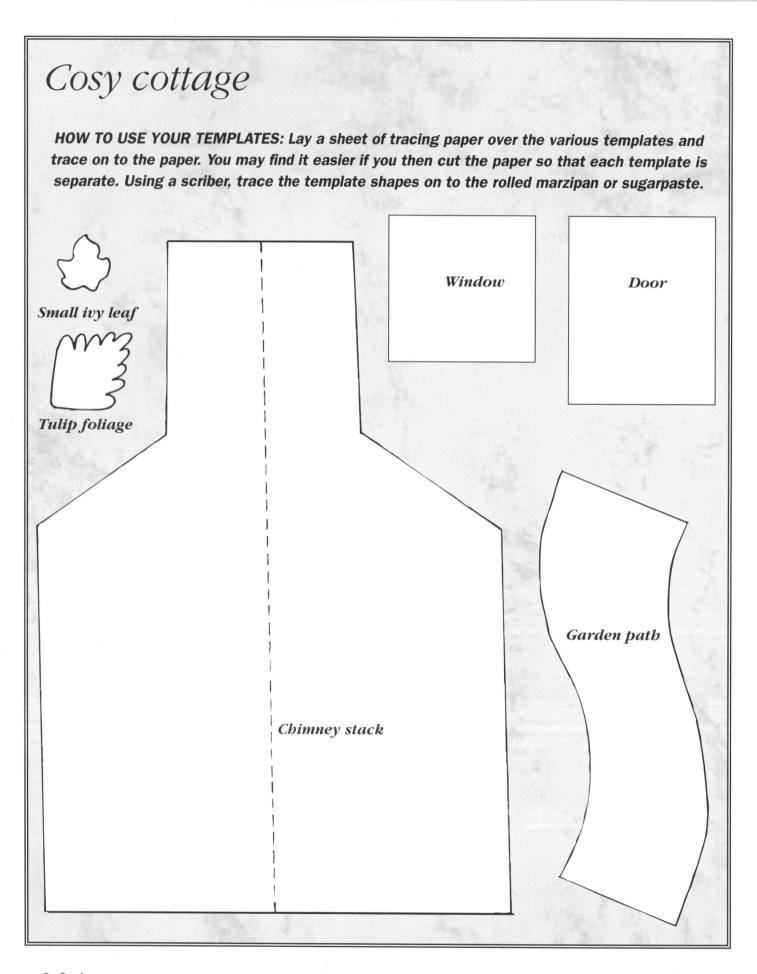

Small ivy leaf

Tulip foliage

Window

Door

Garden path

Chimney stack

Desert island dream

HOW TO USE YOUR TEMPLATES: Lay a sheet of tracing paper over the various templates and trace on to the paper. You may find it easier if you then cut the paper so that each template is separate. Using a scriber, trace the template shapes on to the rolled marzipan or sugarpaste.

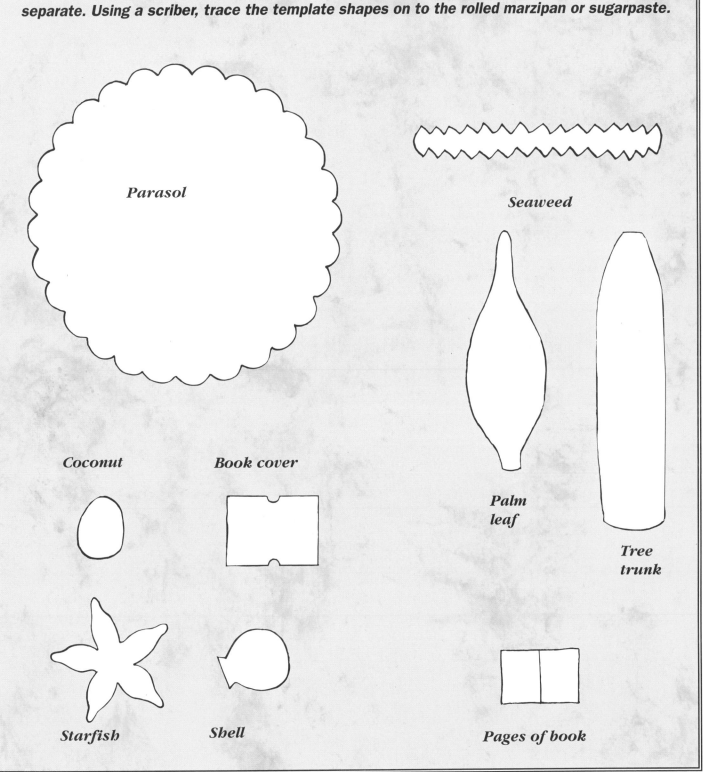

Parasol

Seaweed

Coconut *Book cover*

Palm leaf

Tree trunk

Starfish *Shell*

Pages of book

Easter bonnet

HOW TO USE YOUR TEMPLATES: Lay a sheet of tracing paper over the various templates and trace on to the paper. You may find it easier if you then cut the paper so that each template is separate. Using a scriber, trace the template shapes on to the rolled marzipan or sugarpaste.

Petals

Frill

Leaf

Drum roll

HOW TO USE YOUR TEMPLATES: Lay a sheet of tracing paper over the various templates and trace on to the paper. You may find it easier if you then cut the paper so that each template is separate. Using a scriber, trace the template shapes on to the rolled marzipan or sugarpaste.

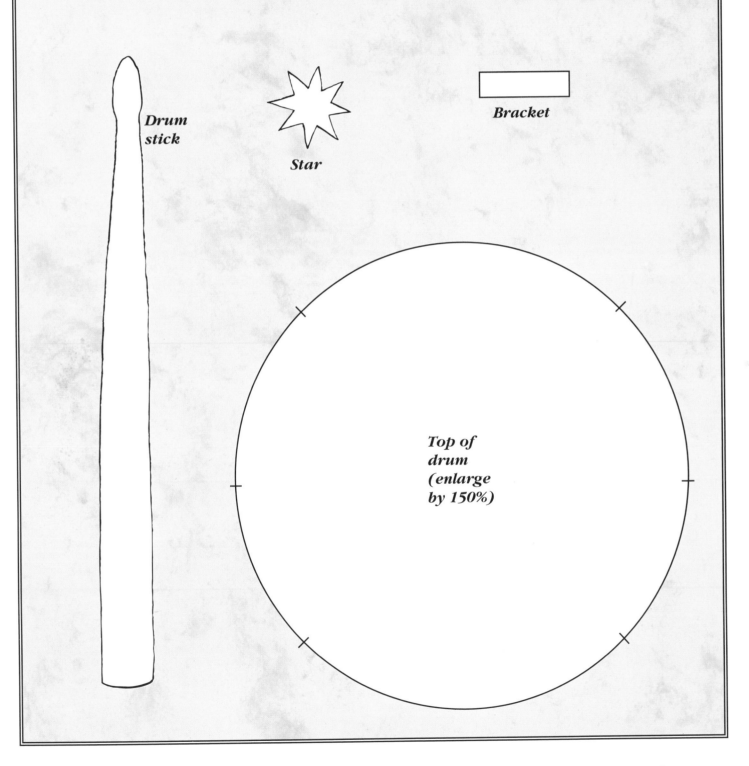

Drum stick

Star

Bracket

Top of drum (enlarge by 150%)

Swimming pool

HOW TO USE YOUR TEMPLATES: Lay a sheet of tracing paper over the various templates and trace on to the paper. You may find it easier if you then cut the paper so that each template is separate. Using a scriber, trace the template shapes on to the rolled marzipan or sugarpaste.

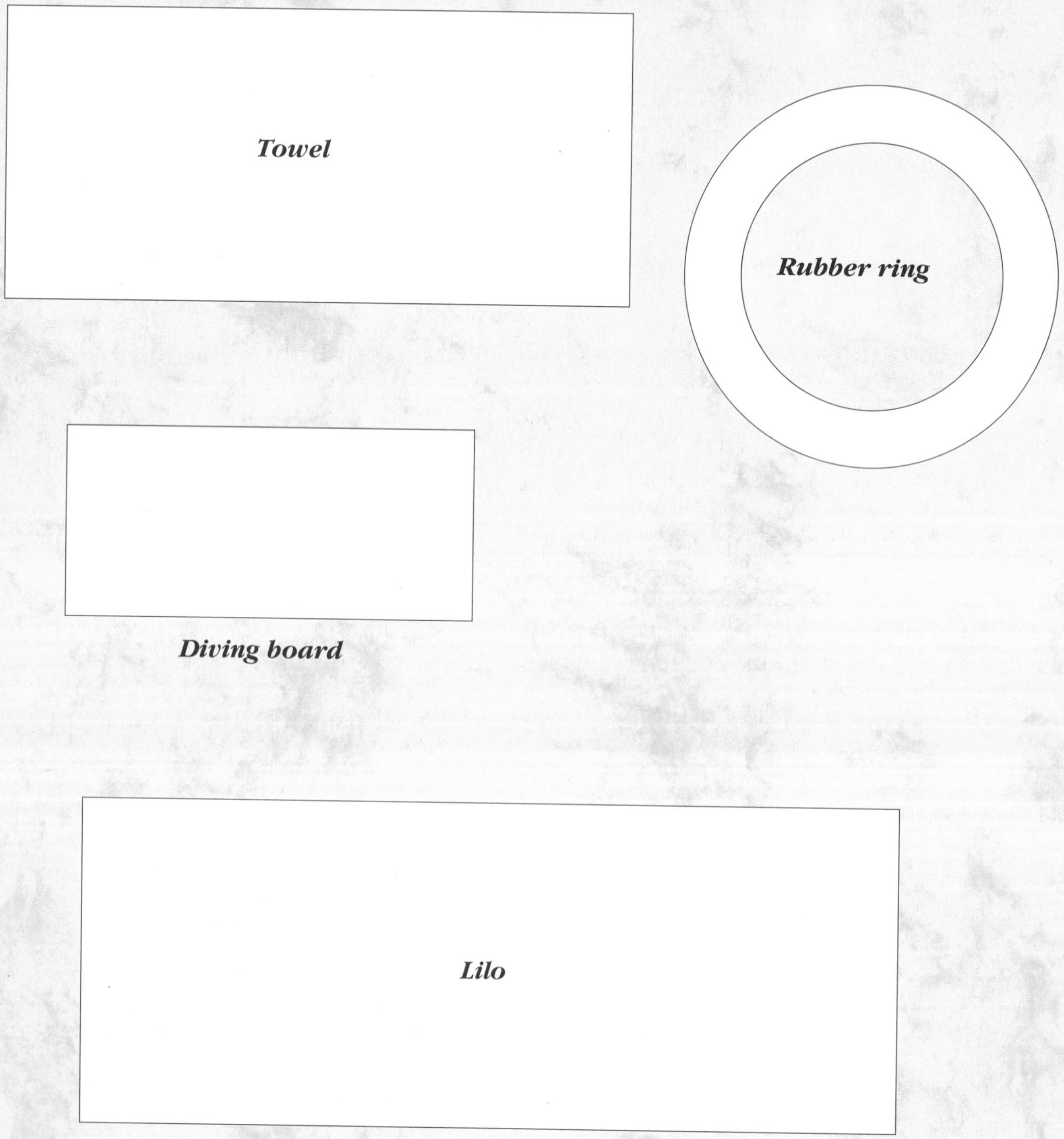

Towel

Rubber ring

Diving board

Lilo